MEDICAL CARE, MEDICAL COSTS

MEDICAL CARE, MEDICAL COSTS

The Search for a
Health Insurance
Policy

Rashi Fein

Harvard University Press
Cambridge, Massachusetts,
and London, England   1986

This book is printed on acid-free paper, and its binding
materials have been chosen for strength and durability.

Library of Congress Cataloging-in-Publication Data

Fein, Rashi.
    Medical care, medical costs.

    Includes index.
    1. Insurance, Health—United
States.   2. Medicaid—United States.   3. Medicare—
United States.   4. Medical care, cost of—United
States.   I. Title.   [DNLM: 1. Economics,
Medical—trends—United States.   2. Health
Insurance for Aged and Disabled, Title 18—history.
3. Insurance, Health—history—United States.
4. Medical Assistance, Title 19—history.
W 275 AA1 F33m]
HG9396.F45   1986   368.3′82′00973   86–7623
ISBN 0–674–56052–3 (alk. paper)

Preface

Health care policy is part of social policy. It is from that perspective that this book explores the growth and development of private health insurance, the attempts, spanning three-quarters of a century, to enact a universal compulsory health insurance program, the history of Medicare and Medicaid and how they function, recent health financing developments, and how we might solve the cost explosion in medical care while assuring a more equitable distribution of health care services.

I write as a political economist, sensitive to economic relationships but also concerned with institutions, politics, history, values, power relationships, motives, goals, and how these affect behavior. These various elements all contribute to the following account of the way we Americans have paid and pay for our health care and to the formulation of my suggestions for necessary reforms.

Chapter 1 explains the perspective from which I write and poses the issue: the need for a control mechanism that would help to contain the expansion in health care expenditures without abandoning our concerns for equity. Chapter 2 traces health insurance developments from 1929 to 1950. It emphasizes the competition in the sale of health insurance, the significance of experience and community rating, the link between employment and private health insurance, and the tax benefits associated with employer-paid premiums. Chapter 3 addresses the issue of government-sponsored health insurance. It covers the efforts to enact national health insurance from the second decade of this century through President Truman's administration. Chapter 4 examines the political history of Medicare and the ideological differences among proponents of alternative proposals to assist the aged. It explains why Medicare, or something like it, was an inevitable outcome of the developments outlined in Chapter 2 and the defeat of national health insurance (Chapter 3).

Chapters 5 and 6 describe the central features of Medicare and Medicaid, how the programs affect beneficiaries and recipients and others in the population, and some of the major problems the two programs face in the coming decade. Chapters 7 and 8 bring the story up to the present. They discuss the pressure for system reform during the early 1970s, the development of health maintenance organizations (HMOs), the explosion in health expenditures, and the impact of these developments on the debate about national health insurance.

The final three chapters return to the issue set forth in Chapter 1: the need for a control mechanism. Chapter 9 discusses the advantages and disadvantages of the competitive market as a control, focusing on such proposals as increases in deductibles, higher coinsurance rates, and taxation of employer payment of health insurance premiums. Chapter 10 defines the right to health care and explains how the concept can be made operational. It argues that the market cannot guarantee the right to health care, but that a universal health insurance program with budget limits can. It also outlines a proposed national health insurance program. Chapter 11 provides a summary and suggests some guidelines for action during a period when we continue to face cutbacks in private and public programs.

This is not an abstract discussion. Health financing policy is, or soon will be, at a crossroads. Our health care insurance system is under stress. Medicare reforms are necessary and will be legislated. Medicaid expenditures will be contained. Private insurance coverage will become less comprehensive. All of us will face a changing and different health care financing world. What each of us thinks about that new world, what we communicate to our representatives, and the policies they support will affect us and our children.

My preference for a universal insurance program derives from my image of a just society. It is an image based on a broadly defined concept of justice and liberty, nurtured by the stories my parents told me, the books they encouraged me to read, and the values they expressed. To them, liberty meant more than political freedom; it also meant freedom from destitution—in Roosevelt's phrase, "freedom from want."

I came to the field of medical or health care economics because of a concern with social issues, because I believed health care was important, and because there were people who feared impoverishment as a result of illness and who lived with the knowledge that they might be denied care because they could not pay the bill. That is the genesis of this book.

The debt to my parents is boundless. Many others (my teachers, students, and those with whom I participated in some of the events described in the following chapters) contributed, formally and informally, to my education and to my understanding of the health sector and its financing. It is impossible to list them all. Who among us is fully aware of the source of an idea, a phrase, a perspective?

But it is possible to acknowledge my debt to some who helped bring this book to completion. The Commonwealth Fund and Milbank Memorial Fund contributed financial support. Shirley Clark provided research assistance and forced me to sharpen the analysis. Marilyn Spellmeyer typed the first drafts, commented on them, and refused to let me give up the task. Susan Holman typed the second draft and Margaret Moroney and Barbara Graham the final manuscript.

A number of friends and colleagues encouraged me to write this book and/or read drafts of the manuscript. Their comments and suggestions considerably improved the result. Harold Luft's critique of the final chapters and Joel Kavet's assessment of the entire manuscript were especially helpful. I also want to thank Melvin Glasser, Mary-Jo Good, George Lamb, Carla Millhauser, Cecile Papirno, and David Willis, as well as my Harvard colleagues Allan Brandt and Harry Marks, who were tolerant of my work habits and generous in helping me guard my time and in providing encouragement and intellectual exercise.

My close friend Eli Ginzberg falls in a separate and special category. Although in a formal sense I was never his student, he has always been my teacher. I am in his debt, not only for what I have learned from him over years of friendship, but also for his concerns with and contributions to this book.

I want to thank Harvard University Press and especially Aida Donald, who believed in the manuscript's merit. Ann Hawthorne edited the manuscript and helped produce a more readable book. Of course I alone am responsible for any errors that remain.

Writing a book is like losing weight. It doesn't happen by itself, no one can do it for you—but you can't do it alone either. My wife and children and extended family provided necessary support, "nagged" most diplomatically, and, by giving up things we would have liked to do together, helped me resist the temptation to put the manuscript aside. I derive a special pleasure from the fact that my children assisted me: Bena contributed her considerable research skills, Karen read the manuscript and forced me to answer her probing questions, and they and Alan and Michael were willing to accord the subject of health insurance a high priority in dinner-table conversation. Their mother, Ruth, made the greatest sacrifice: she not only read the manuscript but had to live with it. I thank them all.

March 1986

Contents

MEDICAL CARE, MEDICAL COSTS

1

The Issues

The American health care insurance system is in jeopardy. The way we provide and pay for medical care, though a model neither of equity nor of efficiency, has yielded immense health benefits to millions. But this structure is fast crumbling. As costs continue to increase, fundamental faults become more evident. The solvency of private and public insurance programs is threatened. If current trends continue, more and more Americans will find it increasingly difficult to obtain good medical care and to pay for the care they receive. Future secretaries of the Department of Health and Human Services may no longer be able to report continuing improvement in health indicators.

Rising medical costs threaten not only Americans' health but also America's economic strength. Labor-management contracts, household budgets, corporate stability, and federal and state expenditures are held hostage to ever-rising health expenditures. The signs of unprecedented difficulty are everywhere and affect everyone:

- Medicare, the nation's largest health insurance program, provides diminishing and less certain protection to its beneficiaries. The program will have to be reformed if it is not to face bankruptcy in the latter 1990s.[1]

- The number of Americans without health insurance coverage increased by 6 million between 1979 and 1984. Thirty-five million Americans under age sixty-five, one-sixth of that segment of the population, had no insurance coverage, public or private, during at least part of 1984.[2]

- In addition to those without public or private insurance for all or part of a year, millions of Americans have very limited protection.

As a consequence, about one in four Americans under age sixty-five (56 million persons) is uninsured or underinsured.[3]

- Surveys of private employers and employees show that health benefit plans have been cut back in recent years. In 1984 over 60 percent of firms required deductibles for hospital in-patient services and almost 60 percent did so for medical services. In 1982, these were required in 30 percent of firms. The number of firms requiring employee premium contributions also increased.[4]

- In 1984 only 40 percent of America's poor received Medicaid benefits. This percentage has remained steady in recent years even as the number of low-income individuals has increased. Thus more and more poor Americans are without Medicaid protection.[5]

- Cost controls are being imposed without systematic assessment of their impact on the availability and quality of medical care. Efforts to shift costs divert increasing proportions of funds, energy, and ingenuity into administrative activities that do not save lives or alleviate suffering.

The days when medical care was a small private matter between patient and general practitioner are long gone and will never return. Today medical care is a large public matter involving patient, medical care system, insurance companies, and government. The friendly doctor with a black bag making a house call and the patient visiting a simply equipped doctor's office have given way to for-profit and not-for-profit hospitals, tax-exempt bonds, third-party payments, premiums, reimbursements, benefit packages, health maintenance organizations (HMOs), specialists, tests, technology, machinery, research, laboratories, and ever-rising costs. Our grandparents' financial or physical well-being, as they related to medical care, did not depend on the views of presidents, members of congressional committees, state legislators, or corporate executives. Today they do.

Government involvement has been forced by advances in medicine and the extension of life expectancy, by the increased costs of medical care, by our desire for greater equity, by the very nature of our society. Government involvement, however, has a corollary: we citizens need to know more.

Each of us faces choices in health care. The private choices of an earlier age—which physician, which course of treatment—remain, but with the growth of medicine the choices have expanded, along with their potential benefits and risks. Today's choices include type of insurance coverage and of delivery system. We can decide among different levels of financial protection and between an HMO or a preferred provider organization (PPO). Choice becomes more difficult.

Beyond these private choices are the many public ones: how the society can reduce barriers to care, how it might improve the way public health care and insurance programs function, how it can help control rising health care expenditures. Those choices cannot be left to the executive branch, to legislators, or to those who administer the various programs. The health care system serves and is paid for by you and me. It is we who are the patients and it is we who provide the funds for research and for construction, who pay the taxes, the premiums, and the bills. Our representatives in government and those who direct private and quasi-public organizations require our guidance, our statement about goals, priorities, and preferences.

Few of us will become involved with detail and fine print. We are not the managers of the enterprise. But the issues before us are not matters of fine print. They are matters of broad policy and of values. The Reagan administration has called for major change in health financing arrangements with which we have grown familiar over the past twenty years or more. Some legislators would reduce government's financial support for health care services; others would expand it. Some public officials call for less insurance and others ask for more. Such changes are not "details." They would affect access, equity, efficiency, the way we pay for care, and even health status. Those of us who are affected by such change—and that means all of us—must help guide the change process.

To do so we must understand where we are and how we got here, the various goals our health care system and financing mechanisms are trying to meet, and how those mechanisms developed. We must examine our private and public insurance system, the increase in health care costs, what has been happening to Medicare and why, what it means to be without insurance—and more. Only then can we consider the potential conflicts among the various goals we seek and how we might deal with the possible policy alternatives.

The story told here is the story of the growth and development of health care financing in the United States. It is a story of success and failure, of old problems met and new ones created. Unlike some stories, it does not end with these pages; all Americans will help to write the next chapters.

As with all description, analysis, and commentary, this is not the only version of the story that can be written. We are surrounded by an infinity of facts and must select among them. Different observers with different skills, interests, biases, and backgrounds would pose different questions, emphasize different events, cite different data, and, perhaps, reach different conclusions. The criteria that must guide all observers are the relevance and importance of events, but disagreement on the application of the criteria is inevitable. We cannot expect consensus from those who study social change and who consider health policy as part of social policy.

How we Americans address matters of social policy, the questions we ask and the solutions we choose, does not derive from disembodied technical models or sets of multiple regression equations with numbers spewed out by computer. The nature of medicine and medical care delivery, of health care finance and policy, is intertwined with social and economic forces and is affected by the experiences, traditions, and values of a society. The choices before us are linked to time and place and all the richness implicit in changing circumstances: the nature and history of evolving institutions and relationships, the attitudes and behavioral characteristics of key participants, the health sector's organic development, the climate of opinion, the traditions of the society, and the goals and values of its members. In a dynamic society, today's attitudes are not the same as yesterday's; 1986 is not 1936 or even 1966. To understand changing attitudes toward our health care financing system, we must consider general attitudes about the state of our economy, about equity and fairness, about efficiency. These factors create the framework within which social and health policies are formulated.

No sector is exempt from the questioning of existing programs, methods, and relationships, of the appropriate roles for government and the private sector, of the nature of our community. The fact that American health care now accounts for over 10 percent of our nation's product and 12 percent of the federal budget forces us and our representatives to ask questions. But the specific questions we ask are determined by the kind of health care financing programs that have developed over time and by the presumed relationship between those programs and the increase in health care expenditures, as well as by prevailing general attitudes.

Today's central policy questions inevitably deal with dollars; they are the leitmotiv of public discourse. Increases in health care costs, the state of the economy, the size of the federal deficit, and the pressure on federal, state, and private-sector budgets have helped frame the concern with health care costs. Can we afford the kind of health system we have created? Can we continue to support our existing payment and financing mechanisms, or have those mechanisms helped create more and new problems? If the latter, what is the best way to improve the situation?

The question can be posed in neutral, academic language: Can third-party (insurance and government) payments for medical care operate in a socially responsible and efficient manner in the absence of mechanisms that encourage all of us to recognize that resources are scarce? But the implications of both the question and its answer are far from academic. The translation of those implications into policy are what the battles to develop new payment mechanisms or to reduce Medicare, Medicaid, and cut back health insurance programs are and will be about. As posed, the question and its answer will not lead to a single new political action committee, campaign slogan, or march on Washington. But the way our leaders and our representatives respond and the policies they advocate to control health care expenditures and to distribute health care in a fairer manner, will do so.

The question seems to be about resources and dollars, but that is an illusion. It really is about people, about 239 million Americans, healthy and sick, rich, middle-income, and poor, young and old. It is about how we reap the benefits and pay the costs of our medical care and how we will choose to do so in the future. It is about what we have accomplished and how we might organize ourselves to accomplish even more.

Blue Cross, Blue Shield, commercial health insurance, Medicare, and Medicaid, the vehicles of our progress, are not experiments. They and similar programs help finance medical care for almost 200 million Americans (85 percent of the population). The Blue Cross concept can be traced back to a modest prepayment program that began in 1929 in Dallas, Texas. Commercial health insurance began its rapid growth in the mid-1940s. Medicare and Medicaid legislation were enacted in 1965. They are integral parts of the medical care financing landscape.

But landscapes change. Blue Cross, Blue Shield, commercial health insurance, Medicare, and Medicaid have changed and will continue to do so. They were designed to respond to the organization of medical care, the medical knowledge base, and the economic relationships that prevailed when they were conceived and built. As the America in which they were embedded changed, the various programs were adjusted accordingly. Today's medical care systems (and the society in which they function) are not those of 1929, when 1,250 Dallas schoolteachers joined a prepayment program that, for an annual cost of $6 per subscriber, provided up to twenty-one days of semiprivate hospitalization at Baylor University Hospital. Today's problems are also different from the ones that existed in 1965, when national health expenditures, the sum of all private and public dollars spent on medical care delivery, construction, and research, totaled $42 billion, about one-tenth of the amount that now flows through the system.[6]

But the fact that things change does not mean that the original programs, altered to meet new conditions and to address new and emerging problems, are tentative or temporary. Those who helped build Blue Cross and other private insurance programs, those who worked to expand and strengthen health insurance protection, those who lobbied and who voted for public programs such as Medicare and Medicaid did not view what they were building as experiments or demonstration programs, things to be tried to see if they might work. Insurance and prepayment, after all, were well-understood concepts. At various times and in limited ways they had already been applied to the delivery of medical services. Presumably they could be extended and made more comprehensive. The expenses associated with medical care could be "covered"; the principles of fire and theft insurance could be applied.

This judgment, perhaps optimistic but hardly naive, was grounded in experience and buttressed by theory. The record speaks for itself: millions of Americans have been protected from the financial burdens associated with illness and, in the process, have sought and received more medical care than they would otherwise have been able to purchase. Every day millions of Americans are the beneficiaries of a health insurance system that has become so much a part of our way of life that until recently it was taken for granted. Convinced that the programs could and would work, their creators did not think in experimental terms. Convinced that the programs did work, their beneficiaries, you and I, do not think of them as demonstrations.

Yet, collectively, these various insurance and financing programs are being tested. The health financing system we have developed is charged with costing too much, inducing a wasteful expansion of the health care sector, contributing to inflation and the enlargement of government deficits, slowing down the rate of economic expansion.

Third-party payment, America's response to the desire for security against the unpredictability of individual medical expenses, is in trouble. It has protected individuals but is accused of having failed society. This accusation, if valid, is no trivial matter. Perhaps America's health payment system was an experiment, after all—something that, over time, would not work as once was both believed and hoped. If that is the case—and many observers of different political persuasions believe it to be—minor tinkering will not suffice. Perhaps it is time for major reform of our health insurance system.

Few Americans would dispute the existence of a health insurance problem. To some, the problem is the lack of universal coverage that would protect all Americans. Others focus on the issues of limited benefits. Some cannot cope with the forms and paperwork. Others are angry because they collect fewer dollars than they had hoped for. Undoubtedly, however, more and more of us are disturbed about the rising costs of care and associated premium increases.

However, increases in the cost of care and in the price of insurance do not in themselves constitute a special problem. After all, we are irritated by many price increases but recognize that most of them are caused by general inflationary pressures. We would like to see a more stable price level and to buy cars, homes, food, and health care at lower prices. The fact that we would prefer lower prices, that we feel that something "costs too much," does not lead us automatically to call for a reorganization of the sector in question.

But health care and its financing arrangements are different from other goods and services. Our irritations with increases in health expenditures stem in part from a feeling that we are captives of some greater force that we cannot control and, further, that we dare not adjust to price increases by reducing consumption. We can shift from coffee to tea, drive fewer miles or in more efficient cars, watch TV instead of going to the theater, encourage our children to attend state rather than private universities, but is it realistic to boycott health insurance, use less medical care, or look for health bargains?

And we are not alone in our discomfiture and irritation about the costs of care. An increasing number of public officials face seemingly inexorable increases in federal, state, or local health budgets. They wonder whether rising expenditures are not an inevitable consequence of third-party payment as we have known it, of uncontrolled financing and reimbursement programs that are inherently explosive.

Yet even if, in the absence of effective control mechanisms, insurance leads to increases in health expenditures, it is not intuitively clear whether we must act or, if so, what actions we should take. Insurance, after all, has many worthwhile purposes, and the achievement of these purposes may outweigh the undesirable side effects. Reasonable people may differ on their individual assessment of the benefits and their associated costs and on the benefits and costs of various alternatives. Thus, if the roads built to provide access to national parks lead to overcrowding, we may choose to ignore the problem, feeling that we can put up with a little overcrowding—but how much will you accept and how much will I? Perhaps we will agree that something must be done, but if we do, will we be able to agree on what that is? Some might accord the elimination of crowding such priority that they would tear up the roads. Others might charge high tolls and admission fees and ration access to the highest bidder. Still others might utilize a lottery or similar distribution system. And some would call for an expansion of the park system. Various options exist. The choice among them requires information on their implications and, in a free society, debate and discussion. So, too, with health care.

Today's facts are the product of yesterday's decisions and of subsequent developments. Thus, the suggestion that the health financing system needs reforming does not imply that the proponents of insurance were wrong in encouraging its development. Who of us would care or dare to be without it? Nor does it follow that the pioneers and builders were wrong in not fully anticipating its side effects or consequences. America today is different from America then, and many of those differences could hardly have been anticipated. We dare not impose our current attitudes and state of knowledge on the past. It is tempting but wrong to suppose that because we do not like today's facts, yesterday's decisions, the precursors of those facts, were mistakes. Many of those decisions, the resolution of conflict between groups with different values and interests, were appropriate to their time. We amend the Constitution, but surely that does not mean that the founding fathers did the wrong thing in 1789.

Yesterday's decisions and events must be assessed in the light of the information and opportunities available then, the problems and attitudes prevailing then. To do otherwise is to convert history to fairy tale, to criticize policymakers because they weren't fortune-tellers. The choices that were made were not the only choices then available, but we cannot assume that the choices then available included those that now exist. Conditions change, and new approaches can help take account of new factors. We cannot assume that because American health insurance is old it is immutable. Nor should we assume that because it is old it is irrelevant.

Health insurance began its growth as a response to changes in the health sector and in the greater economy: rising costs of care and declining personal income. It expanded and continues to flourish, not because we have grown accustomed to it but because it is supported by the vast majority of Americans. Those who need or will need care want protection. Those who deliver care want assurance of payment. At a time when older social programs are being reexamined (regrettably, "reexamined" is in today's world a polite euphemism for the ideological questioning and reordering of budgets and priorities), when economists and policymakers are preoccupied with the possible link between third-party payment and rising health expenditures, it is worth repeating what seems self-evident: insurance met and continues to meet real needs. Blue Cross, Blue Shield, commercial health insurance, Medicare, and Medicaid were not developed by some cabal in Washington or elsewhere. They were not foisted on the American people. They were created in response to social and economic problems.

These problems—illness, a fragmented health care system, the high costs of medical care, an unequal distribution of income and wealth— are still present. The need to share health care costs in a collective fashion persists. The reduction of economic vulnerability and the achievement of better health status continue to be both worthy and realistic goals. The gap between our rhetoric about health care for all and our performance needs to be closed, and not by lowering our sights, adjusting our aspirations, or redefining our goals.

The question is how we might solve the problems that we face, how we might meet our own and our neighbors' needs, and thus fulfill our goals.

2

In Sickness and in Health:
The Growth of Private Health Insurance

Over fifty years ago Dr. Justin Ford Kimball, administrator of the Baylor University Hospital in Dallas, had to find a way to reduce the number of unpaid patient care bills. The institution he headed, like other institutions, incurred operating expenses. It employed people; prepared and served food; used electricity, heat, and water; ordered supplies of all kinds. Each of these resources cost money, and money was obtained from payments by patients and from charitable gifts by donors. Since there were limits on the amount that could be raised through philanthropic gifts, the hospital had to rely as much as possible on generating and collecting billed dollars from patients. Failing that, revenues would not match expenditures, and continuing deficits would threaten the hospital's viability.

A half-century ago hospitals played a less significant role in the provision of health care and were not as central to the health economy as they are today. In 1929 less than one of every five dollars in the health care system flowed to hospitals. Today two of every five are devoted to hospital care. Since fewer patients were hospitalized and since hospital care cost less in 1929, hospital expenditures per U.S. resident (whether hospitalized or not) were only $5.36 per year. In 1984 hospital expenditures came to $644 per person per year.[1]

In 1929 there was no insurance for the costs of hospitalization. Nevertheless, it is reasonable to wonder why there was a problem in hospital finance. Even in relation to 1929 incomes, $5.36 per person per year was not a large sum. The answer, of course, lies in the fact that the $5.36 figure was an average for the entire population. It included those who paid nothing because they were not hospitalized as well as those who paid hundreds of dollars. Like all averages, it is both helpful and misleading. It tells us nothing about variation, about

extremes. It is a "comfortable" figure—we forgot that there were rich
and poor, sick and well, young and old; that, in the absence of an
insurance program in which everyone paid $5.36 and "socialized" the
costs of hospital care, the problem of payment for those who needed
care was real. That was especially the case for middle-income Americans: those too "affluent" to enter the charity ward (where they would
be considered "teaching material") but not affluent enough to pay for
private care.

Absent insurance, patients had to finance their hospital bills out of
current income and past savings. It is therefore not surprising that
many patients were unable to pay for their care. The ledger entry
"bad debts" grew. The red ink flowed. It was under that financial
pressure that Dr. Kimball's plan, initially for Dallas schoolteachers,
was born. The 1,250 schoolteachers were encouraged to prepay their
hospital care at Baylor for 50 cents a month. In return they were
offered twenty-one days of semiprivate care (including use of the operating room and various ancillary services—anesthetic, lab tests) in
a twelve-month period.[2]

Fifty cents a month, $6 a year, meant a lot more fifty-five years ago
than it does today. In 1929 over one-quarter of the 36 million American
families and unattached individuals had an annual income of less than
$1,000, and two-thirds had incomes of less than $2,000.[3] Nevertheless,
given the potential costs of a hospital stay, the "Kimball policy" was
a good buy. It is not surprising that the Baylor plan, though offering
limited benefits restricted to a single hospital, proved popular. The
schoolteachers enrolled and the prepayment method of financing was
quickly introduced to other groups in Dallas. Hospital administrators
in other parts of the United States, facing similar problems, took note
of what had transpired in Dallas. Prepayment, they concluded, might
be the key to a hospital's financial stability.

New social and financial arrangements seldom burst upon the scene
with such success that they are quickly adopted outside the area in
which they are first implemented. More often, these innovations require a period of refinement, adjustment, and adaptation. Furthermore, since it is difficult to change existing relationships and modes
of behavior, there must be a compelling reason to do so: the costs of
inaction must be high and must outweigh the understandable desire
to continue along familiar and accustomed paths. The pressures to act
must be clear; the needs must be compelling; the time must be right.

Dr. Kimball's idea was both acceptable and timely. Already in the last quarter of the nineteenth century there had been health insurance programs called "independent plans." These early plans and others that were developed at the beginning of the twentieth century generally were limited to physician's services, but some did include hospital care. Sponsored by individual employers for their employees or by labor unions, lodges, fraternal orders, and consumer groups for their members, they contracted with individual physicians for services and paid the physician a fixed amount per enrollee per year.[4]

These independent plans faced severe obstacles. They were opposed by organized medicine since they "tied" physicians to contract rather than to fee-for-service practice and "tied" patients to particular physicians. Furthermore, it was nearly impossible for them to grow, since they were not open to the general public and were dependent on a "special" circumstance or relationship: a strong union, forward-looking employer, cohesive immigrant group, or the need to contract for medical care in an area where medical resources were scarce (such as railroads or mines). Finally, these plans were often looked upon and attacked as "alien imports" or as "socialist."

The fact that these types of plans reduced the costs of care by departing from the fee-for-service model hardly endeared them to the larger medical community, which reacted by ostracizing physician participants and by arguing that lower costs were associated with lower quality. Assailed by organized medicine and lacking broad community support, the independent plans were of limited significance. It was not until much later in this century, when their structure had changed to include a broader membership base and when they received government assistance, that they began to flourish under new names (such as prepaid group practice and health maintenance organization). In 1929, however, their structure, history, and sponsorship did not enable them to compete effectively against the far more acceptable Kimball program.

Furthermore, Dr. Kimball's idea, coming as it did on the eve of the Great Depression, was timely. Somewhat similar plans had been tried in 1912 in Rockford, Illinois, in 1921 in Grinnell, Iowa, and in 1927 in Brattleboro, Vermont. But hospital directors were able to ignore these prepayment innovations as long as the economy was growing. National unemployment rates averaged 7.4 percent in 1913–1915, 5.4 percent in 1922–1924 and in 1928–1930.[5] The Rockford, Grinnell, and Brattleboro schemes had little impact because it was possible for hospitals to continue doing business as usual.

Conversely, the Baylor developments in 1929 could not be ignored. National unemployment averaged 16.1 percent in 1930–1932, rose to a high of 24.9 percent In 1933, and did not decline below 10.0 percent until 1941. The 1929 gross national product of $104 billion collapsed to $74 billion (in 1929 prices) by 1933, a real decline of 29 percent.[6] Personal incomes and savings fell dramatically. The problem of unpaid medical bills and hospital deficits was real and pervasive. The pressures on hospital administrators and on patients were mounting. A growing number of unemployed, yesterday's middle-income Americans, could not pay their medical bills. Charity, free care, and a "sliding scale of charges," which in the best of times could do no more than partially address some of the problems of some of the unemployed and poor, were unable to fill the needs of the growing number of persons who found themselves destitute, without jobs, without unemployment compensation and the other social and economic support mechanisms that had yet to be enacted. The Great Depression was not misnamed: millions of Americans were without a present or prospects for a future.

Absent the private savings cushions or public social support programs that exist today, the Great Depression hit all sectors of the society and of the economy. There was a decline in utilization of privately operated hospitals and a shift to municipal and county hospitals, where free care was provided. In Chicago in 1933, for example, 88 percent of government hospital beds were occupied, compared with only 50 percent of all nongovernment beds. In the years 1929–1933, twenty-eight nongovernment Chicago hospitals experienced a decline of 43 percent in service to paying patients. Data from the American Medical Association showed clearly that as the depression continued, fewer patients were admitted to the nation's hospitals and stayed there a shorter time.[7] It is not that Americans were healthier, but rather that an increasing number of Americans could not afford hospital care. An increasing number of beds stood empty, and some hospitals were forced to close their doors.

In this respect, of course, hospitals were similar to countless other economic enterprises whose sales declined and whose revenues could not cover their operating expenses. But there was one major difference: hospitals could erect a private safety net that protected their revenues. Each of the many people at risk could contribute a small sum to prepay the expenses of the few who would need care. Since no individual knew in advance whether he or she would be among the few, prudence—not altruism—would be the driving force.

The principles of insurance could be applied as they had been at Baylor, and the institutions that provided care could be protected. Surely there must have been heads of firms that manufactured shoes or processed food or beverages who wished that they could apply the same principles. But, unlike hospital care, food and shoes were things that all of us needed or wanted, not things that each of us might need but that only few would need. Insurance did not offer a way out for most manufacturers or for the persons who sought their products. It did for hospitals and their patients.

Today we take medical care insurance for granted. It is difficult to imagine a different world. Yet we must do so in order to understand the impact of the Baylor plan and to begin to grasp the problem faced by the millions of Americans who even today are without health insurance. For them even a minor ailment can represent economic catastrophe. Consider how you and I would fare and what we would fear in a world without private health insurance or government health financing programs. Look at your paycheck and ask what it would mean to pay for all health care expenses on an out-of-pocket basis.

It is out of those 1929 beginnings that the ways we pay for care today evolved. It did not happen overnight or in a rigorously planned fashion. There were bursts of activity and periods of relative stability, successes and failures, new and newer programs. But it was at Baylor that the foundation was laid and it was on that foundation that Blue Cross grew.

The sixty-seven Blue Cross plans that today enroll some 80 million Americans are of course quite different from the Baylor and similarly organized plans of the early 1930s.[8] They are not simply Baylor magnified a thousand or ten thousand times. But in several ways their strengths and weaknesses resemble those of the patterns originated at Baylor and copied by other hospitals. The plans were initiated by individual hospitals and provided service benefits in the sponsoring hospital. They were in the nature of a contract for the provision of services by a single institution to a group of subscribing individuals. They offered service benefits (days of care) in that institution only.

This arrangement had the virtues of simplicity and ease of administration. Furthermore, it avoided legal problems with state agencies that regulated the insurance sector since, narrowly defined, these individual contracts for the provision of services were not considered insurance. Yet the disadvantages of this circumscribed and limited arrangement were evident. It did not respond to the possibility that the patient might need to receive care outside of the one institution with which he or she had the contract or that one's physician might not have admitting privileges in the particular institution selected by the enrollee.

Those limitations were real. In addition, single hospital plans were not in tune with the prevailing ideology of "free choice." The public— perhaps unaware that doctors did not have admitting privileges in every hospital—believed that their physician could and did select the "right" hospital for them. The medical community abhorred direct arrangements between a particular hospital and groups of potential patients, for such arrangements called the physician's decision-making power and control into question. Single hospital plans assumed that hospitals would compete for subscribers and that physicians and hospitals would welcome such competition. But the fact is that, as in other sectors of the economy, those who can do business together seldom welcome pressure to compete. It is far riskier to practice competition than to extol it.

Clearly, a new institutional arrangement was required: the development of "free-choice" plans whereby several hospitals in a community banded together to offer prepaid care. This approach, though administratively more complex, had obvious advantages for physicians, who could thus continue in their role as medical decision makers and gatekeepers; for enrollees, whose hospital options were broadened; and for participating hospitals, whose "covered" population base was increased. Multihospital arrangements spread rapidly in the years 1932– 1935, but since these plans were broader in scope and more like insurance, they were viewed as falling within the jurisdiction of state insurance departments. As a consequence, these plans encountered the legal difficulties that the Baylor program and other single hospital programs had avoided.

Then as now, the power to regulate insurance was reserved to the states. In the 1930s that power derived from an 1868 Supreme Court decision exempting the insurance industry from the definition of interstate commerce (today it rests on federal legislation enacted in 1945 to reverse the impact of a 1944 Supreme Court decision that negated its earlier finding).[9] Insurance regulation at the state level required that multihospital plans conform to various state laws and regulations governing insurance companies. In particular, many state insurance commissioners concluded that multihospital arrangements required adequate reserves to ensure that the central or multihospital fund that collected premiums would be able to reimburse hospitals for the service benefits they provided. Concerned about the protection of individual subscribers, insurance commissioners wanted assurance that there were reserves guaranteeing the solvency of the plan. But such assurance could not be given. Reserve funds were not available nor could they be generated. Hospitals did not have pools of cash from which they could contribute to the central fund. Furthermore, many hospital officials (and some state regulators) believed that such reserves were unnecessary except to meet the letter of the law. Hospitals, it was argued, were guided by a different ethic: they had agreed to provide the services and would find a way to do so. Since enrollees received service benefits and were not eligible for cash payments, why keep reserves of cash?

When both the Cleveland Hospital Council and the United Hospital Fund of New York were informed that their prepaid hospital benefit plan would require the establishment of a mutual or stock insurance company with appropriate reserves, another course of development was required.[10] If meeting the letter of the law was impossible, why not change the law? Laws, after all, are created by people. When the law does not serve the people, it can be changed.

In response to the need to create a legal framework that permitted the development of new structures to provide ways of financing hospital care, the New York legislature in 1934 enacted a measure permitting the establishment, under special legal arrangements, of nonprofit hospital corporations, a new type of organizational entity. This legislation conferred special advantages and responsibilities on Blue Cross–like arrangements. In 1936 the American Hospital Association prepared model legislation and actively promoted the adoption of new statutes in the various states. State legislatures responded and Blue Cross expanded: from one plan in 1933 to seventeen in 1936, forty-eight in 1939, and seventy-four by 1943.[11]

The plans were exempt from state insurance legislation and, as charitable organizations, from state and federal taxation. Furthermore, since, without reserves, the hospitals were "at risk," control of these nonprofit hospital corporations was vested in representatives (administrators and trustees) of hospitals and physicians rather than in the lay public. In return for these benefits, the corporations were expected to serve the entire community and to assure the availability of insurance to persons of moderate and low income. Their financial operation and rate structure could be examined by public bodies.

Thus state-enabling legislation made possible the development of hospital association–sponsored plans that offered service benefits (that is, hospital care). These benefits were offered to groups of enrollees since it was far easier to reach groups and since the larger the group, the more likely it was that there would be a balance between those who would need care and those who would not. As with the school-teachers in Dallas, a simple way of defining the group (and of collecting premiums) was to link people through an employer. Since the various plans were regulated by the individual states, they did not cross state boundaries. Thus, employees who moved or who lost or changed their jobs faced changes in and even total loss of coverage. A national and universal plan would have easily dealt with those issues, but Blue Cross plans were neither national nor universal.

Blue Cross and similar plans were brought into being by hospital representatives with active support and encouragement by the American Hospital Association. The AHA and the hospitals assumed leadership and acted in response to the serious problems they and their patients faced: how would hospital bills be paid, how would stable hospital revenues be assured? A patient's potential difficulty in paying for medical care translated into potential difficulty for the hospital if revenues declined. Since hospital service providers developed the payment mechanism, the rules and regulations, and the structure of financing arrangements that helped define and determine the level of payment and reimbursement to the facility that rendered the service, it was clear that the needs and interests of the institutional providers of care would be met.

Blue Cross was created and its governing structure was dominated by hospital representatives and members of the medical community. It negotiated, but hardly at arm's length, with those same hospital representatives, who, although they may have worn two hats, were hardly adversaries. Blue Cross was designed to protect the income of hospitals. In accomplishing that objective, it offered protection to patients and potential patients. It could assure its revenues only by developing a financing system that paid the bills for those who entered the hospital.

The process, then, was much the same as that found in other sectors of the economy. Furniture dealers who wanted to increase their sales developed ways to extend credit to potential buyers. They helped themselves by offering terms that helped their customers. However, the fact that two parties engage in a transaction from which both benefit does not mean that they benefit equally. Both buyers and sellers must perceive advantages or there will be no purchase and sale. But they may derive different gains and in different dimensions. Their interests and their power in the marketplace differ. It is those interests and power relationships that determine where, within the range that encompasses mutual benefits, we strike a bargain and "make a deal."

Blue Cross protected both patients and hospitals, but the terms of protection differed. The relationship between Blue Cross and the hospitals assured greater attention to and concern for hospital revenues than for the subscriber's household budget. Hospital leaders set premiums at levels that assured coverage of hospital expenditures, although the premiums were limited by the requirement that they be "affordable." Premiums tended toward the high end of the range within which all parties could survive. This orientation meant that Blue Cross and its supporters set a high premium and then stressed the fact that insurance was inexpensive (after all, the American public spent large sums on cosmetics and tobacco, and surely hospital insurance was more important). If insurance programs had been organized by consumers, suggested premium structures would have placed greater emphasis on affordability, although premiums would still have had to be sufficiently high to enable hospitals to remain viable. A consumer plan might have set a low premium and then stressed that hospitals could manage and "make do" (perhaps by reducing salary levels or capital investment).

But even though it is clear that the structure of Blue Cross placed little emphasis on hospital economies or on the need for tight fiscal control, we should not exaggerate the impact that consumer-dominated control might have had. There is an important difference between "customers" and patients. As customers we shop and bargain and evaluate. As patients and potential patients we are heavily influenced by our own fears of illness and by the experts in white coats. It is not clear that we would withhold dollars when leaders of the medical community tell us that those dollars would help improve the quality of our medical care. The power of physicians and of chiefs of service in hospitals derives not only from the structure of the health sector but also from our own behavior, our fears and ignorance, and the mystique of expertise.

The issue of high hospital costs is not one of fraud or graft. Nor is it simply that hospital directors and physicians have what has been called an "edifice complex," an equipment fetish, deriving pleasure from being surrounded by costly technology and willing to spend the patient's money to satisfy their personal tastes. The issue is more subtle. It hinges on the fact that patient care is not an exact science in which there is only one answer to every problem. Medical care can be produced in many different ways with different combinations of resources, with different proportions of workers and types of capital. Some equipment may improve care but only infrequently or only marginally. Some equipment may save on labor costs, while other technologies may increase them.

In selecting from among the possible combinations and proportions of the various resources that "produce" medical care, in deciding about levels of investment and operating costs (including expenditures on items unrelated to the quality of medical care though perhaps, as with lobbies and cafeterias, quite related to the satisfaction of visitors, relatives, and others), the emphasis on expansion rather than on economy was apparent. In a society in which more meant better—and few physicians or patients questioned that connection—potential disagreements among hospitals, physicians, and the public tended to be minimized. It was less divisive and appeared less risky to err on the side of generosity, to spend too much rather than too little, that is, to set premiums a little higher rather than a little lower than was "necessary."

Hospitals benefited from hospital insurance; so did subscribers. Those who entered the hospital were not billed for covered-service benefits; those who were healthy felt more secure in the knowledge that they had financial protection. As hospital inpatient care grew in importance—and more patients were admitted in part because hospital care was covered and ambulatory care was not—and as hospital costs increased, the need for and the benefits of insurance also grew. By January 1, 1942, as America entered the Second World War, Blue Cross covered 6 million subscribers (an increase of more than one-third over the previous year).[12]

The expansion of Blue Cross hospital insurance did not go unnoticed by potential rivals, specifically, by firms that had long specialized in insurance. Commercial insurance companies, which for years had argued that hospital care was not insurable, now recognized the market that existed. Previously they had contended that the demand for health care was not actuarially predictable because of "moral hazard": the possibility that the presence of insurance would lead individuals to increase their use of health care services. You and I do not have automobile accidents simply because we have insurance coverage for them. Nor do we arrange for thefts because we have theft insurance. But health care was presumed to be different. In that area, it was argued, you and I—or physicians acting on our and (in a fee-for-service system) their own behalf—would increase utilization as a consequence of the availability of insurance. We would seek care instead of "making do"; they would deliver care instead of accepting lower incomes. Insurance companies thus saw no limit to their potential liability, and especially with service-benefit contracts, under which they could not control either the quantity of services utilized or their price. The expansion of Blue Cross, its favorable experience, and the desire to offer a full range of insurance (health as well as life, property, fire, and theft) to the employer and employee induced commercial health insurers to enter the market. Lacking sponsorship by and ties to hospitals and concerned about their potential liability, they emphasized cash-indemnity rather than service benefits.

Many of us are quite familiar with cash-indemnity contracts. On my desk I have an offer for one such policy, received from the company that provided my gasoline credit card. It informs me that under the highest option I would be paid $60 a day from the first day for any covered hospitalization; under the lowest I would receive $30 a day, beginning after five days of covered illness. For my age group the first option costs $19.80 a month, the second $8.10. This cash-indemnity approach is an extension of traditional insurance principles. It offers the subscriber an agreed-upon sum of money, payable to the subscriber for every day spent in the hospital. This sum may, but need not, be used to help defray the cost of hospitalization and of the various ancillary services.

Cash-indemnity plans have the advantage of limiting the liability of the carrier and thus allow it to offer numerous "tailor-made" plans in which premiums are related to the level of cash indemnity offered and do not—at least in the short run—have to increase as hospital costs or charges rise. The fact that the patient must bear some risks and costs means that unless the subscriber is well informed about hospital charges, he or she may have less (or more) financial protection than desired or "necessary." Many individuals who have cash-indemnity insurance of $50 per day in hospital may be unaware that in January 1985 the average daily charge for a semiprivate room in U.S. hospitals was $213 (with a range from $114 in Mississippi to $281 in California).[13] They may believe that their insurance offers substantial protection, but patently this is not the case.

Perhaps if those with only minimum protection knew the financial risks they bear, they would purchase more insurance. But only perhaps. It may be that the $50-a-day policy, inadequate as it may be, is all they can afford. Although service-benefit plans offer a high level of protection, their premium cost is beyond the means of many Americans. Cash-indemnity plans, on the other hand, can vary their benefits and premium levels to appeal across a wider range of incomes.

Commercial insurance companies started from a base of a mere 15,000 health insurance subscribers in 1934 and had grown to 100,000 by 1938. By 1941 they had enrolled 3.7 million people. Blue Cross covered an additional 6 million. Together with the 3.1 million persons covered by independent plans (and with the purchase of more than one insurance policy by some individuals corrected for), a total of 12.3 million Americans had some form of health insurance, a growth of 8.4 million or 215 percent in a span of three years. And the greatest increase was still ahead.

The Second World War was a period of rapid growth in health insurance. Coverage was broadened and deepened: there were more subscribers and more comprehensive benefit packages. By 1946 Blue Cross enrollment had grown to 18.9 million (a 215 percent increase in five years), commercial insurance had expanded to 10.5 million (184 percent), and independent plans totaled 4.0 million (29 percent). The unduplicated total was 32.1 million (a growth of 161 percent).[14] This rapid expansion was directly related to federal economic wartime policies. These policies contributed to the expansion of the health insurance industry and structured the financing arrangements in the health care sector as they exist today, four decades later.

As the economy was mobilized for the war effort, resources were allocated to war production, to tanks and planes, to ships and arms, to the needs of the armed forces and of supporting activities. Yesterday's unemployed entered the armed forces or found jobs. Women entered the labor force in increasing numbers. The unemployment rate dropped from 17.2 percent in 1939 to 1.2 percent in 1944, GNP increased from $91 billion to $211 billion (almost 75 percent in real terms, that is, corrected for inflation), and personal income after taxes rose from $70 billion to $147 billion (by almost 50 percent in real terms).[15]

Americans had more money, but there were few things to buy. Consumer goods were in short supply and many consumer durables such as automobiles, refrigerators, and washing machines were unavailable. Concerned about the potential of increased incomes to bid up the prices of scarce goods, interested in generating a feeling of collective purpose and effort, the government created the Office of Price Administration (OPA) and adopted measures to stabilize prices and wages. Economic policy was designed to minimize the opportunity for individuals to take special advantage of the war situation. In 1945 12 million men and women were serving in the armed forces. The home front joined in their sacrifice as the government instituted policies of price control, wage stabilization, and rationing and promoted the purchase of government bonds designed to contain inflation by diverting dollars from consumption into savings.

Although wages were stabilized, the War Labor Board permitted management and labor to negotiate changes in employment benefits, including prepaid health insurance. Bargaining over fringe benefits, though limited to 5 percent of payroll, consequently received increasing attention. Furthermore, health insurance packages were especially attractive. Not only did they represent legally permissible ways to increase real income, but their real cost to employers and employees was effectively reduced by the federal tax code. Employers were permitted to consider health insurance contributions made on behalf of employees as a "cost of doing business," and thus, like wages, deductible from what otherwise would have been profits. The consequent reduction in taxes meant that part of the cost of health insurance was paid for by government. And no small part: because of the enactment of wartime special excess profits taxes, the marginal tax rate could reach as high as 85 percent. The real cost, to the employer, of a dollar for health insurance premiums might be as low as 15 cents.

At the same time, to the employee, the value of a dollar for health insurance coverage was greater than a dollar increase in wages or salary (an increase that in any case was illegal). Then as now, the employee paid income and social security taxes on wages but not on the health insurance premium contribution made on his or her behalf by the employer (or on the benefits paid for by the insurance). Thus employees who obtained health insurance coverage paid for by employers received a nontaxable benefit. A dollar contribution to health insurance reduced the employer's federal income tax but did not increase the employee's tax.

This subsidy for the purchase of health insurance provided an additional incentive to its expansion, justifiable on several grounds. Given the rising costs of medical care, the need for health insurance was growing. Economists shun the use of the word "need," claiming that it is an imprecise term involving value judgments. Yet "desire" or "taste" is too weak a word where health insurance is concerned. Economists notwithstanding, there was (and is) a "need for health insurance." A number of powerful interests united to meet that need and to encourage the expansion of coverage. Some undoubtedly wanted to assure the financial solvency of individuals and families and to remove their sense of insecurity. Others may have wanted to assure the financial solvency of hospitals and the incomes of physicians by guaranteeing their cash flows through the availability of insurance payments. Still others may have felt that the encouragement, expansion, and strengthening of private health insurance would help thwart the potential pressure for a government-sponsored health insurance program utilizing a social-insurance approach akin to the already enacted Social Security System.

Despite their different reasons for supporting the expansion of health insurance, these constituencies united in favoring the tax incentive as an instrument of that expansion. And here, as in other areas, tax incentives worked. Though hardly equitable—the tax benefit was of no value to the unemployed or to people whose employers did not contribute to the premium cost and of greatest value to those with higher incomes and in the highest marginal tax brackets—health insurance coverage did spread.

Today wages are not frozen and health insurance benefits are only one of many items on the labor-management bargaining table. Although health insurance premiums paid for by employers remain nontaxable, employees have options and must consider which mix of wages and fringe benefits they prefer. But during the war, with wages frozen and fewer choices, the choice was clear. As health insurance coverage expanded rapidly, more and more people became aware of its existence and desirability. Furthermore, after the war, millions of veterans who had received free medical care, and thus experienced the removal of the financial barrier to the receipt of care, as civilians wanted the next best thing: insured care.

Health insurance coverage continued to expand: from 32 million people covered in 1946, to 53 million two years later, and to 77 million by 1951. In the years 1946–1951 Blue Cross enrollment rose by 18.5 million and commercial health insurance by 29.5 million. In 1951 commercial health insurance enrollment, at 40 million, exceeded the 37 million in Blue Cross.[16] This rapid expansion cannot be explained simply by consumers' willingness (as individuals and as members of groups), to "buy the product" with tax-subsidized dollars. It was the result of a combination of institutional forces and developments.

Of vital importance was the fact that health insurance became a legitimate matter for negotiation through collective bargaining. Those too young to remember the 1940s may find it difficult to imagine how controversial various aspects of the collective bargaining process were in the postwar period. The decision that welfare benefits such as pensions and hospital insurance should be among the bargaining issues was taken by the National Labor Relations Board and upheld in various federal court decisions in the years 1947–1949. An employer's refusal to bargain over health insurance coverage was defined as an unfair labor practice. Only then was health insurance no longer considered a gift by the employer, to be dispensed or withdrawn unilaterally or changed or amended as the employer saw fit.

There were at least four clear advantages to the provision of group health insurance coverage through collective bargaining. First was the monetary advantage gained through group purchase. "Bulk" purchase and sales made possible a substantial savings in marketing, billing, processing, and other administrative overhead costs. Thus group rates were substantially lower than premiums to individual subscribers. In other words, a higher proportion of the premium dollar was returned to group subscribers in the form of benefits. That, of course, is still the case.

Second was the fact that enrollment of groups, and especially of large groups, made possible a less restrictive enrollment policy. Insurance premiums are based on average experience—average levels of health and average utilization of medical services. The issue of whose experience is to be included in that average—whether of the entire population, of all subscribers, or of the employees of the particular employment-based enrolled group—is of critical importance in setting rates. But although the definition of the average may be debated, the concept of an average is fundamental. Clearly, the larger the group, the less significant the individual case. Thus the premium rate for a group of one thousand would hardly be affected by the presence or absence of one high-risk subscriber. When the entire group is enrolled, the few who will be sick are joined with the many who will be healthy.

This, however, is not the case with individual enrollment. Individuals may self-select. At given average premium rates, the individual who anticipates above-average utilization will find insurance more advantageous than will the potential subscriber who expects to be a low user. Inevitably the high-risk user will be more likely and the low user less likely to enroll. When the low user does not enroll, the average utilization of subscribers will rise, as will the premium, which has been based on a mix of enrollees. Insurance companies, necessarily concerned about the possibility that self-selection would increase average utilization, costs, and premiums, attempt to limit their risk exposure by restricting coverage, that is, by not including coverage for "preexisting conditions" and the costs associated with their treatment. Such restrictions are not necessary under group enrollment, where the law of large numbers applies and self-selection is less important.

Group coverage offered two additional advantages over individual enrollment. Health insurance companies offered a range of policies, each with different benefits and premiums. It was difficult to compare the various options and to determine which was a better or best buy. Few individuals are able to assess the impact of demographic variables (such as age and sex), health factors (such as health risks and health history), and the characteristics of the medical care system (such as hospital costs and patterns of specialization) on premiums. Nor can individuals be fully informed about the performance of particular insurers, such as the speed with which they handle claims or their administrative capability. Group enrollment made it possible for an employer or employee representative to gather relevant information, perhaps even to negotiate with the insurer on matters of concern to the members of the group.

The final advantage of group enrollment under union and management contracts related to tax provisions. Because employer contributions to health insurance were not taxable as income, the effective price of health insurance was reduced—but only if one's employer paid all or part of the premium. This advantage to group enrollment via collective bargaining, together with the factors already mentioned, helped foster group enrollment and the employment-based health insurance we have today.

The influence of the way the tax system allocates its rewards and exacts its penalties should never be underestimated. Just as home ownership is stimulated by the deductibility of mortgage interest and local property tax payments, so the development of health insurance was stimulated by the tax code. But in addition the code provided an incentive that shaped a particular (and inequitable) set of institutional arrangements. It did not assist individual enrollment or even group enrollment per se (such as neighborhood, religious, or fraternal associations). Rather, it subsidized the purchase of health insurance only when the employer paid the premium. It thus linked health insurance to employment. In doing so, the tax code molded the nature of American health insurance, its availability and distribution. In extending benefits to some, the tax code discriminated against others.

Greater equity could have been obtained (at the cost of administrative complexity) if the tax code had not had an employment bias. For example, the code might have permitted a tax deduction or, since deductions provide more dollar benefits to individuals facing higher marginal tax rates, a credit for health insurance premium payments individuals made on their own behalf (a tax deduction for part of the cost of health insurance premiums, available to individuals who itemized their deductions, was enacted in 1965 but repealed in 1981). Group enrollees would still have enjoyed lower premiums, and employment-based groups would have remained more attractive; but other groups, community or neighborhood based and appealing to those not linked by employment, might have sprung up. A system that permitted individuals to claim deductions would have made the tax subsidy available to all, including those for whom the employer would not pay. Such a system would not have solved all problems. Low-income earners and the unemployed would not have had the means to pay for comprehensive health insurance (except via a tax credit and treasury payment to the taxpayer if the credit exceeded the tax due). Nevertheless, such an arrangement would have been more inclusive and fairer.

The system that developed did have the virtues of simplicity and of convenience. Insurers already had relationships with employers; organized labor saw insurance as an area within which to expand its bargaining efforts; employers were not averse to keeping the wage base low by substituting health insurance for hourly wage increments (inflation in health costs had not yet hit with force). Above all, there was already an institutional framework. The tax code built upon the past and extended those arrangements. The poor, the unemployed, the employees without health insurance, those who were left out— and they were many—were voiceless. And so it was that employment-based health insurance spread across the land.

The immediate postwar years, a period of full employment and of rapid growth in real incomes, provided a fertile ground for the expansion of health insurance. Furthermore, the perceived need for and utility of health insurance grew at the same time. Medicine was changing. A new knowledge base was being created. The hospital was rapidly being transformed from a largely custodial institution into an institution in which diagnostic tests were performed, interventions were undertaken, and dramatic things were happening.

Hospitals were being built and the supply of beds was increasing. The Hospital Survey and Construction Act (the Hill-Burton Act) was enacted in 1946. This major piece of legislation erected a structure of decentralized state hospital planning activities, and the accompanying appropriations helped fund the capital needs associated with hospital construction. The new or expanded hospitals had more advanced laboratories, equipment, and operating theaters. They had more staff per bed, more employees per patient. They were new and different and more efficient—and they were much more expensive. The costs of care, particularly of hospital care, were increasing, and care was worth having—it could make a difference.

Personal health care expenditures rose from $26 per year per capita in 1940 to $93 in 1955. Hospital care, which had accounted for one-quarter of all personal health care expenditures in 1940, absorbed one-third of the health dollar in 1955.[17] In response to the increase in medical expenditures, the middle class bought more health insurance (especially hospital coverage) to help finance valuable and expensive services. In turn, the presence of insurance helped underwrite and increase the level of expenditures.

Illness which was unpredictable for the individual but predictable for the larger group, interventions which were effective but costly and for which the individual could not budget, rising incomes and standards of living, public policy affecting labor-management bargaining and taxation: all combined to speed the growth of health insurance and especially of hospital-expense insurance.

In a successful effort to derail a proposed state health insurance program, California physicians had developed an insurance program for physicians' services in 1939. Out of this program there grew what is now known as Blue Shield. Supported by Blue Cross, which was especially concerned about the competitive advantage of commercial health insurers, who could cover physician as well as hospital services, Blue Shield expanded in the postwar period. Blue Cross and Blue Shield were similar in some respects (for example, both were provider dominated) but different in others. Blue Shield was not service benefit oriented (except for low-income patients) nor did it attempt to reach out to the total community for subscribers. In part this posture reflected the fact that whereas Blue Cross tried to protect hospital budgets against the risk of unpaid bills, the danger posed by large bad debts to the individual physician was not as great. Physicians could exercise more control and limit risk by encouraging patients who might not pay their bills to seek care elsewhere. In part, the difference between Blue Cross and Blue Shield reflected the fact that the former had been embraced by the American Hospital Association but the latter won only grudging acceptance from the American Medical Association. The AMA had long tried to assure a dominant role for the individual, self-employed physician. In its view, fees were part of the private relationship between patient and doctor.

Commercial health insurance grew even more rapidly than Blue Cross in the postwar period. It had various market advantages over Blue Cross, some of which related to the philosophy and origin of Blue Cross programs. The Blues, sponsored by hospitals and a part of the medical community, offered service benefits: x days of hospital care (say, in a semiprivate room) per year. This service benefit and the premium that paid for it protected the hospital (except for any additional uncovered charges or for any deductible for which the patient might be responsible). Furthermore, service benefits accorded with the medical community's belief that the physician, hospital, and patient should function in a world in which service decisions (at least for the hospital patient) would be unconstrained by their financial implications. But service benefits are, by their very nature, comprehensive and expensive. The commercial insurers, able to offer a range of cash-indemnity benefits at different premium rates, had a clear competitive advantage, which allowed them greater flexibility. They could offer coverage of lesser scope at lower premiums and could maintain stable premium levels during periods of increasing hospital costs.

The structure of premiums gave commercial insurers an even more significant competitive advantage. Blue Cross traditionally had based its rates on the utilization of hospital services in the community of all subscribers. The average included the utilization of high- and low-risk individuals, of sick and healthy, of young and old. For Blue Cross, communitywide pooling of risk, like the provision of service benefits, was a matter of philosophy. True, this mechanism involved a subsidy from some members of the community, generally younger and healthier, to others who were likely to use more medical care. But such a pooling of risk was a virtue. It helped extend coverage to individuals who would otherwise be priced out of the market. Since Blue Cross plans were the beneficiaries of special enabling legislation, they felt, and were felt to have, a special responsibility to extend their program as widely as possible. Community rating, the setting of a single communitywide premium, though not a legal requirement, was one way to meet that responsibility. Also, so long as hospitals felt a responsibility to care for patients regardless of their financial condition, they had an incentive to use a rate-setting system that expanded insurance coverage.

Community rating involved a subsidy. Since the American health insurance system was private and noncompulsory, the subsidy or transfer was also voluntary rather than a tax that all must pay. Voluntary subsidies must be acceptable to those who foot the bill or they must be disguised so that those who pay them are unaware that they are doing so. The conditions that make for acceptability involve attitudes about community and sharing, as well as ethical judgments. Undoubtedly one's willingness to provide help to others will also depend on the size of the subsidy and the ease with which one can opt out, that is, deny help to others while still capturing benefits for oneself. It is, for example, difficult for a voluntary retirement system to build in a transfer from high-income to low-income individuals, since the more affluent may opt out. Conversely, the compulsory Social Security system can provide a minimum benefit in excess of the wage-related level.

When Blue Cross was established, those who wanted to purchase hospital insurance were faced with a community-rating scheme that provided a subsidy to the high-risk members of the community. That is the nature of the community pooling of risk, and Blue Cross had virtually no competitors. As time went on, commercial insurers entered the field and quickly found that they could expand their market share by segmenting the market and basing their premiums on the health experience of the particular group with which they were dealing. If the group was one with lower-than-average risks—if, for example, it included few elderly—the experience-rated premium could be reduced below, perhaps even far below, the communitywide rate.

Imagine that a commercial carrier came to a group of advertising agency employees. These individuals had jobs, were under age sixty-five, were not engaged in a hazardous occupation, and had above-average incomes. Their health experience was likely to be better than that of the community at large or that of all subscribers (some of whom might be unemployed, elderly, high-risk, and low-income individuals). Given the risk selection, the commercial carrier could offer coverage to agency employees at, say, $90 rather than the prevailing Blue Cross community rate of $100. Competition, based on risk selection not on administrative efficiency, had its impact. Individual groups struck their own bargains with commercial insurers. Even if the advertising agency employees, out of a feeling of social responsibility and willingness to define themselves and higher-risk individuals as part of the same community, declined to shift to the $90 premium, there were others who did so. When they did, the Blue Cross rate had to increase. Some of the healthy had pulled out; on average, those who remained were sicker.

The outcome is clear and inevitable. Now the commercial insurer could return to those who once had rejected the lower premium and say: "A month ago we would have charged you $90 while Blue Cross cost $100. Today we're still at $90 but Blue Cross is at $105. Community commitment is an admirable trait, but surely there's a limit." As differentials and, therefore, the size of the required subsidy grew, fewer individuals were willing to provide it.

They could find many rationales to justify their action. Some firms preferred to deal with one insurer for all their insurance (say, life, medical care, disability, and fire). Commercial insurers offered many insurance programs, but Blue Cross and Blue Shield sold only one. Furthermore, many national firms were attracted to commercial insurance companies that operated nationwide rather than to Blue Cross/ Blue Shield plans, which covered individual states (or even smaller areas). In addition, and undoubtedly of great significance, many firms believed that the premium differentials in favor of commercial insurers reflected administrative efficiencies rather than the advantages of risk selection. Free-market ideology argued that those efficiencies should be rewarded.

Undoubtedly there were firms that understood the process of risk selection, the fragmentation of the community that inevitably implied that above-average risks (the aged, the poor, the sick) would face higher and higher premiums. They may have been aware that these were the very people whose incomes were lower than average. They saw the dual problem: low income and high risk of medical expenditures. Yet even as they recognized that their own behavior magnified the problem, they could shun responsibility for its solution. After all, weren't the problems of low-income or high-risk individuals more reasonably addressed by a more comprehensive governmental approach? Why rely on private support from some employers and employees, while others were permitted to shirk their community obligation? Why be a nice guy in a world in which nice guys finish last—or at least have a less favorable balance sheet?

The market competition between commercial insurers and Blue Cross, expressed in the difference between community rating and experience rating, had an inexorable quality. Two philosophies, two approaches, two definitions of society were in contention. One philosophy viewed society as a group of individuals, all searching to advance themselves and maximize their own well-being. In the economic arena this approach called for market competition. Experience rating was the consequence. The other philosophy viewed society as an entity unto itself, composed of something more than individuals, and stressed social well-being. Its community rather than individualistic view argued for cooperation rather than competition and for community rating. Americans (perhaps especially American liberals) have found both views appealing. Sometimes one view dominates, sometimes the other. We have resorted to pragmatism to help resolve our ambivalence.

Commercial insurers were neither evil nor irresponsible. Operating within the American tradition, they offered a product to those who would purchase it at a price associated with the cost of providing it to that defined group. Nor were Blue Cross plans so inclusive that they could be considered paragons of virtue. Even with community rating, many Americans were unable to afford hospital insurance. After all, subsidies provided on a voluntary basis and operating through the private sector could average small differences in risk but could not effectively address large differences in income, employment patterns, or the additional costs of nongroup enrollment.

The competition between experience and community rating took place in the marketplace, in the competition for subscribers. Competition offers a prize to those who win the race. But if we view life as only a race, we are not likely to assist those who lag behind, lest in helping them to finish we lose the prize. It would be years before the impact on the elderly of the competition in the 1940s and the 1950s became clear and prompted government intervention (for government, not the market, is the institution that attempts to further social justice) through the enactment of the Medicare program. Even so, the American free-market orientation, with its emphasis on competition rather than on cooperation, has kept most of us so busy running that we have not fully noticed the many nonelderly (and, even with Medicare, the many elderly) not strong enough to make it on their own.

Behind the actuary's numbers stand definitions. Those definitions—

who is included and who excluded—express our attitudes about community and responsibility to our fellows. Underlying what is considered a technical or definitional issue is a philosophy. And it is not the technician who develops the definition or philosophy. We citizens must determine the goal we seek. At best, the technician can describe the different ways that we might get there.

This account of two contending philosophies—individual versus group, community versus exclusivity, cooperation versus competition—seems to be about to replay itself. We are again faced with proposals for private and for public actions that would segment the market, increase the advantages of risk selection, and penalize those most in need of help. We are still debating the definition of community and issues of social justice. The battle for our minds and hearts continues.

3

The Unrealized Dream:
Government Insurance for All

Losing, we are often told, builds character: such is allegedly the case on high-school football fields. But in the marketplace, survival, not character, is the issue—and it was in the marketplace, where moral victories are irrelevant, that the Blues and their competitors fought their battle. The profit-and-loss statement imposes its own constraints, and survival in a market economy requires selling a product in competition with others, not giving it away. Whatever the differences between experience and community rating, service and indemnity benefits, for-profit and not-for-profit companies, both the Blues and the commercials had to meet the same market test.

Market competition imposed a penalty on those who offered even the limited redistribution inherent in community rating and the broader definition of group risk. It obviously precluded competing insurers from equalizing the impact of income differences on the availability of insurance and on access to care. Insurance companies, like other business enterprises, were not designed to be engines of redistribution. They could not offer coverage to those who could not pay the price. Such individuals would have to seek help elsewhere.

The problems and gaps inherent in a voluntary approach, in the outcome of competition between organizations whose survival required that they sell at prices that covered costs, was clear and had been so for many years. As a consequence, health insurance debates, which had a rich history, did not always assume a purely voluntary, free market approach to the provision of insurance to low-income individuals. Indeed, even before the First World War many social reformers looked to government to develop a medical care insurance program. They discussed and debated the establishment of a system of compulsory health insurance, something that today we might call national health insurance (NHI), arguing that it was one of several important social (not individual) protection mechanisms required to take account of wide income differentials generated in an increasingly industrial society.

Over the last seventy-five years, the various proposals for NHI have taken different forms and have elicited different levels of support. At times the debate was mainly rhetorical, producing resolutions that national health insurance would be "good for America." At times it was concerned with specific legislative proposals. Yet always, though varying in intensity, there was debate. National health insurance has demonstrated a remarkable staying power, leading to two opposite conclusions: that, since the concept of NHI has survived for three-quarters of a century, it can't be all bad; or that, since it has not been enacted over such a span of time, it must be fatally flawed. Indeed, NHI's continuing presence on the public policy agenda is best explained by the facts that those interested in the welfare of all members of society (and in the strength of the society itself) have recognized the limitations of a purely voluntary approach to health insurance coverage but that legislation involving redistribution of resources and reorganization of markets is difficult to enact. None of the advances in protection developed so far—Blue Cross and Blue Shield, commercial health insurance, prepaid health plans, Medicare, Medicaid—has solved the problem of the "have-nots" and, therefore, resolved the debate about the appropriate role for government.

FROM STATE HOUSE TO CONGRESS

The first attempts to enact legislation occurred at the state level. Building upon the successful efforts to institute state workmen's compensation measures designed to provide financial protection against employment-associated accidents and illness, the American Association for Labor Legislation, with initial cooperation from the AMA, actively developed model health insurance legislation. This insurance provided for the costs of medical care, income maintenance during illness, and funeral expenses (hardly offering reassurance about the efficacy of medical care). During the latter part of the decade 1910–1920, health insurance bills were introduced in twelve state legislatures. Optimists anticipated favorable action—if not in all states, then at least in New York and California, where the discussion was most vigorous.[1] As was to be the case time and time again in years to follow, the optimists were incorrect. Why?

When legislation fails, it may do so for many reasons. Some of the factors appear quite accidental: something quite unexpected, perhaps not even germane to the legislation or to its prospects, interferes, distracts attention, or calls for a change in priorities. Other legislation fails because of disagreement about the validity of its objectives or because it is flawed and the debate reveals those flaws. The objectives may be agreed upon but laws are not merely statements of objectives. They define the actions that are deemed necessary to attain the goal. Still other legislation fails because various interest groups oppose it or because it lacks a constituency—a broad base of support, enough people who care enough to say they care—or both. Vocal popular support may not assure political success, but its absence does increase the probability of failure.

That popular voice was lacking seventy years ago. There had been no significant educational effort directed at either the people or their representatives. True, state legislation was supported by various international unions and some state federations of labor, but it was opposed by Samuel Gompers, president of the American Federation of Labor, who believed in gaining benefits through union strength and power, not through legislation. True, legislation was supported by the AMA, but it was vigorously opposed by state medical societies. Harry A. Millis, a former president of the American Economic Association, wrote in 1938:

> The success of the opposition to the proposed legislation was due more to self-interest on the part of many organizations, to fear, to misunderstanding, to wilful misrepresentation, to the charge that it was German [a severe indictment in the period around the First World War], and to the fact that the country had not been prepared by investigation and discussion for a system of health insurance than to any of the weaknesses in what was proposed. Instead of such a system being seen as effecting little more than an assembling of existing costs, it was generally regarded as something that would add an enormous and unsupportable burden. It was denounced as unnecessary, socialistic, un-American, a wrong method of attack—sickness prevention was what was needed. It would beget simulation and malingering; it would involve contract medicine, reduce the income of the doctors, destroy the close personal relationship between doctor and patient, and discourage and undermine medical research. It was not working well in Europe. Such were the more important

sources of opposition and the most frequently voiced objections which, in the absence of a strong, coherent, actively interested group, brought to an early end the first period in an American health-insurance movement.[2]

A system of medical care insurance, it seems, is like cherry pie: many like it in the abstract, but when they taste it some find it too sweet, others too tart, too firm or soggy, too fruity, or too doughy. Legislation requires specific constructs that tell us "how"; introductory "whereas" clauses that tell us "why" do not suffice. But it is around specifics that opposition is mobilized—from those with a differing ideology; from those who believe that, as drafted, the legislation will not work; from those who argue that its benefits will fall short of its costs; from those whose actions would be regulated or constrained; from those who would be unfavorably affected.

Although it is easy to discern various factors that prevented action on state health insurance measures in the decade 1910–1920, it is important to resist the temptation to apply today's analysis of issues and problems to that period. By today's standards, the model bills were limited and hardly radical. Many of the words used were similar to those used today, but their meaning was tied to different attitudes, reflecting a different dimension and definition of the health care problem. The hospital played a smaller role, medical care was less effective and less expensive, and charity care played a greater part.

Although physicians as well as hospitals varied their fees and charges in accordance with their (sometimes accurate, sometimes fallacious) assessment of the patient's ability to pay, charging less to some than to others, the proponents of legislation sensed that the growing costs of medical services would increase inequality in the receipt of care. They also recognized that eventually the increasing effectiveness of medicine would make unequal receipt of care a source of social tension and unequal delivery of care a source of professional discomfort. In 1915, however, these issues were only emerging; they were not yet part of public discourse.

Thus a special opportunity was lost. For, if the problems were not yet severe, neither was the technical complexity required to solve them. A simpler and less expensive health system implied a simpler and less expensive insurance structure. But the political process seems unwilling to address the problems that beset us until they become critical and complex. It is as if simple questions need no answer and complex questions have no acceptable answer; short of crisis we need not act, yet in a crisis we often are paralyzed. Nineteen-fifteen was a time to act—as other nations already had. But the moment passed. In 1918 health insurance was defeated in a California referendum. In 1919 the New York state senate enacted a health insurance bill, but the state assembly refused to send it out of committee to the floor for a vote. The AMA officially reversed its favorable stand in 1920.[3]

In retrospect it seems odd that proponents were so confident of success that they failed to educate the public, build constituencies, and search for allies. Yet various other efforts since then to enact national health insurance have been characterized by the same overconfidence. Apparently it is easy for those who favor particular legislation to be persuaded by the logic of their position, to assume that others will also be persuaded, and thus to believe that logic or a just cause that cannot be denied will translate to votes. Apparently it is easy to forget that the political arena has its own logic and that legislators have their own ways of analyzing public and private costs and benefits. The desire to be reelected does not influence academic "scribblers." It does influence legislators.

The period following the early efforts to enact compulsory medical care insurance legislation was a time of research, study, and education, the necessary (though hardly sufficient) precursors to successful action. It culminated in the establishment, through the support of eight private foundations, of the Committee on the Costs of Medical Care (CCMC) in 1927. This "commission of inquiry" was composed of some fifty members drawn from private medical practice, public health, economics and sociology, institutions and special interests concerned with the medical field, and the "general public"—whose representatives, as is so often the case, were so distinguished that they could hardly be considered representative.

In the period 1928–1932 the CCMC published twenty-eight reports on the health status of Americans, the incidence of illness, and the costs of medical care. Methodologically, these studies were quite different from studies that might be undertaken on similar subjects today. With no computers available, the statistical analyses were necessarily more elementary. Furthermore, the social science disciplines that provided the intellectual framework of the reports were more descriptive and less analytical than is the case today. In 1932 the emphasis was on the "social"; today it is the "science" that receives primary attention. Nevertheless, the CCMC reports strove for and achieved the highest existing professional standards. They represented the most thorough review of the medical care sector and the needs of the population yet undertaken, an organized review that has not since been matched in size and scope.

The final CCMC report was adopted October 31, 1932. It contained five broad recommendations, a list of specific and detailed proposals, two minority reports, and two personal statements. The entire volume was reprinted in 1970 by the Department of Health, Education, and Welfare with a preface stating that the old problems still remained and that "Now is the time for action!"[5]

Many of the CCMC recommendations were accepted by all of the committee members: there was agreement on the need for high-quality care, adequate remuneration of professional personnel, coordination of medical services, and strengthening of public health activities. The committee also endorsed the responsibility of government for veterans, armed forces, and other special population groups (including the indigent); financial support for the expansion of health resources in sparsely settled areas; and the separation, under insurance, of the receipt of medical services from the certification of eligibility.

Unfortunately but perhaps inevitably, the committee split on its two major recommendations. The majority advocated the provision of medical service largely through organized groups of practitioners, but a number of physician members disagreed. Moreover, although eleven members endorsed government-sponsored compulsory insurance, the majority wanted to finance the costs of care through voluntary group prepayment. Yet even while endorsing voluntarism, the majority recognized its limitations:

> Families with low or irregular incomes, even if they are self-supporting while employed, cannot usually be covered by any form of voluntary insurance. The experience with voluntary insurance in other countries has generally led to the conclusion that persons employed in small businesses or self-employed are also unlikely to enter a voluntary plan, unless they see a saving to them personally or a likelihood of better care. For these reasons, voluntary health insurance has been succeeded by compulsory insurance in most of the countries of western Europe.
>
> The use of the state's power of making membership in a sickness scheme obligatory for large groups of persons increases the population served and also reduces the administrative cost of securing and retaining members. The Committee recognizes that the distribution of the costs

of medical care will not become widespread in some communities, or for certain sections of the population in many communities, unless there is legislation which makes the distribution of these costs compulsory.[6]

Nevertheless, having indicted voluntarism and stepped up to the brink, the majority concluded that the time was not yet ripe and turned back: "The majority of the Committee, although aware of the limitations of coverage and the possible difficulties of voluntary health insurance, nevertheless believe that the ultimate results will be far better if experience with actuarial and administrative details, and above all the evolution of group practice units capable of rendering rounded medical service of high quality, precede the adoption of any compulsory plan by a state as a whole."[7]

This latter view prompted Walton Hamilton, an economist and professor of law at Yale, to append a strong personal statement to the report. He argued—in words that those invited to serve on advisory committees would do well to note—that the attempt to achieve consensus was ill conceived:

> The document represents what all who have signed are willing to accept rather than what any individual would have written . . . It is, however, unfortunate that the spirit of tolerance, admirable as it is, should have been so largely indulged. Its manifestation in the treatment of major matters and minor details on the same level, the resort to general but indefinite principles, the setting down of propositions in which the nouns give and the adjectives take away, are far too numerous. If the Committee were a formal agency, charged with the formulation of a constructive program, compromise would be justified as essential to action. But the task of the Committee is to study, to analyze, to investigate, and to report; it has no power to institute a single desirable reform; its labors can be converted into a better organization for medicine only through its influence upon groups who have authority to act. This end, it seems to me, would have been far better served, by cleancut— and even uncompromising—presentation of alternative programs. The sacrifice in analysis and precision to unanimity among the members of the majority may well give a greater influence to the recommendations. But the gain is only immediate, and the problem is likely to be with us for years to come. In the end, the views of the Committee must prevail— so far as they do prevail—not because of the number of names attached, but because they commend themselves to the persons who may come to have the power to act. The gain in immediate appeal is bought too dearly when its price is the sacrifice of more durable values.[8]

In an effort to achieve consensus, the committee had endorsed voluntary health insurance. But Hamilton disagreed:

> So, it seems to me, that the scheme called compulsory health insurance is the very minimum which this Committee should have recommended. Its irregular incidence, and the practical difficulties in the way of budgeting, make necessary some type of collective provision against sickness. Furthermore, we have not as yet found a way to assure to all workers a minimum wage or to abolish insecurity from the economic order; and, so long as income is fitful and uncertain, it cannot provide an adequate basis for the financial maintenance of medical services. Besides, for a long time to come we are to have with us, groups whose meager incomes will permit no contribution to a fund for the maintenance of health. In this scheme I should be disposed to attempt to accommodate the venerable principle of medicine, "to each according to his needs, from each according to his ability to pay," to modern conditions. The service should be available to all, either without charge, or upon the payment of a small fee designed to prevent frivolous use. All members should pay an annual charge towards the support of the service. A person belonging to the lower income group would pay only a nominal amount; a person with a moderate income would be assessed at a rate which would make the venture self-supporting; persons in the higher income groups should be taxed at graduated rates in accordance with the traditional principle of the sliding scale. The whole would represent an accommodation of the traditional system of medical payment to the conditions of the modern world in which we live.[9]

Hamilton's was an articulate but lonely voice. The CCMC behaved as most committees do: it sought consensus through compromise. Yet even so, there was dissent. Those representing the private practice of medicine objected to the recommendation on group practice, and, having won the battle over compulsory insurance, they then opposed voluntary insurance plans unless sponsored and controlled by organized medicine. They argued that the proponents of a compulsory insurance program had documented the inadequacies of the voluntary response, and that those who endorsed the voluntary insurance approach had demonstrated why compulsory insurance would not work. Since neither the voluntary nor compulsory approach was appropriate, the answer, they argued, must lie elsewhere: in actions by the medical profession itself. That minority view was supported by the AMA, whose journal carried an editorial that defined two camps: ". . . on the one side [are] the forces representing the great foundations, public health officialdom, social theory—even socialism and communism—inciting to revolution." In 1915, health insurance had been attacked because it had originated in Germany. In 1932 the country of origin for "alien" ideas was the Soviet Union. Ranked against these alien forces—one would hardly have guessed that they supported voluntary rather than compulsory health insurance and saw only a limited role for government—was a small and lonely band, "the organized medical profession of this country."[10]

The CCMC reports and recommendations of the early 1930s helped thrust the issue of the costs of medical care into the political spotlight. Although the recommendations did not lead to action, they did assist in defining the problem, providing information, and structuring the debate. In contrast with the earlier political action focused on state capitols, this debate took place in Washington. The nation was now in the Great Depression, and Americans had begun to look to the federal government for help. Under Franklin Delano Roosevelt, Washington had become the place in which to address problems that were national in scope. And access to health care was a national problem.

Economic recovery and the reduction of unemployment were the most urgent items on the political agenda, but the crisis of economic insecurity faced by millions of Americans also demanded immediate attention. Private resources and private charities were unable to cope with the dimensions of the problem. The various government buffers that now help protect us, such as unemployment insurance, old age and survivor benefits under the Social Security system, aid to families with dependent children, and food stamps, were not yet part of the American social and economic fabric. The crisis situation spawned executive and legislative initiatives unmatched in quantity and quality before or since, even by the attempt to create "the Great Society" in the mid 1960s.

Roosevelt was inaugurated in March 1933. In June 1934 he appointed a cabinet-level Committee on Economic Security charged with developing a program to deal with "the major hazards and vicissitudes of life which cannot be wholly eliminated in this man made world of ours."[11] The committee operated under a timetable far different from the kind we are familiar with today: its recommendations were received in time to be embodied in legislation introduced in January 1935. Nor did the process slow down at that point: the Social Security Act was signed into law in August of the same year. The crisis situation and Roosevelt's concern "about the offensive against his administration, not from those who thought it was doing too much, but from those who thought it was doing too little," resulted in this burst of speed.[12] Although the original Social Security Act did not include many of the programs that now are part of the Social Security system, the measure was comprehensive in scope: it provided a tax mechanism to stimulate the development of state unemployment insurance programs, aid to the states for old-age assistance, an old-age insurance program (the program most of us think of when we speak of Social Security), federal aid for dependent children, grants for maternal and child-health activities, crippled children's services, and rural child welfare services.[13]

But although some had hoped it would be otherwise, the Social Security legislation did not provide for a general system of medical benefits. Led by organized medicine, the opposition to inclusion of such benefits was formidable, and the cabinet committee and its staff were concerned that the inclusion of health insurance would jeopardize enactment of the entire measure. The committee could go no further than to recommend "a Nation-wide preventive public-health program" and to promise further study and a later report on health insurance. The members set a severe constraint on future recommendations when they noted that "we contemplate no action that will not be quite as much in the interests of the members of the professions concerned as of the families with low incomes."[14]

Human beings have a remarkable capacity to rationalize adversity. Thus, it was argued that old age insurance, providing for cash benefits to an easily defined population, was a significant advance. Though incomplete, it could be built upon and extended. With the Social Security system in place, it would be that much easier to mobilize public support for medical insurance. That, after all, was the logical next step, the remaining priority item. And there were grounds for optimism: did not the growth of voluntary health insurance demonstrate the public's desire for medical protection; did not this suggest that, in time, an aroused electorate would demand action?

The period between the enactment of Social Security in 1935 and America's entry into the war in 1941 was in fact one of considerable activity on behalf of medical insurance. Commissions, committees, and task forces met and released surveys, reports, and recommendations. In Washington as elsewhere, the importance of a problem is often measured by the number of committees appointed to study and discuss it and the number of meetings convened to debate it. By that standard—"of course, it's an important issue; why else would we meet once a week for three years to talk about it?"—health insurance had become important. In 1939 health insurance legislation providing a key role for the federal government was introduced by Senator Robert Wagner, Democrat from New York, whose name was already attached to the Wagner Act, the major piece of labor legislation of the decade.

But again no health insurance legislation was enacted. Supporters of health insurance measures had to derive their satisfaction from the structure of the debate rather than from its outcome. They had to draw strength from the fact that, pressed by social, medical, and economic change, the nature of the debate had changed. From the 1920s through 1932, when the CCMC issued its final reports, the argument had been about the validity, utility, and acceptability of medical insurance. Those issues were settled during the 1930s. With the rapid growth of Blue Cross and commercial health insurance and their acceptance by the American middle class, the question was no longer whether insurance was the answer but what kind of insurance would best meet the nation's needs.

The "whereas" clauses that are the preamble to a law elicit little debate; the "how" clauses that embody the law are what divide proponents and opponents, for underlying them are values and ideologies. One side's favored solution stands in opposition to another's basic principle. Surely, it is an advance to define the issue for debate. It does help if we all recognize and address the same problem. But we are naive if we believe that with that agreement we bury ideology. In the debate over health insurance, questions of sponsorship (government or organized medicine) and of coverage (compulsory or voluntary, universal or income related), matters of principle and ideology, lay at the heart of the controversy.

In 1932 the CCMC report called for voluntary action at the state and local levels. Even then, the recommendations were addressed to the wrong parties. The depression had forced the federal government to the fore, and the debate would be held in Washington, not in the forty-eight state capitals. But Washington in the late 1930s was not the Washington of 1935: the sense of urgency was waning, and so was the president's power. International events assumed priority. By 1939 Europe was at war. On December 7, 1941, Japan attacked Pearl Harbor.

During the war a succession of comprehensive, compulsory health insurance measures was introduced in the House and Senate. Of these, the Wagner-Murray-Dingell bill (sponsored by Senator Wagner, Senator James Murray, Democrat from Montana, and Congressman John D. Dingell, Sr., Democrat from Michigan) received the most attention. It proved useful in keeping the issue of the financing of medical care on the public agenda. Nevertheless, even this distinguished sponsorship could not substitute for presidential involvement, and that was missing. In the United States the war years were not a time for the enactment of national health insurance legislation.

Yet ideas and attitudes were changing. The experience of the depression had caused the voluntary efforts suggested by the CCMC to be superseded by calls for federal grants-in-aid programs to the states. Now the supporters of health insurance were growing disenchanted with the kind of partnership under which the states implemented programs and the federal government paid the bill. The favorable experience with old age insurance under the Social Security Act led proponents of government health insurance to shift their support to a wholly federal program.

Action awaited the end of the war and the personal involvement of President Harry Truman. Thirteen years had passed between the report of the CCMC in 1932 and Truman's endorsement of national health insurance in 1945. The CCMC recommendations on financing were now outdated. New times required and permitted new approaches. The issue of compulsory health insurance, foreshadowed but not joined in 1932, was to occupy center stage. It was to be a vigorous and vituperative debate.

THE "FAIR DEAL" AND HEALTH INSURANCE

On the north bank of the Thames in London, not far from the Houses of Parliament whose members in 1946 enacted legislation creating the British National Health Service, stands the Tate Gallery. In the Tate hangs a painting by an Englishman, Sir Luke Fildes, a painting that played a part in U.S. political history. Today millions of Americans watch British-produced programs on their television sets. In 1950 millions gazed upon reproductions of the painting and read a text that Whitaker and Baxter, a California public relations firm hired by the AMA, had added below it. This curious example of Anglo-American cooperation was part of the successful political campaign against Truman's proposal for government health insurance.[15]

"The Doctor," dating from the 1840s, shows a physician at the bed of a sick child. The hour is late, the room is dark, the only light that of a dim oil lamp. The child sleeps with fevered brow; the concerned doctor sits beside the child watching, thinking, waiting. The parents are in the background. It is a quiet painting, part of a historical record.

The Whitaker and Baxter text does not hang in the Tate. Nor is it found in American doctors' offices as was the case almost forty years ago. It, too, is a historical document, but in contrast with the painting, it is a noisy text—sharp and grating:

> KEEP POLITICS OUT OF THIS PICTURE
> When the life—or health of a loved one is at stake, hope lies in the devoted service of your Doctor. Would you change this picture?
> Compulsory health insurance is political medicine.
> It would bring a third party—a politician—between you and your Doctor. It would bind up your family's health in red tape. It would result in heavy payroll taxes—and inferior medical care for you and your family. Don't let that happen here![16]

The painting and the text formed a central element in the AMA's National Education Campaign against President Truman's proposals. This well-organized and well-funded effort against "socialized medicine" and its supporters, "The Federal Security Administration [the correct word was Agency], the President; all who seriously believe in a Socialistic State; every left-wing organization in America . . . The Communist Party,"[17] was to prove successful.

Truman had endorsed national health insurance in 1945 and supported it in the following years. What the New Deal had ignored, the Fair Deal now embraced. In 1948 it was one of the cornerstones of Truman's campaign against Thomas Dewey and the Republican-dominated "do-nothing Eightieth Congress." When, to the surprise of all the experts, Truman was reelected, compulsory health insurance was assured a place on the political agenda.

The president based his 1948 proposal on a report by Oscar Ewing, administrator of the Federal Security Agency. Today the words "Federal Security Agency" evoke images of investigatory or clandestine activities. Then, "security" connoted things related to the social well-being of Americans: the Public Health Service, the Office of Education, the Social Security Administration, and the Employment Service (except for the last, activities taken over by the Department of Health, Education, and Welfare when it was created in 1953). Truman's health insurance proposal was designed to cover the entire population and to provide a comprehensive set of medical benefits: physician, dental, and nursing-home care; sixty days of hospital care per year; drugs and auxiliary services. Although the proposal described the benefits specifically, it was vague about how the revenues necessary to finance the program would be raised.

This lack of specificity was deliberate. A bill submitted by a member of the House or Senate must be referred to the committee that has jurisdiction over the subject that the bill addresses. The bill may die in committee (with or without hearings) or may undergo substantial modification before reaching the House or Senate floor for debate. Those who propose legislation must consider how their bills will fare in committee.

It was clear that, as with Social Security cash benefits, the many dollars necessary for Truman's health insurance program would have to be raised through a special earmarked tax. Inclusion of a payroll tax (or other tax mechanism) would have moved the legislation to the committees that dealt with taxation (the House Ways and Means Committee and the Senate Finance Committee). Omission of the financing mechanism permitted the bill to be considered as health rather than tax legislation. Aware that the finance committees would be more hostile to the proposal than the committees that dealt with social legislation, the administration submitted the legislation without specifying financing and taxing mechanisms.

Years later, in 1970, a similar approach was used by Senator Ralph Yarborough, Democrat from Texas and chairman of the Senate Labor and Public Welfare Committee, a longtime proponent of national health insurance who wanted to hold hearings on the subject before he left the Senate. Senator Edward Kennedy's national health insurance program, the Health Security Act, S.4297, submitted earlier that year, called for payroll taxes and accordingly had been referred to the Senate Finance Committee, where it languished. Yarborough stripped the Health Security Act of its financing mechanism and substituted a new section, which read: "For the purpose of carrying out any of the programs, functions, or activities authorized by this Act . . . there are authorized to be appropriated for each fiscal year such sums as may be necessary."[18] To be financed out of general revenues, this "new" Health Security Act, S.4323, transformed S.4297 into a health measure. As a result it was referred to the Senate Labor and Public Welfare Committee, where hearings were convened. Yarborough, like Truman earlier, achieved his goal not by breaking but by mastering the Senate rules and procedures.

The measure supported by President Truman in 1948, a revised Wagner-Murray-Dingell bill, was not the only legislative proposal on the agenda. National health insurance was a live issue, one to be treated seriously. Truman's persuasive powers were considerable, and his support for NHI could not be ignored. Moreover, the AMA campaign against compulsory health insurance and its slogans against "socialized" medicine ensured that the issue would receive attention and not be dismissed as a passing presidential thought, something offered simply "for the record." Hence those who disagreed with the administration's approach felt compelled to offer counterproposals of their own.

As early as 1946 Robert Taft, Republican minority leader of the Senate and a powerful conservative leader of his party, had introduced a measure that provided for federal grants to participating states to help finance both hospital and physicians' services for low-income and needy families. This voluntary approach, limited to a narrowly defined part of the population, served as the basis for a number of bills introduced as voluntary alternatives to the Truman compulsory approach.

The battle was joined, and although the outcome was uncertain, it appeared reasonable to assume that some type of legislation would be passed. Yet none of the measures was enacted; no compromise was struck. The vigorous and well-organized opposition by the AMA proved decisive. Whitaker and Baxter, the firm that spearheaded the campaign, had already waged a successful battle for the California Medical Association against a proposal, submitted in 1945 by Governor Earl Warren (later chief justice of the U.S. Supreme Court), for a state government health insurance program. Now it launched its polished and perfected tactics in the national arena. With substantial AMA financing, Whitaker and Baxter organized its campaign through state and county medical societies, through sympathetic local organizations, and through thousands of individual physicians. In addition to this grassroots activity, it solicited support from nonmedical trade associations, national corporations, and civic groups. This support was designed to do more than merely build a file of letters endorsing the AMA's opposition to national health insurance. Instead, the various groups were asked to join the AMA in placing advertisements in the press and on local radio stations. And they did so. As Richard Harris wrote in *A Sacred Trust*:

Thousands of small businessmen went for the idea, including dairy owners ("Selling Milk is Selling Health! . . . Our service to this community has much in common with that of the medical profession"), merchants ("What's Wrong With Freedom? . . . All freedoms stand or fall together. That's why we take our stand today, with the doctors of America, for the Voluntary system"), restaurant, saloon, and soda-fountain proprietors ("There's No Such Thing As a Free Lunch! . . . We want a free America—not the 'free lunch' sort of Government"), and pharmacists ("From Pills to Penicillin . . . This progress is more than statistics—it's people! And the people we know don't want it tampered with!").[19]

It was an effort to influence public and congressional opinion and it worked. Eschewing discussion of the issues, the campaign was designed to generate an atmosphere of fear: fear of a government takeover, fear of a decline in the quality of medical care, fear of interference in the highly personal relationship between patient and physician, fear of "alien" influences and "socialized medicine."

The threat was clear. "Don't let it happen here!" implied that it was in fact happening elsewhere, specifically in Britain, which on July 5, 1948, implemented its National Health Service. The purpose of the British National Health Service Act was "to make all the health service available to every man, woman and child of the population, irrespective of their age, or where they live, or how much money they have; and to make the total cost of the service a charge on the national income, in the same way as the Defense Service and other national necessities."[20] Truman's goal for the delivery of health services, though not for their financing, was similar.

American compulsory health *insurance* was a far cry from a British national health *service*. In America, the health care delivery system would remain in private hands; in Britain, it had become part of government. The Whitaker and Baxter campaign, however, was designed to obfuscate, not illuminate, this difference. The contrast that was described was between American voluntarism—twenty years after Dr. Kimball, the AMA finally made peace with health insurance—and British socialism.

It is useful to recall those earlier times in order to assess how far we have come. More recent debates on NHI have not resorted to the 1950 level of invective nor have they invoked the label "socialism." Recent debates appear to be more analytical. Nevertheless, a residue of the past—and perhaps more than a residue—remains. In the Yarborough committee hearings in 1970 John Veneman, under secretary of the Department of Health, Education, and Welfare, spoke against national health insurance in the following terms: "The deep troubles of the health care enterprise have been nurtured by many factors . . . but I do not believe that past neglect means that we now have to start over *and pursue some course of action that would be entirely alien to our basic traditions*" [italics added].[21] The temptation to play upon the fear of foreign imports (even of ideas that, after all, do not enter into our trade balance) has persisted.

While the AMA's grassroots campaign against Truman's proposal outweighed efforts by its supporters and helped spell defeat for all proposals, several other factors were also important in determining the outcome. First was the fact that, by 1949, 61 million Americans already had insurance protection through Blue Cross, commercial insurance companies, and other prepayment plans. Additional millions were still being enrolled (5 million, an increase of 8 percent over the previous year, in 1949; 11 million, or 17 percent, in 1950; 9 million, another 12 percent, in 1951).[22] Many Americans believed their problems and those of others had been or would be solved through the voluntary purchase of affordable health insurance. There was little middle-class pressure for a compulsory health insurance system. Middle-class voters were reaping the benefits of the postwar economic expansion, of the increase in jobs and employer-provided health insurance.

Second was the fact that the two major alternative approaches represented two fundamentally different philosophies that could not be compromised. Truman's compulsory and universal social insurance proposal and the proposals for a voluntary-enrollment system with federal and state assistance provided only to low-income individuals were radically rather than marginally different. It is possible to reach a compromise on the size of a program's budget and on an appropriation— a little more, a little less. It was not possible to "split the difference" between federal and state, compulsory and voluntary, universal and means tested.

Third was the fact that those legislators—perhaps a majority—who believed that the needs of low-income individuals needed to be addressed were split irreconcilably between two diametrically opposed approaches. Consequently, those who were opposed to either solution were able to wield disproportionate power. While the majority argued among themselves over the merits of building a universal and strong program through social insurance versus the merits of helping some through a means-tested, welfare approach, they did not provide a common front against the American Medical Association.

Finally, of course, there was America's long-standing ambivalence toward government. The Social Security program of 1935 had demonstrated that a federal social insurance program worked. Fire and police departments, parks, and public education were familiar aspects of local government. Yet despite this experience, Americans viewed government as "them," not "us." The fear of government ran and runs deep. Moreover, in 1950, after the trauma of the Great Depression and a world war, America wanted to take life—and issues—easy. Most assuredly it did not want to extend further the role of a federal government that for two decades had grown larger and more powerful. Americans were not willing to repeal the New Deal but neither were they ready to extend it. By 1952 Truman's fight for national health insurance was over. The president was in the last year of his term of office. The Democrats were still trying to put to rest the charge that government support for health activities was socialism. Adlai Stevenson's campaign for the presidency focused on other issues. His discussion of health care in an address delivered October 3, 1952, in Columbus, Ohio, seemed both vague and defensive:

> Here in Columbus you are now building a million-dollar health center; I am told that it has been badly needed for many years. The Federal Government is paying about one-quarter of the cost. Throughout the country, 1,500 such hospitals are going up, or have already been completed—most of them in farming areas which have never before had any kind of hospital service.
>
> Is this socialism? Is this something we can permit the Republicans to wipe out to the last vestige? Of course not.
>
> The hospital-construction program is only a sound beginning toward meeting the medical needs of all our people. I am just as much opposed to socialized medicine as any doctor in this country, just as I would be opposed to socialization of my own profession of the law. I never want to see our physicians on a government payroll, and I'm sure you don't either. You and I know that the United States already has the best system of medical care in the world, but we also know that it is not yet good enough . . .
>
> . . . so far we have found no way to cope with the problem of catastrophic illness, which may spell economic disaster for a whole family. No matter how thrifty, few families can ever protect themselves completely or endure the crushing cost of the accident which disables the

father for life, or the case of rheumatic fever which puts a child in the hospital for months or years. We await the recommendations of the President's excellent Commission on the Health Needs of the Nation, which is now holding hearings throughout the country and will make its report in December.[23]

Stevenson's reference to catastrophic illness, and by implication to catastrophic health insurance, was a far cry from Truman's concern for basic care and early diagnosis and for comprehensive benefits. It was also a far cry from the compromise, an insurance program for the aged, that was already being discussed by proponents of national health insurance and that, in due course, would replace NHI as the focus of attention. In December 1952 the President's Commission on the Health Needs of the Nation, appointed by Truman, recommended that "funds collected through the Old-Age and Survivor's Insurance mechanism be utilized to purchase personal health service benefits on a prepayment basis for beneficiaries of that insurance program, under a plan which meets Federal standards and which does not involve a means test."[24] But the fact that this program for the aged was only one of more than a hundred commission recommendations did little to increase its visibility. Indeed, since the commission submitted its findings and proposals to a president who would leave office in less than a month, the entire report was greeted with massive inattention.

The early 1950s were not a time when compromise appeared necessary to those who had so recently defeated the Truman program. Compromises are struck when the battle's outcome is in doubt, not after victory. It was clear that the momentum for a comprehensive health insurance program had waned. Although the problems of those who had no, or inadequate, insurance remained, the national mood had changed. Those who favored a federal insurance program discussed new initiatives and gathered strength in preparation for the future.

4

The Battle for Medicare

Under normal conditions, the enactment of major social legislation is possible only when a consensus is achieved through sustained political and educational effort under a chief executive's leadership. Sometimes, as during the crisis of the Great Depression or as in the wake of Lyndon B. Johnson's landslide victory over Senator Barry Goldwater following the assassination of President Kennedy, a committed president can force congressional action on measures that have not involved years of debate. By their very nature, however, such crises and overwhelming mandates are the exception rather than the rule.

The election of President Eisenhower in 1952 was not a time of crisis, and if there was a mandate, it was to consolidate old patterns, not to embark on new ventures. Nor was Eisenhower committed to building an informed constituency in favor of national health insurance. His election destroyed any hope that a sustained effort would be built on the debate begun in the Truman years. Indeed, not until 1957, at the beginning of Eisenhower's second term, did the debate about a government health insurance program regain a place on the national policy agenda. And what emerged then was a more limited health insurance program for the aged.

The Eisenhower years were characterized by relative tranquillity; certainly they appear so in comparison with the turbulence of the 1930s and 1940s and of the 1960s and 1970s. But in a nation as large and heterogeneous as ours, change is always present. Below the calm surface there flowed a current. And it was gathering force.

The costs of medical care were rising. The problem of financing care for those who could not afford voluntary health insurance was becoming more severe. The competition between commercial health insurers and Blue Cross needed resolution. Competitive pressures were forcing

Blue Cross to shift to experience-rated premiums that reflected the medical care utilization of the particular enrolled group. The principle of community rating was giving way to the realities of the marketplace.

This shift could be defended as necessary for survival in a harsh competitive world in which price-conscious buyers of insurance shopped for lower insurance premiums. In a voluntary system with multiple sellers, people are free to choose with whom to pool risks and whether to subsidize their less fortunate fellows. An insurer who ignores this reality will lose more and more subscribers and will be left with the poorest health risks.

The inexorable consequence is clear. Those whom the rest of the population would not help would have to make it on their own. Although the high-risk population undoubtedly felt abandoned by the various health insurers, in fact they were abandoned by their fellow citizens who left, or threatened to leave, insurance plans that enrolled high-risk individuals and consequently charged higher premiums. Thus, even as more and more Americans were enrolling in insurance programs, the problem faced by those left out was becoming more critical. Those Americans without insurance today were likely to be without insurance tomorrow; they were the ones who had been left behind. They would have to rely on the vagaries of private charity and, where available, public hospitals.

Many of these individuals had low incomes; others were ineligible for group enrollment and faced high individual premiums. Some were high risks; often they did not receive the advantages (including tax benefits) associated with employer payments for health insurance. And some, particularly the aged, were affected by all of these disadvantages. As the battle over a universal plan waned and as private insurance grew in strength, increased attention was directed at the problem of those who were unlikely to be enrolled under employer-related voluntary arrangements. It was as if the issues involving universal health insurance had been set aside and that America, having opted for the voluntary approach, now had to worry only about those who were unemployed or retired or working at low-income jobs and who would remain uncovered.

Of primary concern were the aged. They were the most vulnerable: not bound into employment groups, they faced higher individual premiums and had no employer contribution to coverage. They also tended to have low incomes and high medical needs and utilization. Their resources were few; their needs were great; and they had little health insurance. Furthermore, this vulnerable population could be defined with ease. Age was an easily measured characteristic. There had not been a single case of an individual who, having reached the conventional retirement age of sixty-five, became younger and, therefore, ineligible in some subsequent year. In contrast, income was potentially susceptible to change: a low income today might become higher tomorrow; high income today did not preclude low income in the future.

A program for the aged had important characteristics that increased the opportunity for and probability of legislative action. The first factor, of course, was that the aged had clear and visible needs. The second was that a massive social insurance program, the Social Security system, already protected the retired aged. The program, functioning and well accepted, could be built upon with familiar and accepted definitions, the same administrative and a similar financing mechanism. One could argue in favor of extending the popular old age insurance program rather than about instituting something totally new. If the argument were won, the principle of a compulsory federal program, albeit for a limited population, would have been established.

In addition, since the selection of age or Social Security status as the criterion for eligibility avoided the use of an income test, the principle of universality would not be compromised. The inclusion of all aged, rich and poor alike, set a precedent for universality. An enrollment criterion that limited the program to the poor set quite another precedent. Coverage for the aged could thus be seen as a first step toward a universal program, one that, by including all Americans, would be stronger and less vulnerable to changing definitions of and attitudes toward poverty.

Furthermore, in shifting attention to the aged, who constituted only 9 percent of the population,[1] the proponents of health insurance could argue that they had compromised, that they were willing to change their proposals. They could cast their opponents as the ones who were inflexible, unwilling to meet their colleagues half-way, simply negative. The battle over the role of government would be fought on a limited front, but a victory on this front would be important. Victory would help a group in need of help, and some felt that it would ensure success in future battles.

Proponents of NHI thus viewed health insurance for the aged as a useful tactical retreat. In a heterogeneous society, with blacks and whites, rich and poor, rural and urban, no single group commanded as much support as the elderly. Whites would not become black, the rich did not anticipate becoming poor, and urban dwellers were not returning to rural areas. But old age, like taxes, affected all and seemed inevitable. Barring catastrophe, today's young would become tomorrow's old; in supporting assistance for today's aged one was helping to erect a program that would provide for one's own tomorrows.

If the rationale of health insurance for the aged was clear to those who favored a compulsory social insurance approach for all Americans, the dangers of the precedent were equally clear to those opposed to NHI. Nevertheless, it was difficult to argue against health insurance for the aged on the ground that it was simply a small version of national health insurance. It addressed the needs of a particular, rather than the general, population and provided help to a group that otherwise could not expect to improve its status. In the late 1940s the AMA and its allies had argued that voluntary health insurance was growing and that, given time, the voluntary approach would prove to be the answer for most Americans. By the late 1950s it had become clear that even if voluntary health insurance continued to expand, it would not provide an answer for the aged. They were a special group whose condition required government assistance, something more than voluntarism. Despite disagreement on how to provide the necessary help, there was a measure of agreement that action was required. Whereas in 1949 many Americans felt that they did not need a government program that would cover everyone, by the latter 1950s they felt that the aged required some support.[2]

In August 1957 Congressman Aime Forand of Rhode Island introduced a bill embodying a social insurance financing approach to health insurance protection for the aged. That bill and its direct successors were to receive sustained congressional attention for eight years. Since legislation is the embodiment of ideas, the history of Medicare begins much earlier than with Congressman Forand or his bill. Nevertheless, it can be said that the legislative chapter that ended with the enactment of Medicare in 1965 opened with the Forand bill in 1957.

The Forand bill struck a responsive chord. In the summer of 1958, five months before the November congressional elections, the House Ways and Means Committee, chaired by Wilbur Mills, held hearings and heard a parade of witnesses. In the process, the public and its representatives were informed about the plight of America's older citizens. With a presidential election only two years away, senior Democrats took note of the issues raised. The years 1959 and 1960 would be spent in sharpening the issue, in mobilizing and organizing support, in doing everything possible to ensure that health insurance for the aged would be part of the 1960 election debate. In pursuing that objective, Medicare's proponents found assistance in an unexpected quarter. The AMA and its supporters mounted a vigorous attack on the Forand bill. They thereby gave it notoriety and conferred credibility.

Thus in 1959 the Forand bill remained in the limelight. The House Ways and Means Committee again held hearings. Although it did not act, the hearings, witnesses, and testimony helped strengthen the emerging consensus that a significant proportion of the aged faced severe difficulties in obtaining health insurance and that some change in existing insurance arrangements, requiring federal action, was necessary. No longer could Forand's opponents argue, "Let's wait and see." They were under increasing pressure to offer an alternative. No candidate for elective office relished the prospect of being charged with callousness and indifference, with being against the aged, only 25 percent of whom had adequate hospital insurance and 35 percent of whom fell below the poverty line.[3]

Nineteen sixty was a crucial year in the battle for health insurance for the aged. Leading public figures endorsed the need for action, and national political leaders were forced to take a stand on the various measures. All who saw themselves as possible presidential nominees tried to position themselves as supporters of some kind of health insurance legislation for the elderly. The reports of a split within the administration (Vice-President Nixon, it was rumored, felt threatened by the administration's continuing delay in offering an alternative to the Forand bill) and the differences between the administration and liberal Republicans in the Senate gave further evidence that health insurance for the aged was now a key item on the political agenda.

It was a year of frenetic political activity. The Eisenhower presidency was drawing to a close, and battles for party nominations were being fought. Power was passing to new figures: Kennedy, Johnson, Humphrey, Nixon, Rockefeller. There were serious attempts to woo important members of the House and Senate and continuing efforts to find a compromise health insurance measure that would command majority support in committee and on the floor of each legislative chamber and not be subject to a presidential veto.

Competing for support were two quite different approaches. There were a number of bills embodying the compulsory Social Security approach and covering those eligible for old-age retirement benefits. Like the Forand bill, these measures proposed to raise the necessary funds by increasing the percentage paid in Social Security taxes by employee and employer and by the self employed. The range of benefits and definition of eligibility differed in the various proposals but, in general, included a specified maximum number of days of hospitalization, nursing-home care, and the costs of surgery. In a vain effort to deflect AMA opposition and in order to limit the costs of the program, the measures did not include physicians' services (except for a limited range, chiefly surgical, rendered in hospitals). Modeled on Blue Cross coverage, it could be claimed that they would put the equivalent of the familiar Blue Cross card into the pockets and pocketbooks of those sixty-five and over.

The second approach, supported by the administration, was a more traditional welfarelike proposal. It provided federal financial assistance to individual states electing to participate in the program. This assistance, together with state funds and premiums from eligible individuals who enrolled, would finance health insurance for enrolled aged persons whose income fell below $2,500 for a single individual and $3,800 for a couple. To be eligible, an elderly person would have to be fortunate enough to live in a state that chose to participate in the program and be unfortunate enough to meet the income limits. To enroll, the individual would have to pay the required premium. To receive benefits, those who had enrolled would also have to pay the deductible: $250 for a single person and $400 for a couple (a sum that exceeded 10 percent of income). After the deductible was met, the patient would be reimbursed for 80 percent of the costs incurred but would have to pay the remaining 20 percent.[4] Although the benefits were comprehensive and extensive (indeed, they provided more days of hospital care than the Forand bill as well as coverage for services outside the hospital), they would be available to a small minority and even then would require large cash outlays by the low-income elderly individual.

The contrast between the plans was sharp and clear. The Social Security type plan offered limited benefits that emphasized hospital care for all. Like Blue Cross, it set a maximum limit on the number of days that would be covered, but the maximum (generally sixty days) was far greater than the average length of stay of about twelve days.[5] The administration plan, on the other hand, offered no assistance to most elderly persons but did offer more extensive benefits, including physicians' services, to the small minority of old and poor who were very sick for an extended period, lived in states that joined the program, and could meet the burdensome, if not prohibitive, out-of-pocket payments. The differences in benefits and in definitions of eligibility were accompanied by differences in administration (federal government versus states operating through private insurance carriers), in method of funding (payroll tax versus general revenues, state taxes, and private premiums), and in basic philosophy (social insurance versus a welfare approach).

Proponents of each approach negotiated among themselves on the definition of benefits and eligibility; but there was little room for negotiation and compromise between supporters of the two alternative solutions. Accordingly, in the first two months of 1960 each group sought additional backing from among the undecided. Each attempted to gain the support of key congressional figures and of the large bloc of Southern Democrats, who disliked a fully federal program yet knew that their state economies could not support a federal-state partnership and that their aged could not finance the premiums and out-of-pocket costs. Unhappy with both approaches, they opposed any legislation.

Wilbur Mills, Democrat from Arkansas, powerful chairman of the powerful House Ways and Means Committee, was the focus of attention. In addition to being the committee that initiated tax, tariff, Social Security, and welfare legislation, Ways and Means was responsible for committee assignments for individual members of the House. The chairman and the ranking minority member derived strength from the fact that they were especially influential in those decisions. Additional committee power derived from the rules and traditions of the legislative process. For one thing, because of the complexity of tax legislation (and the danger of trading votes on the House floor for provisions of importance to individual members and special-interest groups), tax and Social Security changes were generally brought to the floor under a closed rule that did not permit amendments. For another, the committee deliberated in executive session when dealing with legislation for House consideration.

Mills's power stemmed from his expertise in tax matters, his control of the professional staff, his political acumen in welding coalitions and doing favors, and his seniority status under the rules of the House then in force. He could call meetings or postpone them, determine the agenda, and orchestrate the debate. In addition, he served as a bridge between the two wings of the Democratic party: the more numerous and liberal Northerners and the more senior, powerful, and conservative Southerners. Finally, there was the fact that a bill that was popular among constituents back home but unpopular among individual congressmen could be killed in executive session in committee rather than on the floor of the House, where everyone would have to stand up and be counted. Members appreciated Mills's willingness to spare them from the need to cast a public vote.

Yet neither Mills nor the committee had absolute power. Although not all members of the House and Senate participate equally in the legislative process, no single person can exercise power without regard to the views of colleagues. It is a process of complex bargaining made more complex than political systems in other countries because of the checks and balances built in by the Constitution, by tradition, by the independence of individual members of Congress, and by the absence of party discipline. More so than in parliamentary systems, American politics calls for negotiation, a commodity that was abundant in 1960.

Much of the bargaining involved a search for support from Southern Democrats, who were being buffeted by contradictory pressures: their opposition to compulsory insurance; their loyalty to Lyndon Johnson, Senate majority leader, who was seeking the presidential nomination, and to Sam Rayburn, speaker of the House, who was seeking support outside the Southern constituency for Johnson, his fellow Texan; their respect for Eisenhower and for conservative principles, but their need, in an election year, to put some distance between themselves and the Republicans.

Wooed by both sides and under pressure, the Southerners sought a way out. Helped by Mills, they found it in a third alternative. In 1950 the federal government had enacted a program to help the states pay for medical care for the poorest of the aged, welfare recipients who received cash benefits under the federal old age assistance program. Now Mills proposed and the House Ways and Means Committee approved a program that would supplement state funds with federal assistance to purchase medical care for indigent persons over sixty-five whether or not they were on federal public welfare. This provision was attached to a larger bill increasing Social Security benefits. Under the closed-debate rule, the only way to vote against the Mills plan on the floor of the House was to vote against the entire bill. As a result, the legislation passed overwhelmingly.

In the Senate the outcome (though not the process) was the same. Both the Republican and Democratic programs for health insurance for the aged were defeated, the former by a vote of 67 to 28, the latter by a vote of 51 to 44 (with 16 Southern Democrats in opposition). The Senate then turned to a bill quite similar to the Mills approach, sponsored by Senator Robert Kerr, Democrat from Oklahoma. As in the House, the measure was enacted overwhelmingly.

Thus the Kerr-Mills Act, legislation that bore no relationship to either of the approaches that had dominated the discussion, came into being. The years of hearings, the countless witnesses, the studies and the data contributed little to the measure that emerged. Those Americans who had watched what had transpired would have wondered whether this was the deliberative process that their high-school civics texts had extolled.

Nor could they foresee what impact the Kerr-Mills Act might have. Although it provided federal grants to the states to pay part of the costs of medical care for the needy aged and persons on public assistance, the individual states were free to elect whether or not to participate and to determine eligibility and benefits. The benefits of state participation seemed evident: federal assistance. But the costs of participation were equally evident: the impact on state budgets. It was not clear how many states would choose to participate, which of their residents would be helped, and by how much. The states with many poor residents were also the states with the fewest financial resources; the very states most in need were the ones least able to take advantage of the program.

Both Kennedy and Nixon, the two presidential candidates, disowned the Kerr-Mills approach, each arguing that more comprehensive legislation was required. While Kennedy supported a universal social insurance approach and Nixon argued for the administration's welfare-oriented program, neither was willing to call Kerr-Mills a solution. Clearly, the issue of financing medical care for the aged had not been resolved. It would remain on the political agenda.

In January 1961, supporters of a Social Security approach could take heart from the inauguration of a Democratic president who was committed to further legislative action. But President Kennedy's victory was hardly overwhelming. He faced a Congress that was less than fully supportive of his legislative initiatives. He did not have the votes in the House or Senate to enact his rich legislative program. What he did have was the opportunity (if he chose to seize it) to inform and educate the public and the power (if he chose to use it) to keep an issue alive. Kennedy was committed to Medicare (by now that term had become part of the political language), and the public was concerned and interested. It was a potent combination. Kerr-Mills had been enacted, but Kennedy would not permit the issue of health insurance for the aged to disappear from the political agenda.

Indeed, it remained very much alive through 1961 and into 1962. The Republicans offered new alternatives, and Democrats tried to bypass the House Ways and Means Committee by having the Senate add health insurance for the aged as an amendment to a bill that would then go to a Senate-House conference. Nevertheless, there was no final action.

Kennedy hoped that the 1962 election would produce a more responsive Congress. It was clear that Medicare would be an issue in the congressional campaign. Furthermore, Kennedy was quite aware of the existence of a grass-roots organization, the National Council of Senior Citizens, organized to support Medicare. He was, of course, also aware of AMA opposition, perhaps even of the recording of a talk by a California movie actor named Ronald Reagan. Richard Harris wrote:

> To forestall action in Congress, the A.M.A. and AMPAC [the American Medical Political Action Committee] stepped up their campaigns. The women's auxiliary was the first to attack. In a program called Operation Coffee Cup, thousands of doctors' wives held afternoon parties for friends and neighbors, at which they ate cookies, drank coffee, and listened to a recording of a talk by Ronald Reagan. "One of the traditional methods of imposing statism or Socialism on a people has been by way of Medicine," Reagan assured his listeners, and he urged the ladies to write letters, and get their friends to write letters, to members of Congress. "If you don't do this," he said, "one of these days you and I are going to spend our sunset years telling our children and our children's children what it once was like in America when men were free."[6]

In an effort to increase the pressure for action, Kennedy went to the people. Special Counsel to the President Theodore Sorenson noted the flaw in the president's tactic: "On May 20, 1962, nationwide television carried his address to a mammoth rally of senior citizens in Madison Square Garden. It was a fighting stump speech, loudly delivered and applauded. But the President had forgotten the lesson of his campaign, that arousing a partisan crowd in a vast arena and convincing the skeptical TV viewer at home require wholly different kinds of presentation. He already had support from the senior citizens; he needed more support from the home viewers, and that speech did not induce it."[7]

The worst was yet to come. The next day the AMA responded with a half-hour TV presentation from the same arena. Dr. Edward Annis, the head of the AMA Speakers' Bureau, spoke to an empty auditorium;

the drama of the beleaguered physician trying to make his case against a president who had the crowds, the bands, the placards, and the publicity was compelling.

The campaign shifted back to Washington. There, too, the president suffered defeat. In the House, the Ways and Means Committee failed to report out any measures; in the Senate, the vote to attach a Medicare amendment to the public-welfare bill failed by a vote of 48 to 52. Once again there was clear evidence of the split within the Democratic party: 21 Democrats (one-third of the Democratic members) joined 31 Republicans to kill the measure; only 5 Republicans crossed party lines to join the 43 Democrats in its support.

A new Congress was elected in 1962, and the proponents of Medicare were encouraged by the results. Kennedy's words to Congress in his 1963 Special Message on Aiding Our Senior Citizens, in sharp contrast with the views of Ronald Reagan, called for action: "A proud and resourceful nation can no longer ask its older people to live in constant fear of a serious illness for which adequate funds are not available. We owe them the right of dignity in sickness as well as in health. We can achieve this by adding health insurance—primarily hospitalization insurance—to our successful social security system."[8]

Nevertheless, action was not forthcoming; other priority matters, tax-cut and civil-rights legislation, required attention. With Kennedy's assassination in November 1963, Lyndon Johnson became president and carried on the battle.

In 1964 opponents and advocates of Medicare jockeyed for legislative advantage, but the opponents adopted a new strategy. In an effort to preclude enactment of a program of health insurance financed through a Social Security payroll tax, they moved to increase Social Security cash benefits and the Social Security payroll tax that financed those benefits. They argued that the payroll-tax burden could not exceed 10 percent (a maximum of 5 percent on employers and 5 percent on employees). Thus, if the payroll tax were increased to those levels in order to finance cash benefits, there would be no room left within the tax structure for Medicare. The strategy seemed simple enough, but the linkage of Medicare and Social Security gave the proponents of health insurance for the aged a new bargaining chip: Social Security benefit increases could be held hostage to the fate of Medicare.

That happened in the fall of 1964, when, by a vote of 49 to 44, the Senate for the first time passed a Medicare amendment along with an increase in Social Security benefits and a payroll tax scheduled to reach

10.4 percent by 1971. House conferees, however, stood fast in their opposition to the Medicare provision. In turn, President Johnson pressed the Senate conferees to stand firm for Medicare even if that meant no action on cash-benefit increases. He recognized that if no measure was enacted, the debate about Social Security benefits and about Medicare would be resumed in the next Congress; and he was confident that in the November election his coattails would prove longer and stronger than Goldwater's.

The 1964 election did prove decisive. Johnson defeated Goldwater in a landslide. Kennedy had won by 120,000 votes out of 69 million; four years later, Johnson won by 16 million votes out of 71 million. He had his mandate. Furthermore, the Democrats emerged with a better than two-to-one majority in both House and Senate (more senators than at any time since 1939; more congressmen than at any time since 1937).[9] Additionally, they increased their strength in the North, where pro-Medicare members of both chambers displaced Republican opponents. Within a week after the election, Wilbur Mills indicated that the Ways and Means Committee would consider Medicare as soon as the new Congress convened in January 1965. The long battle was drawing to a close.

From January to July 1965, Congress debated. The administration proposal (the King-Anderson bill) provided for payroll-tax funding for benefits and focused on services provided in and by institutions, primarily hospitals. Hospital expenses, of course, represented the most severe financial threat to the family budget, so there was good reason to focus on hospital insurance. It also seemed much easier to design a hospital insurance program rather than one that covered physicians' services: in 1965 there were only about 7,000 hospitals, in contrast with about 250,000 practicing physicians,[10] and hospitals had elaborate bookkeeping, accounting, and data systems. Presumably they could more easily be monitored.

Furthermore, since almost all hospitals were not-for-profit entities, it did not appear necessary to determine what might be considered a reasonable income above costs or to develop new approaches to the issue of reimbursement. All that was needed was to pay for the costs of care of the elderly, to pay the bills the hospitals submitted (after the patient paid an initial deductible of $40, roughly equal to the cost of one day's hospitalization in 1965). Hospital insurance, an extension of Blue Cross, appeared benign. Senator Clinton P. Anderson had argued in 1962 that under Medicare "the Government would assume no responsibility for providing medical services, but would only help older people finance the costs of their most burdensome health expenses through a program of basic health insurance. Aside from the difference in the method of collecting contributions and the fact that the proposed insurance is only for the elderly, what is proposed is very much like what Blue Cross has been doing for years—paying hospital bills without meddling in hospital operations."[11]

Thus hospital insurance responded to the public's needs and appeared easy to administer. Even so, benefits were limited to sixty days of hospital care per benefit period (a period that began with the first day of inpatient hospital care and ended when the patient had been out of a hospital or nursing home for sixty consecutive days). The limit was imposed in order to assure that the Hospital Insurance Trust Fund would remain financially solvent and that acute-care hospitals would not be converted into long-term custodial institutions.

Hospital insurance could hardly be defined as comprehensive health insurance. It certainly flew in the face of the reality of medical care: that there is a continuum of care and that, to a significant extent, hospital and outpatient care are substitutable. If insurance paid for care in the hospital but not in the doctor's office, care in the insured hospital setting would be encouraged. Insuring hospital care would lead to a misallocation of health care resources and, because hospitals used more resources and were more expensive than outpatient care, to an increase in the nation's health care expenditures. The physician could help the patient's (and his own) pocketbook by recommending hospital rather than office care; society's purse would feel the strain.

Though important to experts in and students of health care, these arguments would hardly have led to a broadening of benefits. The search was for consensus, not for the "best" bill but for an acceptable measure. There was fear that expanding insurance benefits to include physicians' services would increase program costs, strengthen AMA opposition, and jeopardize enactment of even the limited benefits of the King-Anderson bill. The Democrats had a substantial majority in Congress, but individual members were free to vote as they saw fit. Without a compromise there might be no majority for a particular measure. Furthermore, the House and Senate are autonomous political bodies. Each has its own committees and procedures; each has its own powerful legislators. There was no guarantee that what was acceptable to one would be looked upon favorably by the other.

Even as the King-Anderson bill was being considered, the AMA and

Republicans led by Congressman John W. Byrnes from Wisconsin, rank-ing minority member of the House Ways and Means Committee, sep-arately proposed their alternatives. The AMA spent almost one million dollars on behalf of its alternative, "Eldercare," in the first three months of 1965. Eldercare was based on Kerr-Mills and called for federal-state matching grants rather than compulsory Social Security funding. It would have assisted fewer persons than the administration measure but proposed out-of-hospital as well as in-hospital benefits (to be fi-nanced through the private insurance sector with federal and state subsidies to the needy). The focus of the AMA campaign was the contrast between the comprehensive nature of Eldercare benefits and those provided by King-Anderson.

Byrnes's alternative also provided out-of-hospital benefits to the elderly on a voluntary basis, but (unlike Kerr-Mills or Eldercare) with federal rather than state administration. The costs of the private in-surance would be met out of federal general revenues and premiums paid by the insured and tied to the individual's Social Security benefits. Clearly, the AMA and the Byrnes's proposal differed with regard to important issues of administration, funding, and eligibility. But both relied on the private insurance sector and provided insurance benefits for physicians' services. The efforts on behalf of these proposals high-lighted the limited benefits provided under King-Anderson and had a significant impact on the legislation that emerged.

The administration had always been concerned that the political process had oversold the program and that the efforts to enact legisla-tion had aroused unrealistic voter expectations. The program, after all, had been misnamed: instead of Medicare, it should have been called Hospicare. Many officials feared the reaction that might follow Medi-care's enactment and the public's discovery that the benefits did not pro-vide for physicians' services. It was even suggested that in an earlier Medicare bill, proposed during President Kennedy's administration, the effective date for implementation of the program had been post-poned from the beginning of the fiscal year, July 1, 1962, to January 1, 1963, not in order to have more lead time in which to set up the neces-sary administrative mechanisms but in order to postpone the wrath of a disappointed electorate until after the November 1962 election.

The Eldercare and Byrnes proposals for out-of-hospital coverage and their stress on the inadequacy of Medicare presented both a prob-lem and an opportunity for supporters of the King-Anderson bill who were concerned about its hospital orientation. Mills responded by grafting a voluntary federally sponsored program, financed by the federal government and enrollees, for physicians' services (Medicare Part B) onto the compulsory payroll-financed program for hospital services (Medicare Part A). Thus the AMA proposal, designed to derail King-Anderson, had an ironic consequence: by emphasizing the limitations of hospital insurance, Eldercare helped build political support for broader benefits. The AMA had managed to convert political defeat into political disaster. Over time, of course, the pain over the political loss was assuaged by the economic gains that accrued to American physicians, whose elderly patients now had Part B coverage for physician services.

And there was more. The discussion of the special problems of low-income persons (nonelderly as well as those covered by the old age assistance program who would not have the resources to pay the deductible and copayments under Part A or the deductibles, coinsurance charges, and premiums for Part B) made possible the development of a totally different program of medical assistance known as Medicaid. Medicaid fitted into Johnson's War on Poverty and replaced and extended Kerr-Mills. Quite unexpectedly, without years of debate on the specific measures, the legislative process yielded a more comprehensive set of programs than had earlier appeared possible.

The spring months saw much activity in the House and Senate. The House enacted its version of Medicare in April 1965 by a vote of 313 to 115. This overwhelming vote (189 Northern Democrats, 59 Southern Democrats, and 65 Republicans in favor; 2 Northern Democrats, 40 Southern Democrats, and 73 Republicans opposed) is, however, misleading. It suggests great strength, but, as is often the case, votes at various points in the legislative process provide a better indication of weakness and strength than does the final vote. In this case, too: before the final vote, the House considered the Byrnes proposal. It was defeated, but by a much closer vote, 236 to 191 (188 Northern Democrats, 38 Southern Democrats, and 10 Republicans opposed; 3 Democrats, 60 Southern Democrats, and 128 Republicans in favor). A shift of 23 votes would have reversed the result. It could reasonably be argued that the comprehensive program that was enacted could not have been passed except in 1965, in a House elected during a presidential landslide, with 65 first-term Democrats, 58 of whom voted against the Byrnes proposal; with the help of a president whose legislative skills were legendary and a chairman of House Ways and Means whose influence was immense.

In July the Senate enacted its version of Medicare. There the battles took place in the Finance Committee, especially around a proposal by Senators Russell Long and Abraham Ribicoff, who had been President Kennedy's secretary of Health, Education, and Welfare, to enact a quite different kind of program. They proposed catastrophic health insurance protection that removed the time limits on hospital and nursing-home utilization but required that patients first pay a significant amount (related to income) essentially as a deductible. Although the measure offered considerable relief to those few elderly Americans who required unusually long hospitalization (especially so if they had low income), most of the elderly would not have benefited and those who did would have received much less assistance than under the King-Anderson or Mills bills.

This fact hardly commended the proposal to most legislators. Having come this far, they wanted to resolve the issue, to "solve the problem," not only for very sick and destitute Americans but also for the large population of elderly who were near-poor or middle class. Furthermore, for reasons that are obvious, individuals who must stand for election tend to favor legislation that offers benefits, even if modest, to the many, rather than extensive benefits limited to the few. Long's proposal was defeated. Removing the limit on hospital and nursing-home care threatened the financial stability of the program. Nevertheless, the focus on patients who needed more than sixty days of hospital care led the Finance Committee to increase Medicare hospital benefits by an additional sixty days (with a copayment provision of $10—25 percent of the $40 hospital deductible—per additional day). Long-term nursing-home care was available to those eligible for Medicaid. The final Senate vote in favor of Medicare was 68 to 21.

The differences between the House and Senate measures were resolved in a conference committee report adopted by both houses. The years of effort, the hearings and the testimony, the process of refinement and amendment, had produced a far broader and more extensive program than Forand had proposed eight years earlier. Eligibility was extended to include 3 million aged not covered by the Social Security system, the maximum number of days of hospital and nursing-home care was increased, a voluntary program extending benefits to physicians' services outside hospitals was created, and the Medicaid program designed to assist many of the nation's poor was separately enacted. The battle for a social insurance program to cover health care costs, a battle begun by Truman and carried forward by Kennedy and Johnson, had finally been won.

The measure now awaited President Johnson's signature. On Friday, July 30, 1965, some two hundred of the nation's leaders assembled in Independence, Missouri, to honor former President Harry Truman, in whose presence President Johnson would sign the Medicare Act. After writing a small part of his signature with each of one hundred pens, the president gave them as souvenirs to the various individuals who had helped bring Public Law 89-97, the ninety-seventh act of the 89th Congress, into being. Johnson, the father of the War on Poverty, had ample opportunity for bill-signing ceremonies, but this one, which vindicated Truman, had a special emotional quality. The fight for compulsory health insurance for the aged had been long and arduous. Now Medicare was law. July 1, 1966, the date for implementation of Medicare (Title XVIII of the Social Security Act) was less than a year away. The executive branch had to begin to organize its efforts to make the program work.

5

Medicare: Proud Accomplishment and Vexing Problem

Medicare as it exists today has changed from the measure signed over twenty years ago. Public Law 89–97 has been interpreted and reinterpreted, amended and extended, and, in recent sessions of Congress, cut back. Nevertheless, its basic character, design, and structure have remained stable.[1] The program that in 1985 covered 30 million aged and disabled Americans (protection for the disabled was added by amendments in 1972) and paid $70 billion for benefits is in large measure the same program that in 1967, its first full calendar year of operation, covered 20 million Americans and paid $4.5 billion.[2]

Now as then, Medicare Part A and Part B cover many, but not all, of the medical care services received by the eligible and enrolled population. Now as then, patients must pay deductibles and coinsurance for covered services. Now as then, the relatively few patients who have unusually long hospital stays or who incur large bills for physicians' services may face financial ruin, since Medicare limits the number of days of hospital and skilled nursing-home care it will pay for and since there are no limits to the total physician coinsurance payments that beneficiaries may face. Now as then, Part A is financed by employer and employee payroll taxes and Part B by beneficiary premium payments and federal government general revenue contributions. Now as then, the Medicare program reflects the complex way in which a law is drafted, enacted, amended, and administered; the struggles between opposing factions; the kinds of compromises struck; the nature of judicial decisions; as well as the interplay between prevailing attitudes held by patients and providers, by the general public, and by those in the legislative and executive branches of government.

Medicare is a complex law. Could the Medicare bill have been written in a simpler fashion? Certainly. Could that "simpler" legislation have been enacted? Perhaps—but only perhaps. The search for votes required negotiation and compromise. The legislative process involved human beings, each with his or her own constituencies, value systems, priorities, information, and expectations. It also involved groups and organizations with different goals, attitudes, influence, and power. Perhaps other compromises could have been reached. Perhaps the benefits accruing to some and the costs incurred by others could have had different dimensions. Perhaps, as in any bargaining and negotiation process, one party overestimated its opponent's strengths and gave away more than was necessary. But compromise and complexity there had to be. The Medicare law is not simple. In our society and under our political system it could not be otherwise.

Medicare was enacted at a point in time. But the law is alive. Its implementation, like that of any law, is a continuing process. That process, too, is one of compromise. Those who suffer a legislative defeat do not leave the field of battle but regroup in order to contain the defeat and limit its consequences. After the bill was signed, the executive branch replaced the legislative branch as the locus of the power struggle and the negotiation effort. Medicare had been enacted; now it had to be interpreted. General principles and broad guidelines had to be translated into regulations. Because the law is amended and evolves, that process, too, made and continues to make for complexity.

The Medicare program was and is heavily influenced by the fundamental characteristic of the act: public dollars pay for services delivered by and in the private sector. Medicare is not a national health service for the aged. It does not own hospitals or employ physicians who render care. Instead, it reimburses institutions and individuals for the costs of care they have provided. Thus the program relies on and requires a cooperative effort. Cooperation cannot be forced nor can it be assumed; it must be obtained voluntarily and sought continuously. Medicare's operation has been molded by the need for that cooperative effort. The reality of the public-private mix is a continuing quest for accommodation among Congress, which has a fiscal and social responsibility; the executive branch, which administers the program; Blue Cross/Blue Shield and other insurers, who participate in its financial operations; health care providers, who deliver the services; and patients and prospective patients with needs and expectations.

The Medicare program was also heavily influenced by the fact that many of its strongest proponents viewed it primarily as a financing mechanism to share the costs of care and were less interested in the nature of the health care delivery system, that system's impact on Medicare and vice versa. Within HEW, the Social Security Administration and its commissioner rather than the U.S. Public Health Service and the surgeon general had the responsibility to formulate, implement, and administer the program. Part of the Medicare compromise was that the program was not to be used to alter the structure of the health care delivery system. Medicare was to be a neutral conduit for dollars. The Committee on Ways and Means had put the matter clearly and strongly when it wrote: "The bill specifically prohibits the Federal Government from exercising supervision or control over the practice of medicine, the manner in which medical services are provided, and the administration or operation of medical facilities."[3]

Defining Medicare as a tax and transfer activity rather than as a health system program made it appear neutral and less intrusive. It was only much later that what was clear to some and what should have been clear to all from the outset was recognized: the program could not afford simply to pay for care without concern for the way services were delivered and how fees were set. It could not ignore the nature of health sector incentives and priorities.

That new perspective was the consequence of the changing environment in which Medicare functioned. That environment included rapid increases in health care expenditures, additional medical care legislation (such as health planning and professional standards review organizations); changes in the organization of health care (such as health maintenance organizations and a renewed emphasis on primary care); a substantial increase in the number of physicians and striking advances in medical science and technology; and changes in demography, the general price level, employment, economic growth, and budgetary constraints. Medicare thus reflects its own internal character and, inevitably, conditions in the external world. To understand how Medicare works and how it is perceived, we must consider both the program and the shifting climates in which it functions.

Such an assessment also requires recognition that Medicare necessarily involves and affects many individuals and groups, each with particular concerns and interests. Since the various parties meet Medicare in different ways, they have different perspectives on the program and its diverse impacts. The views of those who seek care, those who deliver it, those who worry about dollars and budgets, and the countless others directly or indirectly involved will each be different. Each person's perceptions of Medicare's strengths and weaknesses depends on his or her particular vantage point.

DIRECT BENEFICIARIES: THE AGED AND THE DISABLED

Medicare's fiscal difficulties notwithstanding, the first perspective from which to view the program is that of the people whom Medicare was designed to help. How do they relate to Medicare, what do they see, and what are their concerns?

When Medicare began to pay for care, on July 1, 1966, its hospital benefits (Part A) covered some 19 million elderly individuals. That number has risen to 27 million. In addition, Medicare enrolls 3 million individuals who are disabled (and who have been entitled for at least twenty-four months to receive Social Security cash benefits) or who suffer from end-stage renal disease (and are covered by Social Security or are spouses or dependent children of insured individuals). Almost all the eligible elderly and over 90 percent of the disabled elect to enroll in Part B Supplementary Medical Insurance. Elderly persons who are receiving Social Security checks automatically start their Part A hospital insurance at age sixty-five. They are also enrolled in Part B unless they decline that coverage. Others who are eligible, such as nonretired individuals, must apply for benefits. Most elderly people who are not covered by the Social Security program and are therefore ineligible for Part A coverage are nevertheless eligible for Part B coverage. They may purchase Part A hospital insurance (the 1986 premium is $214 per month).

The specific eligibility requirements and benefits provided are described in various pamphlets and brochures published by the Department of Health and Human Services and private organizations. The following summary of Medicare benefits is incomplete and should not be used as a reference guide.[4]

PART A

- Hospital inpatient benefits
    1. Medicare will pay for a semiprivate room (or private room if medically necessary), including meals, regular nursing services, special care units (such as intensive care), drugs, laboratory tests, radiologic services, medical supplies, op-

erating and recovery room costs, anesthesia, rehabilitation services.

2. Medicare will pay for all covered inpatient services received in a benefit period from days 1 through 60 except for the 1986 hospital insurance deductible of $492 (up from $40 in 1966). It will also pay for days 61 through 90, except for a patient copayment of one-quarter of the deductible, or $123 per day. In addition, each enrolled individual has a non-renewable lifetime reserve of 60 days that can be used if the stay exceeds 90 days in a single benefit period. Medicare pays for all covered services for each reserve day, except for a patient copayment of one-half of the deductible, or $246 per day.

3. A benefit period starts when the patient enters the hospital and ends when the patient has been out of the hospital (or other facility primarily providing skilled nursing or rehabilitation services) for 60 consecutive days. There is no limit to the number of benefit periods.

4. Medicare will pay for a total of 190 days of inpatient care in a participating psychiatric hospital in a patient's lifetime.

5. Medicare will not pay for care in a foreign hospital (except for Canadian or Mexican hospitals under carefully defined circumstances).

- Skilled nursing facility benefits

   1. Medicare will pay for skilled nursing inpatient care (not custodial care) under the following conditions:

      a. the patient has been in a hospital for 3 or more consecutive days and is admitted to the skilled nursing facility within a short time (generally, 30 days) after hospital discharge; and

      b. the patient needs skilled nursing or rehabilitation on a daily basis for a condition that was treated in the hospital.

   2. Medicare will pay for up to 100 days of skilled nursing facility inpatient care per benefit period. It pays for all covered services for the first 20 days. For days 21 through

100, the patient is required to pay one-eighth of the hospital deductible, or $61.50 per day in 1986.

- Home health services

  Medicare will pay for posthospital services provided by a home health agency that specializes in providing skilled nursing services and other therapeutic services, such as physical or speech therapy, to a patient confined to his or her home. The care required must be part-time, and coverage does not include general household or homemaker services, meal preparation or the cost of meals delivered to the home, drugs or biologicals, or personal care.

- Hospice care

  Special provision for care in a hospice approved by Medicare is available for those diagnosed as terminally ill.

PART B

- Medicare offers a voluntary supplementary medical insurance benefits program; the 1986 premium is $15.50 per month (compared with $3.00 per month in 1966).

  1. Medicare helps pay for physicians' services, outpatient hospital care, home health services, outpatient therapy and speech pathology services, and various other health services and supplies, including pacemakers, artificial limbs, prosthetic devices, and durable medical equipment (such as wheelchairs). It does not cover routine physical examinations and related tests, routine foot care, eye or hearing examinations for prescribing or fitting eyeglasses or hearing aids, immunization (with some exceptions), or cosmetic surgery (again, with some exceptions). Medicare will not pay for dental care unless it involves surgery or setting fractures, nor does it pay for drugs, eyeglasses, or hearing aids.

  2. The annual deductible for approved charges for covered services is $75 ($50 in 1966), after which Medicare will pay 80 percent of the approved charges for any additional covered services in the rest of the year. Home health services are not subject to deductible or coinsurance payments.

3. Often the approved charge is less than the actual charge billed by the provider. Whether this difference affects the patient depends on the provider's billing practice. Physicians (or suppliers, such as ambulance firms or independent laboratories) may accept assignment. In these cases the charge approved by the Medicare carrier becomes the total charge for the covered service. After the deductible has been met, the carrier will pay the provider 80 percent of the approved charge. The patient is responsible for the remaining 20 percent. If the provider elects not to take assignment, the provider bills the patient directly. The actual charge may exceed the approved charge. The patient is responsible for the entire bill and submits a claim to the Medicare carrier. The patient will receive 80 percent of the approved charge (after any part of the $75 deductible not yet met has been subtracted).

4. Special limits apply to outpatient treatment of mental illness. Special provisions are made for speech and physical therapy. Charges by radiologists and pathologists for inpatient hospital services are also subject to special payment provisions.

The preceding summary describes only the essence of the program, the kinds of services it pays for and the kinds of payments the beneficiary is called upon to make. Clearly, Medicare stands ready to pay for a significant part of the medical care of the elderly population. It accounts for about 75 percent of hospital care expenditures, 55 percent of physician expenditures, and 45 percent of all personal health expenditures (including nursing-home care) for the elderly.[5] It is estimated that in 1983 Medicare Part A, the hospital insurance program, provided an average reimbursement of $5,179 for the 8 million persons who received benefits and that Part B, supplementary medical insurance, provided an average of $950 for the 19 million aged and disabled who were reimbursed under Part B.[6] There is no question that Medicare is vitally important in financing health care for the elderly and the disabled.

Equally clearly, Medicare is not a total program. The individual is liable for premiums, deductibles, copayment, coinsurance, any differences between approved and actual charges, and the cost of a wide variety of noncovered services. To the extent that the aged cannot meet these costs, the gaps—with the largest being long-term nursing-home care—must be filled by other public programs (including Medicaid) and by private charity. Not all gaps are filled. Some elderly do without the care they require. It does not negate Medicare's importance to acknowledge its limitations, the fact that it pays less than half of the total health care expenditures for the aged. "Necessary" does not mean "sufficient."

Although the benefits Medicare beneficiaries receive are real, so are the problems they face as they come in contact with the program. These fall into two categories. The first involves the complex definitions, requirements, and structure of the program. The issue of assignment, for example, is one that physicians but not all beneficiaries understand. In 1983 physicians accepted assignment for only about 55 percent of all claims. Almost 20 percent of physicians always accepted assignment, 30 percent never did, and the remainder decided on a patient-by-patient and procedure-by-procedure basis. The average reduction from billed charges was 23 percent, with the result that the patient's 20 percent coinsurance liability was more than doubled.[7]

I recall being present when, after leaving the physician's office, an elderly man asked the receptionist whether he might sign the Medicare form. The receptionist explained that the physician handled the process differently from the referring doctor: "We will send you a bill and you'll pay us and request reimbursement directly from Medicare." The patient, not aware of assignment or of the difference between the physician's actual charge and that approved by Medicare (which I later found was over 100 percent), responded: "I see. I'll pay and be reimbursed. It all comes out the same." Unfortunately, it doesn't. Consider his confusion and irritation when, having paid the $35 bill, he found that because the approved charge was only $16, the Medicare reimbursement, 80 percent of that amount, was only $12.80. Thus the visit cost him $22.20 rather than the $3.20 he would have had to pay had the physician accepted assignment.

Confusion about insurance coverage is not uniquely associated with Medicare. Who among us copes easily with the complexities in our own health insurance plans? But confusion and irritation about the definition of costs, the scope of covered services, and the nature of reimbursement are surely greater in a population that both uses more medical care and is more vulnerable.

The second problem relates to the personal liability each beneficiary faces. The premiums for Part B, the deductibles, coinsurance, copayments, and the additional sums paid to physicians whose fees exceed the Medicare-approved charges and who do not accept assignment make access to benefits relatively costly. Medicare is a "terrific buy," but it is not an inexpensive one.

Persons who enter the hospital—about 20 to 25 percent of Medicare beneficiaries in any given year—face a first-day deductible of $492 (an increase of 23 percent from the 1985 deductible of $400). Furthermore, the structure of Medicare follows the structure of the private health insurance plans that preceded it in setting limits on the number of hospital days covered. Although these limits, ninety days (with a co-payment of $123 per day for each of the last thirty days) in a particular benefit period, are high and affect relatively few individuals, their existence threatens all beneficiaries. Less than one percent of all enrollees face additional hospital copayment charges in any given year, but the required additional payments may be very large (depending on the length of stay).[8] It is estimated that in 1982, when the hospital deductible was $260, the average hospital insurance deductible and copayment per Medicare beneficiary who used Part A services was $377.[9] Since the deductible now stands at $492, the 1986 liability may exceed $700.

In addition, all subscribers to Part B must pay the monthly premium of $15.50, totaling $186 annually. They also face a $75 annual deductible, coinsurance payments of 20 percent of the Medicare-approved charge, and a liability of 100 percent of any difference between the approved and actual charge. Moreover, enrollees must pay all charges for noncovered Medicare services, such as drugs, dental care, eyeglasses, and "routine" care, all of which may be of vital importance to their health status and psychological well-being.

As a consequence, the elderly face large additional costs for medical care. Some of these costs are paid by Medicaid and other public programs. Some are paid by private insurance purchased by employers or by the aged (often with help from their families). Yet despite these additional supports, the Senate Special Committee on Aging has estimated that in 1984 the elderly faced out-of-pocket costs averaging $1,575.[10] These figures will be higher in 1986 as a result of higher premiums, deductibles, physicians' fees, and other health care prices. In families with two elderly individuals, the average total family liability will exceed $3,000.

High though this amount is, it understates the dimension of the problem some Medicare beneficiaries face. Averages are useful and necessary ways to summarize information, but few individuals are average; some will be required to pay more, others less. The older or sicker or poorer one is, the greater the liability is likely to be. The Congressional Budget Office has estimated that for those with incomes under $5,000, the individual liability (in 1984 dollars) would equal 21 percent of income.[11] Medicare provides yet one more incentive to be young, healthy, and rich—or at least average.

It is not only the concept of the average that can obscure the variation within groups. Even the language used to define groups can do so. "The elderly" is a convenient label that defines the only shared characteristic but ignores many other characteristics. For example, all of the elderly are over sixty-five, but about one-third are sixty-five through sixty-nine, one-quarter are seventy through seventy-four, and a full 40 percent are seventy-five and over. Their incomes differ. Six percent of the elderly had incomes of over $25,000 in 1983, but one-third had incomes of under $5,000. Finally, their needs for health care services differ. Most beneficiaries are not hospitalized in any given year, but 5 percent have a hospital stay longer than twenty days.[12]

The elderly, then, are not a homogeneous group. They have different incomes and resources, different states of health and illness, and different encounters with the Medicare program and the benefits it provides. These differences are important in any assessment of Medicare's role and distributional impact. The program's strengths and weaknesses cannot be measured solely by the contribution that Medicare makes to the costs of care for all the aged or for the imaginary "average" individual; they must be measured by the help it offers to enrollees and beneficiaries at different levels of health expenditure and of income. Medicare's inadequacies are real, especially for the poor and near-poor, for those who need nursing-home care, and for those with long hospital stays and with extraordinary expenses. Medicare reduces but does not eliminate the financial problems of health care for the aged.

Millions of aged and disabled are correct in believing that they have benefited from the Medicare program, but their perception of the dollar value of the benefits may be exaggerated. Medical care prices are much higher today than they were in 1966. As a consequence even with Medicare the elderly pay about the same percentage of their income for care as they did then.[13] This has led some observers to suggest that the elderly would be as well off without Medicare, the presumed cause of the price increases. But that is not the case.

It is true that Medicare's reimbursement structure did permit and encourage medical care expenditure increases. HEW secretary Elliot Richardson described that institutional framework:

> Incentives that have led to inflationary medical costs are not too difficult to discern. When Medicare was introduced, it provided that physicians would be paid their customary fees. Some had been giving care free of charge or at prices below what they considered to be their value, and hardly customary. Hence, there was a rather rapid jump in the cost of physicians' services after the birth of Medicare.
>
> Medicare and Medicaid, as well as private health insurance companies, have been willing to reimburse hospitals at cost, which has become a euphemism for a blank check. There has been little incentive to hold down costs, to search for means of increasing the productivity of health manpower and facilities, or to substitute capital for labor. Our insurance plans also reward people if they go to the hospital for services, and penalize them if they obtain the same services outside the hospital. No wonder, then, that hospitals have been excessively and inappropriately used.[14]

The way Medicare functioned provides a better explanation of Medicare's contribution to health cost inflation than does the narrow economic model (which states that Medicare and Medicaid increased demand and thus exerted pressure upon a fixed supply of physicians and hospital beds). But the fact is that factors external to Medicare were the largest contributors to rising costs. Inflationary price increases have affected not only Medicare but the whole economy since 1965; it is estimated that over 40 percent of the increased reimbursement for short-stay hospital services by the aged can be attributed to general inflation. The improved quality of medical services available also accounts for some portion of the cost increases (estimates run as high as an additional 40 percent).[15] Clearly, inflation in the general economy and in overall health care costs, as well as increases in the quality of care and in the medical knowledge base mean that even if Medicare had not been enacted the aged and disabled would be paying more for medical care (and receiving better care) than they did in 1965. To suggest that the elderly would be better able to cope with inflation or to afford the benefits of modern medicine without Medicare is to do violence both to facts and to analysis.

The sense of security and dignity conferred by Medicare is real. Even those who use few services in any given year benefit from their knowledge that health insurance is available. It is distressing that this sense of security is now jeopardized; millions of beneficiaries are frightened that the program, which has already been cut and whose deductibles and copayment levels have increased in recent years, will be cut back further. The elderly and disabled know that Medicare expenditures have been rising. They read about the impending Medicare crisis and are aware of the large federal deficit. They may not know where Ronald Reagan stood in 1965, but they know where he stands now. Furthermore, their concern is magnified by their observation that many nonaged Americans incorrectly believe that Medicare covers all the medical care costs of the elderly and may therefore believe that requiring the elderly to pay more for their medical care is not unreasonable. They are aware that they will have to fight to retain the program benefits and medicare reimbursement levels that now exist.

INDIRECT BENEFICIARIES: THE POPULATION AT LARGE

Thirty million Americans are eligible for Medicare benefits. However, millions of other Americans are directly and indirectly affected by the program. It could not be otherwise: the elderly and the disabled are part of our community. How they, our relatives, friends, neighbors, and fellow citizens, fare affects us all. Furthermore, the nonelderly use the same medical care system that the elderly do and Medicare helps support this system. Its effects are manifold.

First, many individuals not old enough to be eligible for Medicare nonetheless reap financial benefits. Medicare provides insurance to those at financial risk for costs of care. In many cases, of course, those at financial risk are the elderly themselves. In other cases the risks would be borne and the debts assumed by younger family members. Medicare benefits the elderly who don't want to be a "burden." It also benefits those to whom the elderly would turn. In the battle for Medicare, proponents of the legislation argued that Medicare financing of health care costs would relieve the elderly's middle-aged sons and daughters of a financial obligation and would thus enable them more easily to finance their children's college education. That argument was not mere rhetoric.

Second, many who believe in the biblical commandment "Honor your father and your mother" extend that to all fathers and mothers. They are comforted by the knowledge that our society has developed a collective way to do so. Leaving the elderly to their own resources would offend our ethical sensibilities. We want the nation we live in to organize itself to help the elderly and disabled receive and pay for medical care. We consider such assistance to be one of the attributes of a civilized society, built, in no small measure, by those very aged.

Third, without health insurance for the aged, the American hospital that you and I use would be a far different institution. By assuring the continued flow of funds, Medicare has helped some hospitals survive and many more to expand and improve. Because of permissive reimbursement policies, the nation undoubtedly paid a higher price than necessary for the resulting improvement in quality. Nonetheless, that improvement should not be undervalued. It has benefited all who need and use hospital services.

Regrettably, the benefits that Medicare has brought to the non-Medicare population tend to be overlooked. Few of us understand the health care delivery system, the nature of its financing or organization. We are unaware of the favorable impact of Medicare on America's hospitals. Moreover, since almost two-thirds of the U.S. population has been born since Medicare's enactment or was under age twenty at that time, only a small proportion of Americans—many of whom are over sixty-five and are presumed to have a vested interest and to be "self-seeking"—can fully understand what our society was like without Medicare. We do not appreciate the program's impact because we cannot easily imagine an America in which health care to the elderly would be rationed on the basis of ability to pay and in which our hospitals would be fighting for survival. Yet that is the way things once were and how they still would be without Medicare.

Those under sixty-five derive one additional benefit from Medicare: the assurance that the program will serve them when they grow old. Since none of us really purchases a "policy" that will become effective when we reach sixty-five (or become disabled), the assurance is a political rather than a legal obligation. Theoretically, the political commitment can change and with it the nature of the Medicare program. But that is not likely to occur—if enough voters understand that the aged and disabled cannot bear the risks of ill health without assistance and if that understanding is translated into support for Medicare as a way of expressing the community's commitment to share these risks.

None of Medicare's various benefits comes free. Individuals pay the hospital insurance payroll tax of 1.45 percent (up from 1.35 percent in 1985) as part of their Social Security tax, as well as income taxes for general revenue contributions to supplementary medical insurance. At the 1986 wage base of $42,000, the maximum payroll tax contribution by an employee to the Federal Hospital Insurance Trust Fund is $609 per year (with an equal amount paid by the employer). This contribution will rise along with the wage base.

Even so, the increase in the number of aged, inflation in health care costs, and advances in medical knowledge will increase Medicare expenditures more rapidly than payroll-tax revenues. In time, perhaps as early as 1993, payroll contributions will prove insufficient to finance Part A benefits. It is estimated that the trust fund will be depleted by the late 1990s.[16] Furthermore, the $18 billion general revenue contribution to Part B Supplementary Medical Insurance adds to the federal deficit. Medicare financing needs reform. A better balance must be achieved between expenditures and revenues. This will require the development of new reimbursement mechanisms and legislative action that addresses Medicare's Part A and Part B needs (as well as long-term care) in a comprehensive fashion.

HOSPITALS

For America's 7,000 hospitals, Medicare has provided an important source of revenue. The aged represent only about 12 percent of the U.S. population, but they are hospitalized twice as often and stay twice as long as those under age sixty-five. Thus Medicare accounts for 28 percent of total expenditures for hospital care.[17]

Some proportion of the Medicare dollars that flow to hospitals are not "new" dollars. Even without Medicare, many of the aged would seek and receive hospital care; the bills would be paid by patients or their families. Nonetheless, there is general agreement that without Medicare or its equivalent, that is, without the protection offered the elderly and the dollars available to hospitals through the program, the American hospital sector would be very different from what it is at the present time.

Beginning in fiscal 1984, hospital reimbursement under Medicare underwent a fundamental change. Until then, reimbursement had been based on "reasonable costs," a concept whose definition was complex and whose precise measurement was elusive. Since Medicare reimbursed hospitals in relation to their costs, the definition of what could and what could not legitimately be included as a cost was an important issue. Should Medicare pay for education and research in teaching hospitals, for new construction and depreciation on existing facilities, for a share of hospital bad debts and the free care they deliver (as other payers do)? Should it pay for whatever the hospital felt was necessary, worthwhile, desirable? Each of these and similar questions had to be answered, and each answer affected the number of dollars hospitals would receive and the number of dollar obligations Medicare would incur. Vast sums of money were involved. I recall the anguished look on the face of one person involved in those decisions as he told me that at times he felt that he alone stood between the American hospital sector and all the gold at Fort Knox.

Under the payment mechanism in place from 1966 to October 1983, the total costs to the program were the product of three decisions: who would be paid (that is, which hospitals were eligible), for how many services they would be paid (that is, what controls, if any, would be exercised over utilization and length of stay), and how much they would be paid (that is, on what basis the costs would be calculated). Each of these matters involved important decisions of a highly political nature. In each case the decision arrived at was influenced by government's desire to get the program under way with a minimum of controversy even if that meant compromising other goals. Thus, when Medicare began, the Bureau of Hospital Insurance chose to certify as many hospitals as possible, including institutions whose quality and commitment to desegregation were suspect, and to delegate assessment of utilization and length of stay to the medical profession and peer review.

The compromises regarding cost also tried to minimize conflict. Furthermore, there was a deep belief that hospital expansion was desirable. As a consequence of both factors, decisions were made that helped fund depreciation on hospital plant and equipment, thus making available sums that could be used for future hospital expansion. In turn, hospital expansion added to future operating costs, thus increasing revenues, making possible still further expansion. It is not surprising that today our hospitals have much more capital, larger budgets, and are more expensive than they were in 1965 or than they would have been without Medicare.

The implementation of Medicare was a dynamic process. The definition of costs was critical to that process. It affected the subsequent course of events. Medicare was not and could not be neutral or without influence. By rewarding hospitals on the basis of cost and by defining costs in ways that recognized the cost of capital, Medicare encouraged hospitals to grow and costs to increase.

One former hospital director tells the story that in pre-Medicare days he kept a list of capital equipment in his desk drawer, items the medical staff wanted and felt would help improve patient care. If a potential benefactor appeared, he would try to match the donor's interests to an item on the list. After the implementation of Medicare a wealthy benefactor, a close relative willing and able (as some would put it) to sign a blank check, did appear: Uncle Sam. In turn, the shopping list disappeared.

Medicare helped stimulate capital growth at a time when Americans believed in the benefits that growth would bring. Regrettably, it did so by enabling individual institutions to expand without reference to community needs and priorities or regional planning efforts. In helping individual hospitals to accumulate capital and depreciation funds, Medicare discouraged a planned and controlled growth of the hospital sector. Redundancy and duplication of facilities and programs, all fueled with health insurance dollars, added to operating costs and to overall health expenditures. In some cases this duplication had a negative impact on the quality of care, since it reduced each hospital's load and since some medical and surgical procedures are much better done by staffs who perform them frequently.

Although many of those who regret the magnitude of this expansion view Medicare as the culprit, Blue Cross and commercial health insurance were driving the system in the same direction. Insurance and the guarantee of payment by both federal and private third-party payers removed the constraints that hospital decision makers otherwise faced in their quest for dollars to support expansion. Of course, it can be argued that Medicare had a special responsibility and opportunity to exercise control. The program was large and new; it was adding dollars to the health care system. But Medicare was not all-powerful, and Congress feared the medical establishment. It would take years of cost increases before pressure for a different system for paying hospitals would receive congressional support.

Administrators and physicians were not involved in a boardroom conspiracy to which the rest of us, had we but been aware, would have raised objections. Far from it. The expansion plans were public, and the new construction and equipment offered a measure of security to prospective patients and were a source of pride to the community. They were supported by a population that welcomed the technological advances, believing that the products of research and development would improve the quality of care. Given the funding mechanisms, these resources appeared free, but it cannot be assumed that had their real price been known, substantially less growth would have occurred. The hospitals that HEW secretary Joseph Califano later viewed as "obese," others, including patients, felt were "pleasingly plump."[18]

Hospitals had to pay a price for the benefits that Medicare brought in increasing and guaranteeing hospital money flows and in reducing bad debts and the need to offer free care. They had to establish new accounting procedures and detailed record-keeping systems. Since Medicare did not pay hospitals an inclusive rate but reimbursed separately for each item of patient care, the required data were extensive and voluminous.

In 1969 John Knowles, then director of the Massachusetts General Hospital, dramatized the nature of this reimbursement mechanism to members of the Joint Economic Committee. Knowles opened his testimony by rising from his seat with a thick stack of computer printouts in hand and asking for the assistance of a clerk. After a delay that served to heighten the sense of drama, a clerk appeared and Knowles asked him to take a corner of the printout and walk up the aisle to the back of the auditorium, unfolding the printout as he went. When the aisle was covered with a carpet of white, as if in preparation for a wedding procession, Knowles began to read the computer printout: "medication, $1, medication, $2; day nurse, $35; clinical labs, $1; . . . anesthesia, $90; clinical laboratories, $1," and so on.[19] The bill was for one patient.

Knowles's point was clear: this was an inefficient way to bill and reimburse for care. Medicare wanted the data for reimbursement and auditing purposes, but because it was inundated with paper it could not perform the audits. Money and effort were devoted to generating bills and records in an efficient manner. Little thought was given to the fact that the inefficient design of the larger payment system was what required all the paper and all the detail. Knowles's presentation was a masterful performance, yet nothing changed. The paperwork continued, although the familiarity bred by years of experience reduced its costs.

A more positive effect of Medicare was the development of a peer review process to examine hospital utilization. Since the sums the program would pay depended on the number of days of patient care, government wanted to eliminate any unnecessary days. Hospitals were therefore required to institute formal utilization review procedures to justify decisions to keep the patient in the hospital beyond a fixed number of days. While all payers for care, commercial health insurers,

Blue Cross, private noninsured patients, should also have wanted to monitor and control excess or unnecessary days of care, Medicare provided the first organized national attempt to address the issue of utilization. In no small measure that was the case because Medicare was a single large national program with much at stake while other payers were smaller and fragmented and each had less to gain from control efforts.

Initially many hospital directors felt that utilization committees represented an additional bureaucratic structure that would bring few benefits. Furthermore, many physicians resented the implication that they might keep their patients in the hospital longer than was necessary and resented the involvement of a review body, even if composed of their peers, in matters of patient care. They felt frustrated and harassed when the patient no longer needed hospital care but could not be discharged because alternative facilities or home health services were not available. As time passed, however, utilization review committees became the accepted norm and their procedures were taken for granted as part of the institutional fabric.

The dollars Medicare, Medicaid, and private health insurance provided to American hospitals and the conditions under which they were provided had profound effects on all parts of the health care sector and its expansion. But the golden age could not be sustained. As economic growth slowed but health expenditures continued to increase, all payers—often led by Medicare—grudgingly and haltingly at first, more actively later, began to develop new reimbursement policies, incentives, and control mechanisms. Hospital directors might speak of loss of freedom, constraints, and interference, but the world had changed. Old and comfortable relationships and dollar flows were no longer sustainable.

Constraints on hospitals and concern about rising expenditures developed at the very time (and not by accident) that there was a growing skepticism about the efficacy of various medical procedures and interventions. Some of this skepticism, expressed in cost-benefit and cost-effectiveness language, came from academic medicine, some from economists and health service research analysts. It also coincided, again not by accident, with the growing skepticism about the effectiveness of all kinds of social interventions, expressed in the slogan "Nothing works." A host of contributing factors (including Vietnam, the oil crisis, and inflationary pressures) led to a change in attitudes toward experts, including those in medicine, and their supposed expertise. We began to question both experts' plans and the planning process, and we became more acutely aware that resources are scarce and that there are limits.

It is therefore hardly surprising that today more attention is given to matters of organization, reimbursement mechanisms, incentives, cost effectiveness, and the total costs of care. That attention and the change in government's priorities and in its sense of power have altered Medicare's attitude to the hospital sector. Today legislators and Medicare administrators have a different perception of their task than in 1966. Then the task was to implement a program, to make it acceptable and to make it work; today, with the program established, the task is to develop incentives that would help contain its costs.

As a result, in fiscal 1984 Medicare began to phase in a new reimbursement system under which hospitals would no longer be paid on the basis of "reasonable cost."[20] Instead the Health Financing Administration has defined 467 different diagnostic categories and reimburses hospitals a predetermined number of dollars per patient with a particular diagnosis. Since various adjustment factors (such as geographic location, area wage rate, and cost of medical education) are taken into account, hospitals do not receive the same sum per diagnosis. Nevertheless, each has an incentive to search for efficiency and to conserve resources, since the amount it will receive per diagnosis will be fixed in advance.

The incentives that a set price provides as a stimulus to efficiency are obvious. So, too, however, are the dangers to the quality and distribution of care.[21] The fixed price may lead to undertreatment and rapid discharge. Furthermore, hospitals will have an incentive to treat patients with diagnoses for which the "fixed price" is likely to prove profitable. Since the diagnosis-related group (DRG) payment system does not fully take account of severity of illness, there is an incentive to shun patients who are very ill and whose costs of care are likely to exceed the level of payment. If cleaning companies received a set sum for cleaning an apartment, they might be more careful in their use of soap and dustcloths and might work harder to accomplish the task in less time. Yet they also might cut corners and do the task less adequately. Surely they would shun large apartments and ones they feared would be especially dirty and demanding. The risks are apparent.

Hospitals, of course, have varying senses of mission. They are sponsored and supported in different ways (government, community-at-large, medical school and university, religious denominations). Some

are profit oriented and investor owned. Others are not-for-profit institutions. Public city and county hospitals will continue to serve all
patients, including those "dumped" by other institutions. In many hospitals, the trustees' sense of a community service mission and the staff's
ethical standards will protect against undesired and undesirable side
effects. Nevertheless, there is reason for concern: as hospital budgets
grow tighter, as the search for efficiency assumes priority, and as
increasing numbers of hospitals become answerable to stockholders
rather than to the general community, power will shift to financial
administrators. The three-piece suit and attaché case will replace the
white coat and stethoscope. When the hospital becomes a "business"
and the patient a "satisfied customer," there will be a temptation to
cut back on free care and community obligations. The justification will
be the need for a favorable bottom line. The desire to flourish and the
need to survive can lead to a reassessment of the hospital's sense of
mission.

The degree to which the new diagnostic-related reimbursement system will prove effective over a sustained period in changing behavior
and inducing efficiency (and at what costs to quality and access to care)
are not yet clear. The system will have to be modified if it is to preserve
equity among hospitals and protect patients. It will have to adjust for
severity of illness and take account of the high probability that many
patients, especially in the aged Medicare population, enter the hospital
with multiple and interrelated medical problems. Nevertheless, the
new way of reimbursing hospitals represents an important conceptual
break with the past. It can be assumed that if payment by diagnostic-
related categories fails to constrain costs sufficiently or affects care
unfavorably, Congress will try a different approach, perhaps something akin to the negotiated prospective budgets under which Canadian
hospitals receive a predetermined annual sum (not tied to particular
diagnoses or specific patients) with which to carry on their activities.[22]
The new concern with costs, the pressure for control and constraint
and for limiting hospital cost increases, will continue to guide policy.

PHYSICIANS

Medicare Part A helps pay for hospital care, Supplementary Medical
Insurance (Part B) for physicians' services. Medicare is required to
assess the physician's "usual and customary fee" and its "reasonable-
ness" with reference to prevailing charges in the community. Medicare

determines an allowable or approved charge for a particular procedure by selecting the lowest of three amounts: the customary charge prevailing in the community, the usual charge by the particular provider, or the actual charge billed. Approved charges, which vary by procedure and provider, are updated annually.

The Medicare-approved fees are not determined by a process in which government decides the total it will spend and, through negotiation with physician groups, develops a fee structure that exhausts the available budget resources. The fees that are approved reflect the fees that physicians have charged in an earlier period. Physicians complain that Medicare-approved fees lag behind general fees and that annual increases are limited by a Medicare economic index. Nevertheless, they have considerable opportunity to affect the Medicare-approved fee structure. The fees they have set in recent periods increase today's approved fees and reimbursement.

In addition, physicians retain the power to attempt to maximize income by taking or not taking assignment. The option of not taking assignment and billing the patient directly for an amount set by the physician (not by Medicare) was developed as a response to physicians who, for ideological reasons, refused to deal with or accept payment from government. In 1965, when physicians were threatening to "strike" and to refuse services to Medicare patients, such an option seemed imperative.

It is clear that the greater the difference is between the Medicare-approved charge and the physician's desired charge, the greater the incentive will be to bill the patient directly. This phenomenon shifts costs from the Medicare program to patients' pocketbooks. Thus government's power to contain the amount the elderly must pay for physicians' services and to restrain increases in total health care costs (or in physicians' incomes) is limited.

The question of assignment has been at issue as the federal government has attempted to limit physicians' fee increases. In 1984, for example, Congress considered freezing Medicare-approved fees for fifteen months (July 1, 1984, through September 30, 1985). While it was recognized that this would help contain Medicare expenditures (unless physicians, in an effort to make up for the price freeze, increased the number of services billed for), many legislators feared that physicians would simply shift costs to patients (by not accepting assignment and by billing them directly).

As a result the final legislation, part of the Deficit Reduction Act of

1984, provided incentives for physicians to accept assignment and penalties for shifting costs to patients. Physicians who agreed to accept assignment for all patient claims were defined as participating physicians and listed in directories and in other reference sources available to Medicare beneficiaries. They were to be reimbursed more rapidly and were permitted to submit their actual charges to Medicare. The information on their customary and prevailing charges would be used to update their approved fees when the freeze was lifted (originally on October 1, 1985, but then postponed). Fee increases for nonparticipating physicians would be postponed for an additional time. Furthermore, physicians who did not participate and who increased their charges to beneficiaries beyond the amounts charged from April through June 1984 could be subject to a civil penalty of up to $2,000 for each violation and might be excluded from the Medicare program.[23] This compromise permitted physicians to continue to charge patients more than Medicare would pay but did not permit an increase in these additional charges during the freeze. In adopting this legislation, Congress recognized that a freeze on Medicare-approved charges without incentives to encourage participation and penalties on cost-shifting would hurt Medicare beneficiaries. It also recognized that requiring all physicians to accept assignment at Medicare-approved levels below the market price would increase the risk that physicians would refuse to accept Medicare patients.

Beyond not taking assignment, physicians can increase incomes under Medicare, as under other insurance programs, by increasing the utilization of medical services—asking the patient to come back for one more visit or to return in three rather than six months—and by being aware of and reacting to the structure of relative fees approved by the program. The prevailing fee structure is not a logical necessity but a reflection of historic patterns and attitudes. Historically, insurance programs have paid more amply for procedures (particularly surgical ones), laboratory tests, and X rays than for time.

Though troubled about the loss of personal care, most Americans and most physicians have welcomed the increased emphasis on medicine's scientific component and on measurement as science. Physicians receive much of their training in hospitals, where, pressed for time and hardly knowing their patients (and knowing them even less as the length of hospital stays declines), they turn to technology to provide presumably objective information. Patients, too, place great emphasis on "doing something," and tests and procedures provide seeming evidence that someone is doing something. The fee structure does not countervail but reflects and supports the pressure to probe with instruments, not with questions. More procedures and more tests are the inevitable consequence. So, too, are higher costs.

Physicians have benefited from the Medicare program. Notwithstanding their historic opposition and early negative or hostile attitudes, Medicare has had at least two favorable effects on their practices. The first, of course, is financial. The availability of health insurance for the aged has increased the effective demand for care, with obvious implications for physicians' incomes. In addition, the guaranteed Medicare payment under assignment or, at the minimum, the assistance provided to beneficiaries via the partial reimbursement of physician charges, has increased collection rates and reduced bad debts as compared with the pre-Medicare years.

It is true that these revenues can be obtained only under conditions of accountability that require paperwork. However, there is no reason to believe that physicians would choose to forgo the income derived from Medicare in order to reduce the paperwork. Physicians can do so, if they so choose; no physician is required to treat Medicare patients. The fact that few choose to withdraw their services not only reflects physician-patient relationships but also offers evidence that the conditions set by Medicare are not viewed as entirely onerous or unrewarding.

Medicare has had a second and even more important effect on physicians. Although Medicare does not provide complete coverage or payment and thus still requires substantial patient cost-sharing, the program has partially freed physicians from the need to ration services on the basis of the patient's income. This benefit may be overlooked by physicians under age fifty, who, having entered practice since the establishment of health insurance for the aged, do not ask themselves how things might be without it. It may even be forgotten by older physicians who now take Medicare for granted and who do not choose to remember pre-Medicare conditions.

Before July 1, 1966, when medical care was less costly than it is today, physicians had to ask themselves whether a particular patient could afford the intervention and treatment they deemed appropriate. Some of the gap between what good care cost and what the patient could pay was filled by private charity, often provided by the physician. Even so, many patients went without the care that medicine could and did offer to the more affluent. Today medical practice has become both more complex and more expensive. Physicians can, and often must, call upon the laboratory, new diagnostic tests, and hospital and technological resources to achieve the kind and quality of care that they believe would benefit the patient. Without health insurance and Medicare, the gap between what was deemed necessary and what was affordable would be far wider and the problem faced by both patient and physician far more acute.

Physicians' willingness to contribute their time and to reduce their fees to help individuals without health insurance is no longer enough, as the nation has learned in recent years of high unemployment. Physicians would be confronted with the need to select a therapy consistent with the individual patient's ability to pay. Medical ethics and traditions suggest that physicians would find it repugnant to allocate care (perhaps life itself) to elderly patients on the basis of their individual incomes and wealth. Yet that is what they would have to do. Medicare has liberated physicians, and the value of this freedom should not be underestimated. Though hidden, the benefits associated with Medicare (and other third-party programs) are real.

One physician summarized this point in a letter to me: "I do not want to go back to the pre-Medicare days under any condition whatsoever. I would hate to face again the situation when we didn't give high quality care to our elderly citizens who couldn't afford medical care even in the days when it was relatively inexpensive, let alone now when it is incredibly costly."

PRIVATE INSURANCE COMPANIES

Patients and providers are not the only ones involved in the day-to-day operation of the fiscal aspects of the Medicare program. Title XVIII requires that the payment and reimbursement part of the program be contracted out to the private sector, to "intermediaries" for Part A and to "carriers" for Part B. These organizations receive the requests for payment for services rendered by care providers and make the disbursements that, under the prevailing standards and guidelines, are deemed appropriate. It is with intermediaries and carriers, most often Blue Cross and Blue Shield, that patients and providers deal on financial matters involving payment.

This arrangement involving the private sector was part of the initial Medicare compromise. Since the federal government was not experienced at claims review and the Blue Cross/Blue Shield system and the commercial insurance companies were, it seemed reasonable to build on their experience and on already-existing relationships. Government wanted to make certain that the program would work and was willing to pay a long-run price for short-term gains. Furthermore, government wanted to reassure providers (and patients) that they would be protected from government intrusiveness, that they would deal with organizations with which, on the basis of previous association and experience, they would feel comfortable. Naturally insurers who were experienced in processing claims welcomed arrangements (akin to self-insurance) that would pay their administrative costs without requiring them to bear the risks of underwriting.

The mechanism that was developed is complex, cumbersome, and often duplicative. The intermediary disburses government funds and must carry out various reviews and audits. In turn, government requires accountability and has its own review and auditing procedures. For some purposes, the patient deals directly with Medicare; for other purposes, with the intermediary or carrier in the geographic area where he or she received the service. Furthermore, there are different intermediaries and carriers in each of the states (and sometimes in subareas of a state) and generally also for Parts A and B. The system is not easily explained or understood.

Today it is clear that government underestimated its strength and competence while overestimating providers' abilities and willingness to remain outside the program. Moreover, it is also clear that government overestimated the diligence that intermediaries would bring to the review and auditing activity. Government put up the dollars, relying on the intermediaries for cost control and cost containment. Unfortunately, this divided responsibility was not a prescription for effectiveness. Cost control was not an item of high priority on the agenda of the various private insurers. Their dollars were not at risk, and guarding someone else's dollars was not of special interest.

The intermediaries and carriers (most often Blue Cross for Part A and Blue Shield for Part B) welcomed the opportunity to be involved with Medicare. It placed them in a powerful position to help mold definitions, criteria, and regulations—especially in Medicare's early days. After all, they had the day-to-day responsibility for administering the program and they were experienced. Their views on what would work and what would not were not easily disregarded. Since intermediaries and carriers continued with their other health insurance activities, they found it advantageous to be able to influence Medicare and to be part of the system. Furthermore, their role brought three potential monetary benefits.

First, they would be paid for processing the countless pieces of paper. Second, they would have the opportunity to shift some portion of their normal administrative costs, which otherwise had to be met out of premium dollars gathered in their regular insurance activities, onto the Medicare program. Third, through the reimbursement policy they could shift some of the hospital's costs, which otherwise had to be paid for by non-Medicare patients, some of whom were their subscribers, onto Medicare.

The cumbersome arrangement for intermediaries and carriers, no longer justified by administrative need, has been institutionalized. The private insurers have hired employees, purchased computers, and developed the required systems. An infrastructure has been built as a result of the flows of money. It would be as difficult to redirect Medicare's flow of dollars as to redirect the Mississippi's flow of water.

Private insurers are affected by Medicare in two additional important ways. The first is a consequence of the structure of Medicare benefits: the deductibles and coinsurance and the limit on hospital days lead to gaps in coverage. These gaps have provided insurers with an opportunity to sell supplementary insurance (Medigap policies) that help meet out-of-pocket costs and that pick up coverage where Medicare leaves off. This type of insurance has proved popular: about two-thirds of aged Medicare beneficiaries (the percentage, of course, varies by income class) have private supplementary coverage.[24] Building on the base provided by Medicare, private insurers have once again been able to tap the aged health insurance market.

The costs of such supplementary insurance policies have been rising rapidly under the pressure of two forces: the continuing increase in health care costs and the increases in Medicare deductibles and copayment, which translate into greater patient liability. Thus private insurers have been offering a more valuable and necessary product, but one that has become increasingly expensive. Chief executives of insurance companies who remember the pre-Medicare days are aware that without cost control and in the face of Medicare cuts they may once again find that their product has been priced out of the market.

Private health insurance policies can complement but cannot substitute for Medicare. A Medicare program that covered less and less and was subject to continuing erosion would destroy the mass market for supplementary insurance. In 1965 private insurers knew they needed

Medicare. Today, too, they recognize the stake they have in general cost containment and in a strong Medicare program.

Private insurers also are involved with Medicare in the area of cost-shifting. This is a complex matter related to hospital accounting and billing practices; yet it can be put simply. As Medicare (and Medicaid) tightened their reimbursement policies, they paid hospitals less than the hospitals believed was a fair share of total hospital expenses. Hospitals reacted by increasing charges to other payers, especially to commercial insurance carriers, in order to cover the shortfall in total receipts. In turn, private insurers have had to raise their premiums in order to, as they would put it, "subsidize" patient care only partly paid for by government.

Concerned that both federal and state government will continue to tighten reimbursement regulations and limit expenditures, private insurers fear that differentials will widen and the cost-shifting phenomenon, the "hidden tax" on their subscribers, will grow. The point is clear: the health financing system is like a balloon. Pressure on one part of the balloon does not reduce its volume; it simply causes the balloon to pop out elsewhere, affecting the private sector and subscribers. Thus the private insurance sector has yet another interest in Medicare's and Medicaid's well-being: a reduction in government programs and smaller government payments means more extensive cost-shifting and requires larger private payments, not only by the aged, disabled, and poor, but by all payers.

THE FEDERAL GOVERNMENT

The final set of perspectives on Medicare is that of individuals in the federal government. They deal with Medicare in different ways and around different issues. They have one responsibility in common, to guide a federal program now deeply embedded in the American health care system and in the federal budget.

Executive Branch   The Health Care Financing Administration, part of the Department of Health and Human Services, is responsible for administering Medicare, for making the program work on a day-to-day basis. Those administrators have the task of translating the law into operational terms and into regulations, but within the constraints set by the legislation and by its legislative history: congressional perspectives revealed in debate and committee reports. Few of us who are over age fifty recall any discussion of regulations in our high-school civics courses. We learned that bills were enacted by House and Senate, reworked in conference committee, again enacted, then signed or vetoed, and, if vetoed, might still become law. The implication was clear: the story ended when a bill became an act.

Today we are aware that when the legislative battle is over, a new round of activities involving the development of regulations begins. The words in the Medicare Act—"hospital," "physician," "reasonable cost," "customary charges"—must be defined and the definitions must be clear and precise. They cannot be made on an ad hoc basis, subject to the individual, perhaps conflicting, interpretations of the various persons faced with Medicare-related problems, questions, issues. We are a society of laws. It follows that we are necessarily a society with regulations.

Because it would be impossible for Congress to spell out every detail, to address every contingency either before or after it arises, government officials draft a host of specific interpretations and regulations in an attempt to bring order to what would otherwise be chaos. These are the persons who are called bureaucrats. Often they must do their work under unfavorable conditions: with fewer resources than are required for efficiency, with conflicting objectives and criteria for measuring their effectiveness (such as paying claims quickly versus investigating claims fully, or setting high standards for hospital participation versus maximizing the number of approved hospitals). Furthermore, they must discharge their responsibilities under changes in leadership, and thus in priorities and goals: since Medicare was enacted, there have been five Presidents and twelve secretaries of HEW and its successor, the Department of Health and Human Services (DHHS). Finally, perhaps the most difficult problem faced by administrators is that every decision they make and every regulation they draft has distributive implications, bringing benefits to some and costs to others. Such decisions inevitably create controversy.

The administrators of Medicare are part of the greater society. They read the newspapers and books we read and see the movies we see. Although they tighten and loosen regulations partly in response to the views of their superiors, their interpretations also inevitably respond to broad shifts in social attitudes, goals, and priorities. In balancing their perceptions of the public interest, the legislative history, and the pressures from interested parties, administrators are not engaged in a purely technical process. Their regulatory decisions are the product of judgments that are neither immutable nor infallible.

Rule making is a political process in which individual citizens and organizations (and those who speak on their behalf) are free to voice their views, to appeal to their representatives in Congress, and to use the pressure they can command to alter regulations and their application. Medicare administrators cannot help but be aware that the relatively few providers are better organized than the many beneficiaries and that "free speech" does not mean equal control of and access to the microphone and loudspeaker. Some affected parties speak with louder voices than do others, and the volume may bear little relation to the merits of their case.

Given the difficulties that program administrators face, it is vital that they receive recognition and support from superiors, especially since these administrators are anonymous and their effectiveness will seldom be recognized except by peers and colleagues. Few of us know the names of those who helped make Medicare work or understand the formidable task they had to undertake in the less than twelve months between the signing of PL 89-97 and what came to be known as M-Day, July 1, 1966. The Social Security Administration, the agency then responsible for Medicare, had to develop reimbursement and payment mechanisms and criteria. A central automated record system had to be established to record eligibility for each of the two plans (Part A and Part B), payment of premiums, and utilization data. Four million persons not on the beneficiary rolls had to be located. In addition, it had to contact and enroll the almost 19 million persons eligible for benefits. Each had to indicate whether he or she wanted to enroll in Part B. Two million forms a week had to be mailed and the replies processed. Followup mailings were necessary. Medicare handbooks describing the program had to be translated into twenty-two languages. Every eligible person had to receive an identification card. Mailings to beneficiaries and providers totaled in the hundreds of millions. According to Somers and Somers, from whose book *Medicare and the Hospitals* this brief account is taken, President Johnson said, "the preparations for the program constituted the largest management effort this nation had undertaken since the Normandy invasion."[25]

Today the program is fully implemented. Nevertheless, it does not run itself. Periodic legislative changes and amendments, as well as the process of learning from experience, necessitate or suggest revision of procedures. Unfortunately, those who administer Medicare no longer receive the recognition accorded them by Johnson. Presidential candidates and elected chief executives, appealing to the American suspicion of central authority, have found it advantageous to campaign against government and to criticize and belittle government employees. Effective administration has been weakened by low morale. While the well-being of federal employees may not be a matter of concern to most citizens, all of us want government programs to be well administered. We want Medicare to enroll beneficiaries expeditiously, to reimburse them speedily, to answer their questions quickly and correctly. An environment that undervalues administrators and encourages able officials to leave government service inevitably reduces program effectiveness. In turn, the public loses confidence in government's ability to govern.

It is true that not all administrators are able individuals whose goal is to serve the public and serve it well. But valid and appropriate criticism is very different from the easy quip and thoughtless joke about foolish, ineffective, and bumbling government. The former alerts us to work to improve government; the latter helps to destroy it.

Congress   Responsibility for Medicare also belongs to Congress, the 435 members of the House and 100 members of the Senate, each with his or her own interests, priorities, and constituencies. Since health insurance for the aged is only one of many complex policy issues that legislators face, it is not surprising that only a few members of Congress, as a result of their committee involvement and staff interests and capabilities, are versed in the details of the Medicare program or are especially knowledgeable about emerging health care problems and issues. Nevertheless, all legislators, wherever they come from, whomever they represent, whatever their individual and particular concerns, are affected by the Medicare program. It provides important benefits to their constituents and in doing so expends over $70 billion annually. To members of Congress these are two important pieces of data.

Most members of the present Congress have not had occasion to participate in a broad Medicare debate. Few of them served in the House or Senate in 1965, when Title XVIII was enacted. Furthermore, the Medicare program does not require an annual appropriation or periodic reauthorization. None of us, therefore, knows whether a majority of both houses believes in the social insurance principle on which the program roots. But we do know that a minority is prepared to repeal a Medicare program that works.

Congressional attitudes and perceptions can be divided into three broad categories. There are those members who are convinced that the 86th Congress made the correct decision when it rejected a program of federal financial support for state means-tested health insurance programs. They believe that the best protection for the middle-income and the needy aged is a universal program. They also believe that the best protection for the program is its basis in principles of social insurance. The fact that, in recent cutbacks of social programs, Social Security and Medicare have fared better than Welfare and Medicaid, reinforces their convictions. If Medicare did not already exist, they would vote to enact it. Since 1986 is not 1965, the nuances and compromises would be different, but the essential character of the program would be the same.

A second group of legislators is less committed to the principles of social insurance but aware that Medicare helps to solve problems that call for and require government intervention. They recognize that in enacting Medicare Congress was trying to meet a real problem and that the program has done so. They understand that if Medicare disappeared, the earlier problems—magnified by inflation and by the increase in the number of those age sixty-five and over—would reappear. Even if they question whether Medicare was the optimal solution, even if they wonder whether they would have voted for it in 1965, they are aware that the choice is not between Medicare or a purely voluntary system but between Medicare or a different kind of government program. The lack of a consensus on an effective alternative reinforces the existing program. The fact that Medicare has worked means that to replace it, members of Congress would have to choose between a successful program that their constituents know and accept and an unknown program that might or might not work. Given that choice, it is not surprising that they support the basic character of the existing program.

Both the first and the second groups recognize the need for reform of Medicare in order to assure its survival and to increase its effectiveness and efficiency. A third group of legislators has strong doubts and reservations about a Medicare program that helps all the aged and disabled, that is compulsory and universal rather than voluntary and means tested, and would repeal the legislation. What others define as the helping hand of government, they view as the destroyer of individual initiative and responsibility. Yet they are aware that their constituents rely upon the benefits and reimbursements provided by Medicare for two decades. They know that Medicare is so important and so large, so deeply embedded in the fabric of American medicine, the budgets of hospitals, the income of physicians, and the quality of life of patients (indeed of all Americans), that they dare not vote for its outright repeal. Given their aversion to government assistance programs, they are willing to cut benefits, increase deductibles and coinsurance, shift costs to the private sector, and add elements of means testing. They label those changes as fine-tuning, as marginal, or as useful or necessary adjustments. They would destroy the program while claiming to improve it.

The fact that in the next decade the Medicare Hospital Insurance Trust Fund expenditures will exceed revenues and reserves will be depleted provides these legislators with an opportunity. They know that these fiscal realities mean that within a few years there will again be an important Medicare debate, one that may be as fundamental as the 1965 debate. The battle in that debate will be for the votes of those members of the House and Senate who are not experts and who hold no strong ideological commitment, the legislators in the second group. Absent a knowledgeable, watchful, and vocal electorate, absent enough citizens who understand Medicare's accomplishments and who express their belief in equity as well as in cost control, Medicare may be radically changed. As many Americans have learned in recent years, it is easy (and dangerous) to underestimate the power of an ideological argument, particularly if it is cast in pragmatic terms.

In a world of cutbacks and budget deficits, Medicare is and will continue to be at risk. In the near future the greatest risk is not outright repeal but a continuing nibbling at the edges, which, over time, would emasculate the program. Each cutback and change would appear small, one that does not do violence to the program or to the benefits of current (in contrast with future) beneficiaries. Nevertheless, the cumulative changes could destroy the program.

Today Medicare survives. To survive, however, is not the same as to flourish. There can be little doubt that the legislative perspective on Medicare has changed. In its early years the program was extended, benefits were increased, and criteria for eligibility were broadened. In 1967, for example, the number of days of covered hospital care was increased by the addition of the lifetime reserve of sixty days. In 1972 coverage was extended to the disabled and to those with renal failure.

Furthermore, Congress was aware that the program was incomplete (for example, it did not provide any benefits for prescription drugs outside the hospital), and there were numerous efforts to include additional benefits.

In recent years, however, these efforts have been replaced by cutbacks and by talk of even further reductions. In an effort to reduce outlays, Congress has increased premiums and deductibles and has enacted legislation designed to shift some Medicare costs back to the private sector. The Gramm-Rudman budget-deficit legislation protected Social Security but did permit limited reductions in Medicare expenditures. Despite the broad commitment to the program, a new tone has crept into the discussion. Much, though not all, of the new thrust derives from concern with the size of Medicare expenditures.

Health care has become more costly and hospital care especially so. Expenditures for Medicare (Parts A and B) service benefits have grown from $36 billion in 1980 to $70 billion today. These increases are large, and, worse, further increases appear inevitable. There is little in the system, a system that pays for care delivered in and by the private sector, to make these increases self-limiting. Diagnostic-related reimbursement for hospital care and the freeze on physician reimbursement may prove effective in slowing increases in expenditures, but it is far too early to be certain whether that will be the outcome or whether— given the growth in the number of aged and the expansion in medical science—the savings generated will be sufficient.

We pay a price for the compromises struck in 1965, compromises that called upon Medicare to pay the bills but gave the program no authority to rationalize the health care system. Thus, concerned about the future costs of benefits and averse to increasing the payroll tax or using general revenues to raise the necessary funds, Congress casts about for ways to control costs without doing violence to the program.

Concern with scarcity has replaced concern with distributive justice. That many of today's political leaders see Medicare as a frustrating problem rather than as a magnificent achievement should not surprise us. The general climate of opinion has altered radically.

For decades economists had tried to convince the public that resources were scarce, that every nation, even the United States, faced limits. It was a difficult task, for members of the politically dominant white middle class saw their society as one in which an expanding present would lead to a fully satisfying future. The Other America, the America of poverty, which Michael Harrington described in 1962, was invisible.[26] It was not difficult to respond when John F. Kennedy and Lyndon Johnson used the power of the presidency to bring the problems of the disadvantaged to public attention. In a growing economy, few voters asked how much they would have to give up to provide help to others who were needy. As long as the economy continued to create plenty, to generate an ever-larger GNP, its riches could and would be shared by all. We could engage in redistribution and still leave everyone better off because the pie was growing. Americans believed that a growing economy could be compassionate.

Today economists continue to deal with the allocation of scarce resources. They still draw "production possibility curves," graphic representations of the need for choice, for tradeoffs. But Americans no longer have to be convinced that scarcity and limits are realities. The Zero-Sum Society has displaced the Affluent Society.[27] The view that others can gain only at your or my expense has replaced the view that we can all advance together. Many Americans believe that a compassionate economy cannot grow.

Perhaps we will come to recognize that growth and compassion are not mutually exclusive. Perhaps we will recognize that expenditures for social programs, including Medicare, can be stretched by government fiscal policy, including a tax increase. Perhaps we will realize that substantial cuts in taxes and substantial increases in defense expenditures are only two of a large number of political choices and are not preordained. For the present, however, the emphasis on scarce resources and on the impoverishment of government is pervasive, and that perception helps guide public policy. The resulting dialogue, with its emphasis on how to limit public expenditures while increasing private spending, applies to Medicare as to other activities of government. Controlling expenditures, especially in entitlement programs, which provide benefits whose costs grow as prices rise and as the population ages, becomes a high priority.

Yet although Congress views Medicare as a program that should be carefully scrutinized for potential cost-cutting efforts, it also views it as an important safety net. Thus, although Medicare has been cut back, it has not been emasculated. Protected by its universality, the central issue in the debate over its enactment, the one issue that could not be compromised, it has been weakened but not gutted. To continue to survive in a world of adversity is no mean accomplishment—and Medicare survives.

Budget Experts   Those in both the executive and legislative branches who are especially concerned with budget matters—the size of the federal deficit, the level of expenditures throughout the federal government, and issues of tradeoffs among various departments and activities—have yet another perspective on Medicare. The director of the Office of Management and Budget (OMB), the secretaries of the executive departments, and members of Congress, especially those who serve on the finance and budget committees, are forced to deal with the fact that Medicare is a large budget item, that it contributes to the federal deficit, and that it competes with other programs for support.

Since Medicare Part A is financed largely through compulsory payroll taxes while 75 percent (some $18 billion) of Medicare Part B is funded as a federal contribution from general revenues, the program can be viewed both as one of a number of tax-collecting mechanisms and as one of a number of expenditure programs. Those concerned with budgets see two Medicare problems, one with immediate, the other with intermediate, implications.

The immediate problem arises from the fact that every dollar saved in Medicare helps reduce the federal deficit (or becomes available to help finance other federal programs). Until fiscal year 1969, Social Security expenditures and receipts (including Medicare hospital insurance and supplementary medical insurance) were not included in the unified federal budget as submitted by the president. Therefore, Medicare activities did not affect the size of the reported budget deficit. The exclusion of its trust fund operations from the unified budget offered Medicare (and Social Security) some shelter from fiscal policy decisions. Although, as a result of Gramm-Rudman, Social Security receipts and expenditures are again off-budget, Medicare remains part of the unified budget and subject to the congressional budget process adopted under that legislation.

The 1969 changes, supported by many economists who saw them as "technical" improvements, had important political and policy repercussions. Before 1969, changes in social insurance legislation had to be justified in relation to the program they were designed to affect; they were judged by their impact on the program and on its financing rather than by their impact on the total budget deficit (or surplus). The Social Security and Medicare programs were viewed as contracts between the government and the people. A change in conditions affecting the integrity of the program might require or permit a renegotiation of the contract.

The depth and strength of Americans' feelings about the importance of protecting the integrity of such programs were evident in the early 1960s, when some staff members of President Kennedy's Council of Economic Advisers informally expressed misgivings that a Social Security tax rate increase was scheduled to take effect during a recession: raising taxes was hardly an appropriate antirecession policy. Within hours the rumor had spread that the council was considering postponing the scheduled payroll tax increase. The response was clear, strong, and immediate: raising taxes might be bad economic policy, but using the Social Security system for fiscal policy purposes was even worse. The integrity of the system was at stake. One did not tamper with a contract.

That, however, was two decades ago. Today, partly because of the unified budget and the new budgeting procedures in Congress, partly because of the sheer size of the federal deficit, Medicare is vulnerable to the perceived requirements of macroeconomic policy. Medicare (and Social Security) revenues exceed expenditures. One of America's best-kept secrets is that the programs do not add to the deficit but help offset it. Nevertheless, if contributions were maintained at present levels while benefits were reduced, the deficit generated elsewhere in the budget would be reduced. Thus, controlling social insurance expenditures has become a matter of priority for reasons that, in the short run, have little to do with the effectiveness and financing of the social insurance programs.

Medicare's expenditures also affect officials who are responsible for programs that compete with Medicare for scarce budget dollars. The closer a particular program lies to Medicare in terms of constituencies or in terms of activities that promote health, the more directly and visibly its budget may be affected by what happens to Medicare expenditures. More "health dollars" for Medicare may mean fewer such dollars for other activities of any kind in DHHS and in other government departments.

Thus some officials in the Pentagon may feel that the defense budget is threatened or has suffered significantly because of Medicare. Certainly, many staff members at the National Institutes of Health, the U.S. Public Health Service, the Veterans Administration, and the Department of Education believe their budgets have been affected by Title XVIII expenditures. They know that at OMB their programs compete with Medicare for the scarce resources to be devoted to social welfare. They must justify their budget requests and plead their case in both executive and legislative presentations. They are frustrated by, and irritated with, a Medicare program whose expenditures grow automatically and are not subject to the same review processes. Medicare spends the sums required to meet obligations incurred as a consequence of billions of private decisions to seek and to render care at prices largely determined in the general medical marketplace. It hardly seems fair to be forced to compete under such unfavorable terms, to operate on a budget when Medicare operates on a blank check.

Of course, it is not obvious that if Medicare expenditures grew less rapidly, more funds would be allocated to competing social programs. The savings could be used in a variety of ways. Nevertheless, Medicare's presence in the unified budget permits policymakers to invoke the rising costs of health care as an argument for the need to contain other programs. As a result, administrators of other health programs and other social service programs tend to feel that their activities are hostage to Medicare and to the health needs of the elderly and the disabled.

This view is especially evident in OMB and in the congressional budget committees, which are concerned about the sum of all program expenditures. Budget analysts are acutely aware that even in the best of economic times, federal expenditures are limited and not all wants can be satisfied. In recent years, and partly as a planned result of President Reagan's policies of tax cuts and increased defense expenditures, budget dollars for social programs have grown ever scarcer. The immediate Medicare problem is the outgrowth of these policy choices.

The frustration felt by those who construct the federal budgets is similar to that felt by individual citizens who, with periodic increases in their private health insurance premiums, are left with fewer dollars for other expenditures. However, to draw an analogy between government and "the household" and to view their problems as similar in kind though different in size can only lead to faulty understanding and analysis. Government has far more control over economic events and the state of the economy than do individuals. Individual citizens can do far less than government to lower unemployment and thereby increase Medicare payroll-tax revenues, or to control inflation in health care prices and influence the structure of the health care delivery system in order to decrease Medicare expenditures.

The immediate Medicare problem stems from the federal deficit. The intermediate problem is even more severe: sometime near the end of the next decade the Medicare program is likely to face a financial crisis. If medical care prices, particularly those paid for hospital care, continue to rise at substantially higher rates than increases in the general wage level, the Medicare Hospital Insurance Trust Fund will be exhausted. Ways will have to be found to increase Medicare receipts and/or to reduce program outlays.

Which of the numerous possible options that would bring the trust fund into balance is selected—indeed, which options Congress will examine and consider—will not be determined by technical analysis alone. The options chosen and the solutions offered will reflect goals, values, and perspectives, the way the president, members of Congress, and the public view the role of government and its relation to citizens. The choices made will be based upon a vision of society.

The power implicit in the language of a budgetary recommendation stating that the nation "can no longer afford Medicare" should not be overestimated. Words frame and limit the agenda for debate. They can be used to advance recommendations that would shatter the foundations of the program. To say we "can no longer afford" rather than we "choose not to finance" would suggest that although various proposals might be unfortunate, they are necessary. Were we to elect not to pay for Medicare, we could hardly justify that action by arguing that we had no other choice.

Furthermore, packaging the argument in the (presumably) value-free language of fiscal responsibility contributes to a sense of urgency. In such a climate there would be pressure to eschew discussion of the equity goals of Medicare, of the many options that would strengthen the program's financing while promoting those goals. We would be left with a debate that emphasized changes in fiscal relationships rather than in program strengths and in the nature and organization of the medical care delivery system. It is true that fiscal relationships can be changed far more rapidly than the behavior of medical care providers and patients. Nevertheless, we dare not neglect the latter. We cannot expect to solve Medicare's problems in an equitable manner if we address only Medicare financing and again, as in 1965, ignore the incentives of the medical care system of which it is a part.

When debates about money displace those concerned with principles, it is the bookkeeper who dominates the discussion. Such debates, with their focus on the "practical," tend to ignore the vision of the kind of society and medical care sector we seek. Unless we guard against this kind of practicality, we run the risk of becoming the sort of people of whom it might be said: "Talk to them of Jacob's ladder, and they would ask the number of steps." There is a time to be practical, but the time is after, not before, we have determined our objectives.

6

Medicaid: Can Separate Be Equal?

On November 6, 1964, three days after the election, President Johnson's Task Force on Health (of which I was a member) submitted its report to the victorious incumbent. The eight-member group, convened in late August, had been asked to consider America's health needs and to recommend a legislative program to meet those needs. During that meeting the president emphasized the importance of a long-term vision. He did not want us to recommend only what we felt was politically feasible within a year or even within a presidential term. Instead, we were to decide what health measures were desirable for the nation over the next two decades and to recommend legislation that would enable America to fulfill its promise. It was the president's job to translate legislative proposals into action; the members of the task force were not to play at being politicians. What we rejected as bad politics, the president might believe to be advantageous. He reminded us that we were amateurs and he was the professional.

Even so, the task force split into two camps. A majority felt that it was foolish to ignore political reality—that if the task force was too visionary, its recommendations would be considered irrelevant. A minority argued that if our recommendations were limited to those we thought politically acceptable we would have misled the president, who had asked that we do more.

Such clashes are inevitable. Committees, task forces, and individuals who advise policymakers want to offer sound advice but also want to be realistic. They often feel a need to temper their analysis of required actions by injecting their views of political reality. If they do so, they may contaminate the advice they offer; if they do not, they may invite disdain and be ignored. The ability to achieve a balance between the two competing pressures—not to compromise too soon but to understand the need for compromise—is one of the distinguishing characteristics of successful and effective policy advisers. Such skills are rare indeed.

As individuals, several members of the task force possessed these skills. However, the composition of the task force (which included some administration officials who perhaps were reluctant to recommend more than they felt they could deliver) made it difficult to respond to the president's directive to think without pragmatic inhibitions. This was especially the case in the area of health services financing, where the administration already had supported the limited program of hospital insurance for the aged.

The task force analyzed the structure of health insurance in the United States and concluded that "the aged and the children in low income families face the greatest financial barriers to access to good health services." It recommended enactment of hospital insurance for the aged (along with some additional benefits but not including physicians' services), expansion of maternal and child health programs to serve children living in poverty, and appointment of a "committee of experts . . . to examine the feasibility and cost of programs to provide assistance to needy persons not otherwise adequately provided for."[1] These recommendations, together with additional comments from two members who felt the recommendations did not go far enough and who favored a universal insurance program protecting all Americans, went to the president. The amplifying comments attempted to alert the president and his staff to the fact that the task force had not in fact looked beyond a time frame of one or two years.

The basic conservatism of the task force document is demonstrated by the fact that within eight months Congress enacted a more extensive set of financing programs than the report had recommended. Instead of developing hospital insurance only, Congress established a Medicare program that included physicians' services; instead of appointing a committee of experts to consider health care for the poor, Congress enacted legislation establishing Medicaid. Nineteen sixty-five was a year of opportunity. Those who recognized that the health needs of the poor were real, that the existing Kerr-Mills program for the aged poor failed to meet those needs, and that additional action was required seized that opportunity. Further study and more deliberation by a "committee of experts" would probably have produced a more effective piece of legislation, but it is doubtful whether such legislation could have been enacted, since after 1965 congressional attention was increasingly riveted on Vietnam.

Title XIX of the Social Security Act, Medic*aid*, was adopted at the same time as Title XVIII, Medi*care*. The difference in the names even though both programs paid for medical services conveyed a symbolic message. Medicare and Medicaid are organized and funded differently, serve substantially different populations (though with considerable overlap), and evoke different responses from the general public, providers, and elected representatives. In fact Medicare and Medicaid can be considered as a test of two different approaches to the provision of assistance in meeting the costs of medical care. It is as if for twenty years the United States has conducted a massive social experiment that asked which approach, Medicare or Medicaid, operates more efficiently, effectively, and equitably. In examining possible directions for the future, it is useful to consider what lessons can be drawn from these two decades of experience.

Medicaid is a complex federally and state-funded program (a few states also require local funding) administered by the individual states. In fact it is a collection of fifty-six separate programs, one in each of the fifty states and the District of Columbia and, under different regulations, one each in Puerto Rico, Guam, the Northern Mariana Islands, American Samoa, and the American Virgin Islands.[2] The federal Medicare program, although it uses different intermediaries and carriers to process and pay claims, has a single set of rules that apply nationally to all beneficiaries. In contrast, Medicaid operates with different rules, eligibility requirements, schedules of benefits, and administrative structures in the various states.[3]

Each state must meet various specific federal requirements in order to receive federal funding, but within those basic requirements each is free to define eligibility, the structure of benefits, reimbursement and payment levels, and administrative and organizational mechanisms. Who will be assisted, for what, and by how much are therefore determined by both the federal government, which pays a portion of the costs of the state program and has a stake in the responses, and by the individual states, which also bear part of the costs. As a result few Americans know and understand how Medicaid works. At best, recipients, providers, and legislators know the program in a specific state. Their attitudes toward Medicaid are derived from that limited exposure and experience.

The federal government's contribution to a state Medicaid program is determined by calculation of the federal percentage share. The formula used compares state and national per capita income and provides a higher federal matching share to poorer states. The calculated percentage—the 1980 minimum of 50 and the maximum of 77.55 percent were reduced by up to 4.5 percent as a result of the 1981 Omnibus Budget Reconciliation Act—is applied to actual state Medicaid expenditures to determine the federal dollar obligation.[4] Thus the dollar amount of federal support is a function of a state's relative level of income, the state's decision about the size and scope of its own Medicaid program, and private provider and recipient behavior.

State levels of spending for Medicaid are a function of the nature of the state program: once a state has determined the groups that will be eligible and the services that will be covered, expenditures will depend upon the level of fees and of utilization, that is, upon prices and quantities. Medicaid expenditures are not predetermined by a budget or appropriation but are open-ended. Medicaid is considered an entitlement program, and the payments made are those required to meet the obligations written into current law (which of course can be amended at either the federal or the state level).

If a state elects to participate, it must provide coverage (that is, pay providers for the services delivered) for individuals on federal cash-assistance programs: those covered under the federal Supplemental Security Income (SSI) program that assists the blind, disabled, and aged; members of families eligible for the Aid to Families with Dependent Children (AFDC) program; and certain categories of pregnant women. States may elect to cover other defined groups and receive federal assistance to meet the cost of their medical care. The largest group among these are the "medically needy," individuals who are not otherwise eligible for cash assistance but who have incurred such large medical expenditures that their income, net of those expenditures, falls below a predetermined "welfare" level. States may also include, but without any federal cost-sharing, still other groups (such as able-bodied individuals who do not meet SSI or AFDC eligibility criteria, that is, who are not blind, disabled, old, or in a household with children but who meet state income criteria).

It is clear that state discretion makes for widely different eligibility standards, particularly for individuals who are not covered by the SSI program. States can impose more stringent (but not more liberal) definitions of income (what will and what will not be counted as income, such as work-related expenses) and standards for AFDC than are required by federal law, as well as their own definitions of an AFDC-eligible family (such as whether it must be female headed or whether an unemployed father can be present). They decide whether to cover the medically needy (two-thirds of the states do so) and, within federal limits, the income criteria to be used to define "need." They also determine coverage for those not receiving any federal cash assistance. As a consequence of the various federal and state eligibility criteria, the interplay of income standards, state of residence, age, and family structure become critical variables in determining the total number of Medicaid recipients (almost 22 million in 1984).

Many Americans think of Medicaid as a program that pays for medical care for the nonaged poor. That perception is incorrect. Although 69 percent of the individuals (and 61 percent of the households) who received Medicaid assistance in 1983 were poor, most of the poor do not receive assistance. In 1983 Medicaid covered only 40 percent— with very wide variation among the states—of households that fell below the poverty line of $5,061 for a one-member household and $6,483 for a two-member household (the U.S. median income in 1983 was $10,747 for single-person households and $21,065 for two-person households). Nearly half (48 percent) of all poor children under age five did not receive Medicaid assistance. Most shocking is the fact that between 1977 and 1983 the number of Medicaid recipients declined by 1.3 million (6 percent), while the number of poor persons grew by 10.5 million (43 percent).[5]

Medicaid is not a program for all the poor or for only the poor. Nor is it limited to the nonaged. Although 70 percent of recipients in 1983 were AFDC eligible, the services they received accounted for only 26 percent of the dollar expenditures (44 percent were dependent children, accounting for 12 percent of expenditures). Despite the existence of Medicare, 16 percent of Medicaid recipients in 1983 were age sixty-five and over, and payments made on their behalf accounted for 37 percent of total payments (another 35 percent were for services for the disabled).[6] Medicare beneficiaries receive Medicaid assistance, in part because of the "buy-in" provision that permits states to purchase Part B Medicare for Medicaid-eligible individuals unable to pay the required premiums, deductibles, and copayments on their own. Furthermore, Medicaid covers services not provided under Medicare (especially, but not limited to, long-term care).

Another public misconception is that once an individual has attained eligibility, Medicaid will pay for all the medical care received. States have wide latitude in determining the list of covered services they will pay for. As with eligibility, so too, with benefits: some are mandated by the federal government (although states may set "reasonable" limits to their utilization), while others are optional and states will receive federal financial assistance to finance them. Inpatient and outpatient hospital services, skilled nursing-home and home health care services (for those age twenty-one and over), physicians' services, laboratory and X-ray services, and early and periodic screening, diagnosis, and treatment for those under twenty-one are among the mandated services, but states may limit the number of services they will pay for (such as the number of hospital days or physician visits) and the conditions under which services may be utilized (by requirements for various review procedures). In addition, states may include still other services (such as intermediate care, dental care, drugs, and eyeglasses) if they wish. Here, too, they may set limits and require copayments.[7] States do not provide the care that Medicaid recipients might seek. They pay providers for services rendered. Recipients must find the care they need. If, as sometimes occurs, the care is unavailable (for example, if physicians in a particular community refuse to enroll in the Medicaid program), the fact that the services are mandated becomes irrelevant.

The differences among states in eligibility criteria, in the range of covered services, and in the limits placed upon those that are covered make for wide variations in the definitions and treatment of Medicaid recipients. The probability of receiving Medicaid assistance if one is poor varies widely across the nation, as does the amount of help one might receive once eligible.

Whereas eligibility for Medicare is easily determined, eligibility for Medicaid (as well as for particular services) requires periodic review and assessment. People move on and off the rolls as their incomes, places of residence, or ages change or as state or federal eligibility criteria are altered. This process has three effects. First, it adds to the administrative costs of the program. Resources which are allocated as health care expenditures and which we believe are paying for needed health services are devoted to determining recipient eligibility, "error rates," whether federal matching applies, and so forth. Complex laws— and Medicaid is complex—are expensive to administer. Second, health care providers (physicians, hospitals, and others) are never quite certain whether the individual with whom they establish a relationship will continue to be eligible for Medicaid benefits, or for how long. Third, because the patient is also unsure about his or her present or future eligibility, it is impossible to maintain the continuity of care regarded as so important by American health professionals and valued by so many of us.

These problems are exacerbated by the fact that Medicaid is an on-off program: below a given line individuals receive full benefits; above the line they receive none. Thus even slight increases in income may lead to the loss of all benefits. Yet those who barely cross the mandated income thresholds remain unable to finance the care they or their children need.

Society proclaims the virtue of work and of low marginal tax rates as a way to increase work incentives. Its actions on behalf of lower-income groups belie those proclamations. The Medicaid program contains significant deterrents to work, particularly for AFDC parents and most particularly for women. The Medicaid program in effect places a heavy marginal tax (the loss of Medicaid benefits) on what often are small increases in earnings. This marginal tax rate can exceed 100 percent. In many cases, mothers receiving welfare assistance want to work but are reluctant to accept employment because they fear losing the Medicaid health benefits their children need.

In addition to the Medicare-Medicaid distinctions concerning the populations covered—a single national eligibility standard versus eligibility standards that vary by state, permanent eligibility versus periodic eligibility review, and a nationally defined structure of benefits versus state-determined levels—there are additional significant differences between the two programs. One that is of critical importance in affecting many state decisions relates to funding patterns. In contrast with Medicare's insurance (and trust fund) approach, Medicaid depends on appropriations at both federal and state levels. In periods of budget stringency, the program becomes more vulnerable.

Nor is the problem simply one of fluctuating budget stringency. Every state Medicaid program is dependent upon that state's willingness and ability to raise the required funds. Although poorer states find that the Medicaid program is a "good buy," since the federal government will contribute about 75 cents of every program dollar spent, poorer states have fewer state resources and more poor people than do richer states. The 75 percent that they receive from the federal government is a big help, but only if they can find the matching 25

percent. Consequently, some states may find themselves in the same
position as a poor individual who is offered a substantial discount on
an expensive car or advance information about an excellent investment:
the bargain or the knowledge is of little use to someone too poor to
take advantage of the opportunity. As a result of limited state resources and massive needs, the poor who live in the poorest states
may in fact receive the least generous Medicaid benefits.

The more affluent industrial states had more generous health programs for the poor in pre-Medicaid days. Thus, federal matching funds
relieved them of some of the state, county, or local expenditures they
were already incurring and induced them to erect more liberal Medicaid
programs. With rapid increases in health care costs and Medicaid expenditures and downturns in their industrial bases they too are hard
pressed. As a result of these various influences, and especially of state
attitudes toward the poor and toward their medical care, state levels
of support for Medicaid differ widely. As with other welfare benefits,
needy individuals are likely to fare better (if the debilitating psychological effect of being poor in an ocean of riches is ignored) if they live
in a relatively affluent state but not in one so affluent that the needy
become invisible.

The contrast between Medicare and Medicaid is pervasive. As the
first chairman of the HEW secretary's Medical Assistance Advisory
Council (which dealt with Medicaid), I observed firsthand the enormous
disparity in federal interest, commitment, planning, monitoring, and
administrative resources devoted to the two programs, and this despite
the fact that in many important respects Medicaid was a much more
complex program needing more, rather than less, attention. Medicaid
was, and remains, the "poor relation."

The two programs reflect society's attitudes toward the population
groups assisted and the political power of those groups. Medicare, the
program for the aged, was designed as a federal social insurance program with some administrative responsibilities *delegated* to carriers
and intermediaries; Medicaid, the program for some of the needy, was
designed as a welfare program and *relegated* to the states. Those who
are part of the Medicare program are classified as "beneficiaries,"
individuals who receive benefits which they presumably have paid for
and have earned and which are financed by payments into a social
insurance trust fund. In contrast, those enrolled in the Medicaid program are termed "recipients," individuals who are granted assistance

as a matter of public charity. Their benefits are not considered to be earned. They rely upon the milk of human kindness and know that it may curdle.

Both federal and state expenditures for Medicaid have risen rapidly. The total reached $37 billion in 1984. In the past decade most of the increases in federal and state costs have been the consequence of rapid inflation in medical care prices (the number of Medicaid recipients declined by 6 percent between 1977 and 1983 while vendor payments increased by 99 percent). The fact that Medicaid spending has grown far less rapidly than Medicare (187 percent) has not made the increases palatable.[8] Both the federal government and the individual states have felt the pressure to search for changes that help contain expenditures. Since total expenditures depend on only a few variables, only a few options are available: reducing the number of eligible recipients, the kinds of services to be paid for, the level of utilization of services, the prices paid for services, or the share Medicaid pays for services.

At various times the federal government and the individual states have tried each or several of these options. There have been significant reductions in AFDC eligibility (both through state actions limiting increases in AFDC benefit standards and through federal action mandating new definitions for AFDC eligibility), in state coverage for the medically needy, and in coverage for the aged, through federal action making it more difficult to become eligible for nursing-home care by transferring one's assets and thus becoming impoverished. Similarly, there have been changes in the structure of service benefits as the federal government removed the requirement that services provided to one Medicaid-eligible group had to be provided to all eligible groups and as individual states set limits on the utilization of services (such as the length of hospital stays or the number of physician visits per year). There have also been attempts (stimulated by recent changes in federal requirements) to control hospital reimbursement and to limit physicians' fees.

But even though states have considerable discretion to change the regulations under which their own Medicaid programs operate—especially as a result of federal legislation adopted early in the Reagan administration—there are limits to what they can do to cut expenditures. These limits are set by the basic nature and structure of Medicaid, the needs of the population at risk, and the pressure of providers, as well as by the fact that Medicaid is only a part of the total health care system. The prices it must pay and the pattern of service that its recipients utilize are determined in largest measure by forces that lie outside the program.

When Medicaid was enacted, health officials proclaimed that charity medicine had been abolished. Thus, when state governments set lower reimbursement rates for the care of Medicaid patients than are paid by Medicare or by private insurance companies, health care providers inevitably and understandably resent the fact. They may conclude that Medicaid is trying to save money by shifting the obligation once assumed by the total society back to the limited number of individuals and institutions that deliver care. The lower reimbursement often leads to unwillingness to treat Medicaid patients.

Nonetheless, despite the difficulties of administration, program changes, restrictions and cutbacks, Medicaid has had and continues to have a significant positive impact on the lives and health of millions of people: on pregnant women and their babies, on young children in need of care, on the elderly whose Medicaid dollars help them buy into Medicare or enable them to enter long-term care institutions. Critics who argue that Medicaid's billions of dollars are not used in a manner that exerts leverage on the health care system, that all they do is pay for care, are correct, but the indictment is inappropriate. Medicaid was not designed to change the American health care system, but to enable millions of people with limited access to that system to buy into it.

Given the economic and political strength of the existing medical care delivery system, as well as the decentralized nature of the Medicaid program, this limited goal was not an unreasonable one. There are real limits on the leverage that a program designed to assist a vulnerable population whose service needs compete with those of the rest of the population can exert. The harder the Medicaid bureaucracy might push to alter the conditions and arrangements under which Medicaid recipients would receive services, the more likely it is that service deliverers would reallocate their time and effort away from Medicaid patients.

Medicaid did not try to erect a new kind of health care system. Its goal was to give Medicaid recipients what other patients covered by private insurance or by Medicare possessed: freedom of access to all health care providers, and thus, freedom of choice in their health care arrangements.

Free choice is a highly charged political issue because it involves a conflict of goals. When Medicaid was enacted, its proponents insisted that recipients have the right to seek services wherever and from whomever they desired (subject to the usual and well-accepted requirements regarding licensing and accreditation). The goal was to open the entire health system to low-income patients and to do away with two-class or two-tier medicine—a situation in which the poor received their care from a limited number of providers, under different conditions (such as without appointments), and in different surroundings (such as in hospital outpatient clinics).

Some observers did point out that since information on the quality of care offered by different providers was not available, the right to free choice conferred the right to make bad choices (albeit unknowingly). Under those circumstances the average quality of care received by the low-income population might actually decline. This could occur if, for example, Medicaid recipients chose to receive their care from incompetent physicians or in (presumably lower quality) community hospitals instead of in (presumably higher quality) teaching hospitals affiliated with medical schools, which in pre-Medicaid days often treated large numbers of impoverished and nonpaying patients.

This argument, however, spoke to an issue that affected all the population: the need to inform choices through standards, review, and dissemination of information on quality. It did not speak to or negate the concept of free choice: the right, whatever the level of information available, of individuals (including those in need) to make their own decisions, the right of and opportunity for Medicaid recipients to make the same, sometimes wise and sometimes foolish, health care decisions that others make.

In 1965 the concept of free choice was viewed as compelling. Medicaid, after all, was not only health legislation but also social legislation. It was enacted by a Congress much of whose energy was devoted to expanding civil rights. That Medicaid granted rights in addition to financing health care should not surprise us.

It is true that in enacting Medicaid instead of providing the eligible poor with a higher level of income maintenance, society had already narrowed the choices available to those with higher income. Society, after all, could have given the eligible population the most basic resource, dollars, and thus permitted recipients to choose between medical care or other goods or services. Instead, Congress chose to offer its assistance specifically for the direct purchase of health care only.

This decision can be explained on many grounds: the long tradition of assistance in kind; a concern that cash assistance might be allocated to nonhealth expenditures and that society would still have to pay for the health care of sick low-income persons even if they had "misspent" their income; a societal concern about health care as a priority item and a willingness to offer assistance for medical services but not for other goods and services; a recognition that health care involves "externalities" (improving your health also improves my health—a situation particularly evident in but not limited to cases of communicable diseases); the political visibility and power that derived from the emotional concern with health care in contrast with an abstraction such as income. In essence, the body politic said that it accorded health care a priority, although within the field of health it was prepared to have the patient decide from whom and when to seek care.

While for some legislators free choice was an expression of lofty aims and high ideals, for others it was a pragmatic response to the medical community's fear of government interference as well as to the recognition that government had to let patients make decisions because it did not possess the knowledge or the ability to do so for them. That view has changed. It is not that those in federal or state government are necessarily convinced that they can make medically better or wiser decisions than recipients or that, even if they could do so, they would be justified in abrogating free choice. Rather, those who control the purse strings are convinced that they would make less costly choices. The effort to control Medicaid expenditures and the knowledge that some providers and organized systems of care are less expensive than others has led policymakers to reopen the question of free choice of providers.

If medical care could be delivered in only one way, the issue of costs and free choice would not be related; society would not be confronted with a dilemma. The "simple" question would be, how much assistance federal and state governments would be willing to continue to make available, given the medical care cost explosion. The operational dilemma arises because all of us have learned that the level of health expenditures and the quality of care are not directly related and that the health care system can provide care at widely varying costs. Some hospitals are much less expensive than others without any apparent differences in results; some hospitals have less complex and less expensive technology or do not allocate resources to research and education; visits to the physician's office are less expensive than visits to emergency rooms or hospital outpatient departments; some physicians order fewer tests or are less likely to recommend surgery or hospitalization; utilization patterns vary widely with no apparent explanation (except that physicians have different styles of practice); fee-for-service care seems to be more expensive than other care arrangements; generic drugs are less costly than name-brand prescriptions.

These and other variations affect total health care costs and expenditures for individuals with private health insurance or with Medicare coverage as well as for recipients of Medicaid. There is no question that total health care costs and health insurance premiums could be reduced if more of us were prudent buyers, if variation in physicians' treatment patterns were narrowed, and if the delivery system were rationalized. Indeed, employers, unions, and insurance companies are trying to bring their collective pressure to bear on medical care providers and on the organization and structure of the health care system in an effort to reduce health care expenditures. However, both because of its federal and state funding out of general revenues and because it deals with a more vulnerable population (benefits obtained under collective bargaining and "earned" rights are one thing, "charity" is quite another), it is within the Medicaid program that the dilemma between excessive cost and free choice has been most directly posed.

Since we don't go to physicians for the pleasure of the visit but because we seek results, shouldn't the focus of attention be on treatment outcomes and results? If that is the case, isn't society justified in restricting the Medicaid recipient's choice to providers or systems that offer comparable quality (that is, good results) at the lowest cost? If quality can be guaranteed, why should Medicaid pay for the additional psychic benefit of free choice? But how can similar (or acceptable) standards of quality be guaranteed? How can those standards be sustained if there is a two-class health care system: one for people of means and/or with insurance, the other for Medicaid recipients? In the real world, can separate be equal? If it can, how long can it remain so?

The dilemma faced by legislators and Medicaid administrators—absent a comprehensive restructuring of the health care delivery and financing system that serves all Americans—is very real, for it exists in the context of fiscal constraints on taxpayers and the various levels of government. Assuming a given amount of money for Medicaid, is it preferable to offer medical care and the principle of free choice to fewer persons or to restrict choice and, by thus cutting costs, offer more medical services to more people? Is it preferable to have brand-name drugs, teaching hospitals, emergency rooms, and fee-for-service

for some or generic drugs, community hospitals, and HMO-type arrangements for many?

Does the answer hinge on an assumption of comparable quality?
What if the less expensive arrangements improve quality? Alternatively, what if they lead to a slight reduction in quality of care? What
does "slight" mean? How good must care be to be "almost as good"?
How do we define and measure "good"? What is the tradeoff between
quantity and quality? Finally, does our reaction to the dilemma depend
upon the population at risk? In other words, do those of us who are
not Medicaid recipients have a different emotional and intellectual
response to the restriction of our choices and the choices of all Americans—government tax dollars, after all, subsidize everyone's medical
care expenditures—than we have to restrictions on the choices of some
Americans?

Today the debate about free choice largely involves Medicaid. Soon
that debate will involve the systems of insurance that serve the rest
of us who also face rapidly escalating costs for health care. Employers
are not immune from budgetary pressures. They, too, will want their
dollars to stretch as far as possible. But the debate in the private
sector will be cast in different terms. Whereas the Medicaid debate
involves the imposition of legislative restrictions on choice, the debate
in the private sector will concern economic incentives that induce and
encourage us to economize.

In a market economy, free choice is necessarily constrained by personal income. As medical care becomes more expensive and market
oriented, as health insurance premiums increase and economic pressures exert themselves on employers and persons of moderate and
even higher income, all of us are likely to discover that "free choice"
is an inadequate description of reality, that the medical care choices
we can truly make (that is, afford), like other economic choices, are
limited.

Thus the issue of whether the Medicaid population should be told
where to get their care rather than encouraged to search for lower
costs is but an early legislative formulation of a much larger economic
question. We can broaden choice by inducing system and institutional
change that would benefit not only the Medicaid population but all
Americans. It is clear that the health care system needs cost-control
mechanisms. But the kind we need must work equitably and not depend
so critically on legislative and economic constraints, on forcing coercive
regulations and hard choices on persons with less income while exerting

less visible pressure on those with higher income and greater resources. The development of different systems of health care for persons of different income is one of the consequences of rising costs. It
need not be that way. None of us should accept the inherent inequities
with equanimity. The rules that we make for low-income persons today
will someday be made for us as well.

Undoubtedly the decisions made in the political arena will depend
in part upon whether the potential dollar savings and efficiency gains
associated with the restriction of free choice are trivial or large. Clearly,
they should also depend upon whether or not the quality of medical
care services can and will be maintained and monitored. Therefore,
the most effective protection for the Medicaid population would be its
enrollment in systems of care (such as HMOs) available to and utilized
by the population at large. Given the fact that most Americans are
not able to assess the quality of care they receive, we dare not assume
that the general population makes wise choices. Nonetheless, a one-
tier delivery system does offer some reassurance.

The issue of free choice for Medicaid will remain controversial. Forcing Medicaid recipients into modalities of care that are rejected by the
rest of the population will exacerbate those tensions. Even if such
modalities are cost effective, and even if they diligently guard against
diminution of quality, they will be perceived as, and are likely to
become, second-class medicine.

As long as Medicaid exists as a separate program, its expenditures
will remain high, because of the pattern of care that it finances. Thirty-
six percent of Medicaid expenditures is for nursing-home care. Those
dollars go to assist aged and disabled persons who, having substantially
exhausted their resources, require financial assistance for long-term
care. These expenditures, which account for 43 percent of the income
of nursing homes, are difficult to contain.[9] Noninstitutional alternatives
to nursing-home care are not sufficiently developed in the various
states to encourage the hope that even the prudent-buyer principle—
whereby the states would pay only for care that is produced efficiently—would permit substantial savings. Nor does the projected
rapid increase in the number of the very old indicate that the need for
care will decline.

The inevitable costliness of a program serving such a population (as
well as the millions of poor adults and children) makes it even more
imperative that we get "value for money." Today's Medicaid program

needs reform. Our twenty year experience with a program that serves diverse populations and finances different types of care has taught us much. We must recognize that the old are not the young, nursing homes are not like doctors' offices, chronic care is not the same as acute care. There is urgent need for a rationalization of federal and state responsibilities. We must assure greater equity across state boundaries—a problem that the federal government is uniquely qualified to address. Finally, and in the context of federal standards, it is time—it has long been time—to deal with the needs of those millions of Americans (the low income, the working poor, the unemployed) who require assistance in meeting their medical care expenses but who do not meet the restrictive eligibility standards of the cash-assistance programs.

How much of the unfavorable image of Medicaid results from the belief that it serves poor people for whom the rest of us must pay, in contrast with Medicare retirees, who have paid their own way, and how much results from the difference in the structure, administration, and funding of the two programs is unclear. Yet the lessons that emerge are clear: social insurance programs are stronger than welfare programs; federal standards for eligibility and benefits are more equitable than varying state standards; administration by a single authority is more efficient than a federal and state sharing of administrative responsibility. Operating a program that is primarily for the poor (a changing population) is difficult and administratively cumbersome and expensive; mounting a program that is part of the welfare system further increases its vulnerability. Such a program is subject to continuous attack as wasteful, unnecessary, bureaucratic, and designed for "freeloaders." Thus it is not surprising that welfare and Medicaid for the poor have been at greater risk and, in recent years, have been cut back more (when we take into account inflation and increases in the population served) than Social Security and Medicare. Programs for the poor tend to become poor programs. The needy are better served by universal programs in which their fate and that of other Americans are inexorably intertwined.

The problem that Medicaid attempts to address, the need to pay for care for those who cannot do so themselves, is as real now as it was in 1965. The problem is not dispelled by rhetoric; slogans are not substitutes for dollars. Cutting assistance to the millions of our citizens who are helped by the Medicaid program will not make them healthier or more affluent. Institutions (both nursing homes and hospitals) that serve the Medicaid population—and especially those that serve a disproportionate number of Medicaid recipients—rely upon Medicaid reimbursement for their survival. Weakening Medicaid weakens the nation's health and the strength of its health delivery system. Medicaid cannot be replaced by voluntarism. In the absence of a universal health insurance program, Medicaid will remain necessary. It needs to be reformed and strengthened.

7

System Reform: A New Emphasis

The enactment and implementation of Medicare and Medicaid helped address the health care financing problems of many Americans not covered, or not adequately covered, by private health insurance. Yet, if there were members of Congress who believed that health system and health financing issues could now be set aside, they were to be disappointed. New issues concerning efficiency and costs and older ones involving equity would continue to demand attention.

Inevitably and predictably, there were various amendments designed to clarify or adjust legislation so far-reaching and so new in structure. But the need to devote time and energy to modifying ongoing programs is inherent in the legislative and administrative processes. The unexpected outcome was that the implementation of Titles XVIII and XIX did not enable the American medical care agenda to become more focused and more circumscribed. Indeed, the opposite occurred. The issues that public and private policy had to deal with grew more numerous and more complex.

And yet in retrospect this outcome, too, was predictable. Congress had constructed a partial solution to the problems that parts of the population had in financing health care. It had added to its earlier concerns for veterans, members of the armed forces and their dependents, federal employees, and other special population groups. It had helped meet some additional important unmet needs. But it had not provided any answers for Americans who had problems in financing care yet were excluded from the various assistance and insurance programs. Most persons, after all, did not meet the specific eligibility requirements for Medicare or Medicaid. Although the majority of Americans had private insurance, that coverage was neither universal or comprehensive: many individuals were without any protection, still others could afford only a minimal benefit package, and many policies had wide gaps in coverage. It was inevitable that attention would be drawn to the availability and adequacy, the structure and performance of private insurance.

Furthermore, Medicare and Medicaid expenditures were large and growing. Responsibility to beneficiaries and recipients, as well as concern about budgetary impacts, helped shift the perception of government's role from that of bill payer to that of service purchaser. It was not enough simply to assume that beneficiaries and recipients were receiving value for (government) money. Nor was it enough simply to have intermediaries and carriers mail checks to hospitals and physicians and let the sum of countless private decisions determine the level of public expenditures. At the very minimum, government, the payer of the bill, was required to ask why the bill was what it was; at the maximum, whether the bill needed to be that large, whether what was purchased could be obtained at less expense or, indeed, needed to be obtained at all. The story goes that Charles Dawes, the first director of the U.S. Bureau of the Budget in 1921 (now the Office of Management and Budget), once said that if Congress passed a law requiring that garbage be spread on the White House steps, the bureau's regrettable duty would be to tell the executive branch and Congress in an impartial and nonpartisan way how the largest amount of garbage could be spread most expeditiously and economically. A narrow role, perhaps—one could ask why the garbage should be spread—but, even so, a role that goes beyond that of keeping ledger books on receipts and on expenditures.

The same concern with economy applies to all programs. Medicare and Medicaid review began with auditing; it moved to utilization review and to a concern with the efficiency of the health system that served the people whose bills were being paid. Since that system was the same one that served all Americans, it was inevitable that government become involved with issues of system reform.

The interest in the nature of the health care delivery system was strengthened by the growing recognition that third-party payments both by government and by private insurance could not be distributed in a purely neutral fashion. The sums involved were so large that they would inevitably have a substantial impact on arrangements for the delivery of and payment for health care. If the expenditures were not disbursed in ways that provided incentives for and stimulated system change, then they would help rigidify existing relationships. Third parties—and government was the largest and most powerful third party—learned that they were not bystanders to a drama but key actors. The way they interpreted their role would either change or freeze the nature of the play.

Moreover, there was a steady growth in total health care expenditures and in the share of GNP absorbed by the health sector. Medical care prices increased more rapidly than the consumer price index, and medical care expenditures rose even more sharply than medical care prices. Individuals who paid all or part of their health insurance premiums and medical care costs; employers who financed all or some of their employees' health coverage; local and state government, which funded Medicaid as well as other medical programs and health facilities; and the federal government, with its numerous health-related programs, all faced a cost explosion. Each percentage increase in expenditures was superimposed on a larger and ever-growing base. As health expenditures exerted an ever-greater effect on both the private and the public economy, the issue of controlling and containing increases in health care costs assumed growing importance and received more and more attention.

Yet the most important factor that kept America's attention upon health care issues was the most predictable of all: the dynamic nature of our society. Our mobility, changing population and economic characteristics, new products and new ways of performing old tasks, mean constant evolution in each sector in the society. Change has meant new issues, challenges, and opportunities, adapting old and adopting new ways of looking at and dealing with traditional and emerging wants and needs. Above all, change has meant a new agenda. Thus issues related to the characteristics of private health insurance, system change and reform, and rising expenditures and cost containment were added to the older concern about the development of a universal and comprehensive national health insurance program that promoted equity.

Equity and fairness are simple concepts. They are also rather vague and general, the sort of terms that each of us agrees with as long as we are not required to accept the next person's precise definition of their meaning. Some policymakers have argued that as health care costs rise it is more equitable to increase insurance deductibles than to raise premiums. The deductible affects the users of the services; the premium affects everyone. Although that may sound "fair," another way of putting it is that the deductible affects the sick and the premium spreads the costs among all enrollees. Isn't that one of the purposes of health, automobile, fire, and theft insurance? Yet it seems clear that equity and fairness mean different things to different people.

Nor is that the only problem. All of us recognize that in a real sense "life is unfair," and some (perhaps many) of us wish it were otherwise. That shared desire, however, does not mean that we will all agree that a particular problem need or should be addressed by government. Government cannot do everything; it, too, must set priorities. We may therefore disagree about whether a particular injustice is sufficiently important to merit national attention and action.

There are still other potential areas for disagreement even among those who share priorities and who concur that achieving greater equity is warranted. Individuals may differ on their estimates of the costs associated with various solutions. Furthermore, there may be disagreements about the best way to reach a particular objective. The disagreements may be especially sharp if we assume, as we must, that our society is constantly changing and, therefore, that today's preferred solution should take account of tomorrow's possible new conditions.

National health insurance, not surprisingly, was an issue to which different parties brought different definitions of the needs to be addressed; different attitudes about the appropriate role for federal, state, and local government; different estimates of the costs and side effects of action and inaction; and different views about the future. It was not a proposal around which a consensus could easily be developed. Nor, since it involved relationships between the private and the public sectors, was it an issue on which differences could easily be reconciled. Indeed, as we shall see, over the years compromise became more difficult as the debate grew more complex, as the goals of a national health insurance program expanded, and as both the economy and the health sector changed.

Debate about national health insurance began anew only a few years after the enactment of Medicare and Medicaid. This time, however, new goals were added to the old objective. National health insurance was still concerned with equity and universal and comprehensive coverage, with helping make certain that all persons had access to the American health care system. But the new national health insurance proposals, unlike those of the 1970s, were constructed to do more than achieve equity.[1]

These added dimensions are instructive. At the minimum, they remind us that legislative proposals reflect existing institutions and knowledge and prevailing attitudes at a particular time and that all these are being constantly modified. At the maximum, they illuminate the structural and attitudinal changes that set constraints on available options.

Discussions of national health insurance as it might exist in America are and need to be tied to reality, and our reality is the United States, whose health system embodies its own sets of relationships and flow of funds. It is shaped by general economic conditions and events, characterized by an apparent disenchantment with government, and influenced by information and misinformation about health insurance programs here and in other countries. Reality is described by data in tables but is also a function of our impressionistic conclusions. However much analysts may deplore the discrepancies between the data and the impressions, those discrepancies are part of the reality.

The dominant, almost the exclusive, rationale for comprehensive universal health insurance in the debates that predated Medicare was to provide coverage for individuals who did not have and could not afford insurance. The issue was one of fairness, of concern for persons who might be denied care because they could not finance it, of the need to create a system by which the total society helped finance care for all its members, care that would be available under conditions of dignity and on an equal basis regardless of individual health risks and individual circumstances.

The task was to assure that all members of the population had insured protection. Issues of universality, means testing, benefits and contributions, the relationships between the various levels of government, the role of voluntary insurance, and centralization of funding mechanisms were part of the technical and ideological debate about the best way to achieve the goal. It is true that individuals who were concerned about the distribution of physicians, the decline of general practice in the face of specialization, the usefulness of organized, structured, and planned delivery systems, and the quality of care also championed national health insurance. They saw NHI as the way to correct the deficiencies in the private fee-for-service health delivery system.[2] Nevertheless, the national health insurance issue was primarily defined as one of equity. "Fairness" was the rationale for the legislation, and the political debates were cast in the language of fairness.

The enactment of Medicare and Medicaid reduced political pressure for a single and universal national health insurance program. Those opposed to NHI could argue that the two programs had addressed the needs of the two largest and neediest population groups and that other groups and individuals could best be helped by America's traditional approach: tailoring specific programs to fit particular population groups and their situations.

Why enact national health insurance? Private health insurance, though employment based, was growing. It covered more and more individuals and families, and its benefits were increasingly comprehensive.[3] Medicare and Medicaid could be expanded. Why not solve the few remaining problems and fill in the remaining gaps with ad hoc measures? Why create a new, complex, universal program to serve 100 percent of the population when only 15–20 percent were without insurance? This estimate of the size and nature of the remaining problem did not take account of the needs of the insured who had inadequate coverage. It also failed to recognize that those who had no or inadequate insurance were a heterogeneous population: the unemployed, low-income earners, persons not in the labor force for a wide variety of reasons. These individuals could not easily be reached by the traditional American approach, which focused on particular beneficiaries and their characteristics (such as merchant seamen, veterans, the aged, the disabled, and tubercular patients). Nor could these have-nots easily be organized or organized around.

The argument that private insurance was doing a bigger and better job and that all we needed were a few patches here and there and the health insurance quilt would protect everyone, carried significant political weight. So, too, did the argument that shifting the billions of dollars now in the private insurance sector to a government universal program would require dismantling existing relationships among subscribers, employers, and insurers. Enacting such a program would be difficult and politically unrewarding. Private insurance had grown from $1 billion and 9 percent of all expenditures for personal health care in 1950 to $10 billion and 22 percent by 1967.[4] The new and growing private health insurance dollars had become an integral part of the health system. The economic and political power those dollars represented had to be reckoned with.

The richer justifications offered for national health insurance reflected the growing recognition that the flow of health care dollars affected the medical care delivery system, that the medical care system was wasteful, and that all Americans—whatever the source of financing for their health care—were paying for this waste. They also reflected the increasing concern that insurance, including third-party payment under government programs, did not guarantee care, but only payment for the care the patient managed to obtain. The structure of third-party payment (such as the fact that reimbursement rates were higher in urban than in rural areas) could exacerbate resource maldistribution and make it harder, not easier, for some to find the care they sought.

Supporters of national health insurance could therefore argue an old point but accord it greater priority: by concentrating payment through a single payer in one universal program or two (if Medicare were kept separate), national health insurance would have sufficient leverage to help reform the health care delivery system. In its new construct NHI was more than a program to assure equity; it was also a mechanism that could be used to rationalize medical care delivery.

Translated into operational terms, the resulting NHI program would stress regionalization and planning of facilities, monitoring of performance, and encouragement (through economic incentives) of the growth of organized delivery systems that departed from traditional fee-for-service reimbursement. The last goal, of course, went to the heart of American medicine's prevailing payment mechanism. Most hospitals and most physicians increase their incomes by filling beds, seeing more patients and seeing them more often, performing more tests and procedures. There are no monetary rewards for not filling the hospital bed, not ordering the test, or discharging the patient. The incentives of the fee-for-service and hospital reimbursement systems (excluding Medicare's diagnosis-related prospective payment system) are to do more and more. These incentives and the structure of physicians' fees lead to more tests and procedures, more surgery, more interventions.

These facts do not mean that physicians are interested only in making money, that they are prepared to order care they know is unnecessary and a waste of the patient's or the third party's funds. Medical care is not an exact science with published and well-accepted precise standards of care that are related to differences in patient psychological and physical characteristics. Medicine is part science but part art. It needs not only its protocols but also individual judgment calls. The issues involved in the mechanisms for payment run deeper than the doubtful ethics of a few physicians.

The more pervasive issue is related to the fact that for marginal decisions—one more day in hospital, one more test, one more procedure, one more visit—the various pressures and incentives all work in the same direction. American physicians and patients have come to define intervention and more medical care as better medicine. This is particularly the case under third-party payment, which is perceived as costing nobody anything or as costing everybody only a minute amount. If there are potential benefits and few risks associated with doing more (a significant "if"), if the fear of a malpractice suit leads to more tests (suits are not brought for doing a test that is unnecessary—for harming the patient's pocketbook—but for doing it badly or not doing it when it might have been useful—for harming the patient's body), if patients and third parties are willing to defer to physicians' judgments and simply pay the bill, if physician and patient view payment as a "painless" matter, the result is a set of pressures for expansion rather than restriction. The problem is that the fee-for-service reward system does not countervail these pressures but adds its own incentives to do a little more.

Fee-for-service, of course, is the mode of payment for TV technicians, plumbers, and automobile mechanics—and explains why so many of us seek additional information, opinions, diagnoses, and estimates from friends, neighbors, and other service providers (our suspicion is converted to concern because paying the bill requires opening up our own wallets). Yet health care is different because of the nature of the relationship between physician and patient, the difficulty patients have in evaluating and comparing potential variations in quality of treatment and performance; the difficulty physicians face in predicting the required course and duration of treatment. Health care is different not merely because medicine is not an exact science. We do not view illness and a malfunctioning garbage disposal in the same terms. We view physicians differently from how we view plumbers. There is an important element of trust in our relationship to the profession.

Even if we deplore the incentives created by fee-for-service, we cannot be certain that doing too much is less risky than doing too little. Nor are we certain which of the many alternative payment mechanisms would be preferable. We sympathize with hospital directors who are lectured about society's interests in reducing unnecessary bed occupancy but face a payment mechanism that rewards them for filling beds. The abstract societal interest conflicts with their concrete self-interest. We understand the problem of the physician who is told to order fewer tests but is paid per test performed. Sympathy and understanding, however, do not help structure a new reimbursement mechanism.

As a consequence of the health sector's growing impact on government and employer expenditures, on household budgets, and on the national economy, the pervasive and perverse fee-for-service incentive structure became more widely understood. In turn, the desirability of system change became one of the important arguments for national health insurance. NHI—defined as pluralism in the delivery system but as fiscal centralization through a single system of payment—was seen as the vehicle by which system change could be stimulated (or coerced). Unlike Medicare or Medicaid, national health insurance was not supposed to accept the prevailing medical care system and operate within it. It was to use its considerable fiscal power to change the system. The old goal remained: to make certain that everyone in the society had insurance protection and that it was financed in a way that took account of ability to pay. But a new goal was added: to make certain that the system that paid for care would be structured to provide new incentives promoting efficiency and quality in the delivery of care.

The battle for national health insurance was reopened under conditions far different from those that prevailed during the Medicare debates. Rising costs had forced proponents of NHI to meet the argument that the nation could not afford to finance care for everyone in an open-ended system. They responded not by compromising on the goal of universality but by constructing a program which would have a defined budget and which would stimulate new ways of reimbursing and delivering care—in other words, a program that would close the open-ended system.

One of the arguments by Medicare's proponents was that it would not change the health sector; one argument advanced for the Health Security Act, the national health insurance bill proposed by Senator Edward Kennedy in 1969, was that it would stimulate change. The contrast with the "permissiveness" of Medicare was clear in Kennedy's words: "The organization and delivery of health care is so obviously inadequate to meet our current health crisis that only the catalyst of national health insurance will be able to produce the sort of basic revolution that is needed."[5] Indeed, the AMA proposals for a tax credit to offset the costs of purchasing voluntary insurance—tax credits, though not creating a single unified payment system, could be designed to be as progressive in their distribution of benefits and costs as anyone might desire—were faulted, not on grounds of equity, but because they would leave the existing insurance and delivery system in place and freeze relationships and incentives.[6] Many in Congress and throughout the nation had learned a lot from the growth in private health insurance and from the Medicare experience. Health insurance to finance an inefficient and uncontrolled delivery system would no longer suffice.

But whereas the earlier "simple" Medicare-like social insurance approach that only paid the bills appeared unnecessary to the many Americans who had private insurance, an NHI program that tried to restructure the delivery system appeared threatening. The centralization of power in Washington ran counter to the prevailing climate of opinion. Replacing the private insurance system and also altering forms of payment and of organization seemed doubly threatening to millions of Americans who had insurance, felt that the system was serving them well, and were fearful that their relationships with their physicians would be jeopardized.

Nevertheless, when Senator Kennedy introduced the Health Security Act, which offered incentives to prepaid group practice, many (presumably) astute observers who were close to the health sector predicted speedy and favorable action. They expected that out of the give-and-take of the legislative process there would emerge some form of NHI that would cover additional individuals and groups, provide comprehensive benefits, and (perhaps hesitantly at first, but with gathering force) address some elements of system reform.

In retrospect, we can understand why the predictions proved incorrect. The judgment of those closest to the health sector was colored by their very closeness. Their lack of perspective caused them to underestimate the attention that other pressing national issues would receive and to overestimate the concern of the average American with the "crisis in medicine."

Influenced by the enactment of Medicare in 1965, the proponents of NHI viewed the fight for national health insurance as a continuation of a war that they had already won. But Medicare was a victory in a battle (and not as overwhelming as was suggested by the final vote), not in a war, and the victory was not necessarily unconditional or permanent. It was easy for the experts to forget that traditional divisions and sharply conflicting views still remained. National health insurance had not yet gone through the years of building coalitions, of education, of debate—even the years of legislative defeat on the floor of Congress. The experts knew so much and talked and listened so much to each other that they forgot that others did not share their concerns, analyses, or conclusions. They were so taken with studying and understanding the issues that they failed to consider that the American people had not done so.

Surely, they forgot that major social legislation—and NHI represented the most important and complex reform proposal since the enactment of the Social Security Act more than three decades earlier—moves forward only with presidential leadership. Given that the president can use his press conferences to structure the national agenda and to instruct the nation, one useful litmus test of the chief executive's commitment and of NHI's serious political prospects would have been questions about it at three successive presidential press conferences. The questions were never asked that consistently.

Senator Kennedy's statements received coverage and attention, but he was not the president. Furthermore, the fact that Kennedy was expected to seek the presidency both added to and reduced his power. Although many Americans and legislators wanted to assist a future president, others wanted to make certain that the senator, if he became the actual nominee, would not be able to take credit for a legislative success.

National health insurance still faced the same complex committee structure that Harry Truman had had to deal with. As chairman of the Health Subcommittee of the Senate Labor and Public Welfare Committee, Senator Kennedy could hold hearings on the health crisis facing the nation and, by asking adroit questions, could use those hearings to discuss how things might be improved were NHI in place. But both his colleagues and the witnesses knew that because he was not a member of the Senate Finance Committee, he could not use that forum to move the legislation forward.

Absent presidential involvement, absent years of mass education and organization, absent the urgent and visible crisis that required action to help middle-income Americans; and present an issue that seemed "old," present a proposal that was more complex than any health or social insurance legislation previously enacted, present a direct threat to existing financial and medical care relationships, and present Medicare and Medicaid that helped relieve the pressure for millions of Americans, the wonder is not that national health insurance was not enacted rapidly. The wonder, rather, is that so many reasonable and intelligent persons thought it would be.

Yet although the Health Security Act never even came to a vote on the floor of either House or Senate, it was discussed. There were speeches and rallies, hearings and committee meetings, negotiations and political maneuvers. There was a process of education: books, magazine articles, high-school debates, forums, lectures, even a "CBS Reports" documentary, "Don't Get Sick in America." The increased understanding (in Congress and throughout the nation) of the issues, including the need for system reform, did not result in NHI. But it did contribute to the enactment of various legislative measures designed to improve the way the system functioned and the way it allocated resources.

The most significant of these, the Health Maintenance Organization Act of 1973, was structured to assist the growth of organizations that would link insurance with the delivery of care: for a predetermined monthly premium, a group of care providers would agree to deliver all covered health care services to a group of subscribers. As both insurer and deliverer of care, the HMO (in the final instance, the defined group of providers) would assume the risks entailed in guaranteeing care to the defined group of subscribers. The assumption of financial risk would encourage the HMO to seek out economy and efficiency in the delivery of care and, thereby, reduce the costs of care. Furthermore, once the premium had been paid, the financial threat to the individual or family budget was eliminated, since HMOs typically limited their out-of-pocket costs to modest copayments (such as a small set fee for a physician visit) and did not have deductible or coinsurance charges.[7]

The term "health maintenance organization" was new, but the organizational structure had been part of the American health landscape for many years. It had taken two basic forms: the prepaid group practice (PGP) and the independent practice association (IPA). Of these, the former was by far the larger and more widespread. It also was rejected by organized medicine. PGP physicians were accused of practicing contract medicine and often found it difficult to secure hospital privileges.[8] Yet, though viewed in many circles as "radical and left-wing," the PGP had demonstrated its effectiveness and its survival power.

Nevertheless, only a small fraction of Americans were familiar with the characteristics of prepaid group practice and an even smaller fraction were enrolled in the relatively few PGPs that then existed. There was little reason to expect PGPs or IPAs to expand rapidly without federal assistance. Concerned about rising health care costs, interested in offering an alternative to Kennedy's Health Security Act, and influenced by advisers who came from California and were familiar with the Kaiser prepaid health plan (an important part of West Coast medicine), President Nixon in 1971 endorsed an HMO initiative designed to offer the help needed for growth. Universal and comprehensive national health insurance would wait, but its system reform component was embraced, and the generic term "health maintenance organization" was adopted in an effort to mute criticism from those in organized medicine who found PGPs distasteful.

The years since the enactment of the first HMO legislation have seen numerous changes in the original program and in the level of financial assistance made available to assist HMO growth. They have also seen rapid growth (from a small base) in the number of HMOs and in the number of individuals enrolled. From mid-1971 to January 1985 the number of operational HMOs increased from 33 to 377 and the number of subscribers grew from 3.6 million to 16.7 million (although this figure was still only 8 percent of the U.S. population).[9] While some of the growth can be attributed to factors other than the federal HMO program (such as changes in employer and insurer attitudes and the influx of private capital), there can be little question that the federal effort has had a substantial impact. It provided financial assistance, overrode state legal barriers, required employers to offer an HMO option (when available) to their employees. Above all, it conferred approval, legitimacy, and status.

HMO arrangements represent an important break with traditional insurance and delivery systems. In general, private health insurance is molded by the way the health care system functions. It accepts and adjusts to the prevailing patterns and incentives of the delivery system. In sharp contrast, the health maintenance organization (and especially the prepaid group practice) is designed to alter and adjust delivery system incentives and provider behavior in an effort to control costs and create a better match between the kind of financial protection subscribers desire and can afford and the delivery of care.

In attempting to change provider behavior and to stimulate cost-efficient care, HMOs do not take the prevailing patterns of resource allocation generated by those who deliver care (especially physicians) as given. The fact that delivery and insurance are linked, that the organization operates within a budget and therefore has a control mechanism, alters behavior, delivery system priorities, and resource allocations. Controls affect the supply of personnel and hospital beds, the utilization of ambulatory and hospital services, the patterns of care and costs. HMOs have an inherent economic logic. As a model of a controlled system, their significance extends far beyond the fact that they offer comprehensive protection to millions of enrollees.

In the PGP arrangement, the health plan either employs physicians to deliver health care services and pays them individual salaries or contracts with a group of physicians to deliver the medical services required to deal with subscribers' health problems and pays the group a predetermined sum. The plan's income depends on the number of subscribers and the monthly premium, not (as under fee-for-service arrangements) on the number of services and procedures delivered and billed and paid for. Accordingly, the plan estimates its expected premium income and budgets its expenditures within the constraint imposed by the anticipated revenues. If the number of subscribers were to fall short of expectations, revenues would be below budget and the plan would be unable to meet its financial commitments to providers. Conversely, if the number of subscribers were to increase unexpectedly, the plan would have more revenues but would be unable to meet its service commitments to the individuals who had enrolled. Thus, anticipated plan income and expenditures as well as the number of subscribers and the resources required to serve them have to be matched. As with any organization that seeks to survive, the task is to turn projections into reality.

Individuals who join a PGP enroll in a delivery system. As members they become eligible to receive the various medical services specified in the membership agreement. They do not have to pay additional amounts when they use the delivery system they joined, that is, when they receive services from providers who are associated with the plan. Although they are free to seek care outside the plan with which they have contracted, they must pay for such care themselves (except in specified situations, such as emergencies). Thus their monthly premium does not purchase traditional insurance coverage but the right to receive services that are offered by the organized delivery system.

The prepaid group practice plan provides something conspicuously lacking in other parts of the health care system: an organization that guarantees and arranges care, makes certain the necessary care providers are available, and assumes responsibility for the care rendered. No longer does the patient visit individual physicians, each with his or her own speciality, each self-employed and operating under fee-for-service arrangements. Instead of that fragmented approach, the member of a prepaid group practice plan meets providers who operate under an organizational umbrella. The vast majority of Americans who are

not members of HMOs can complain about, but not to, the American
health care delivery system. The system, after all, is an abstract construct; it has no officers or bylaws. In contrast, HMO members have
an organization to which to take their complaints. The difference between individual and independent practitioners who are reimbursed
on a fee-for-service basis for the care they provide to those who walk
through their office doors and an organization with a fixed income, a
budget, and contractual obligations to a defined population, its members, cannot be greater.

Since the PGP plan contracts for services with a group of physicians
or employs physicians on a salary basis (in both cases, perhaps with a
bonus arrangement related to the plan's economic performance), physicians' incomes are not increased by increases in utilization. There is
no economic incentive to perform more procedures, to generate extra
visits or additional days of hospitalization. Instead, salary and bonus
arrangements and budgets provide incentives and pressures to economize. The resulting economic gains may be shared by personnel in
the form of higher incomes or shorter hours and by those who pay for
and those who use services (such as employers and employees) in the
form of lower premiums and/or a wider range of benefits. In for-profit
HMOs, whose rapid growth reflects their access to capital, the economic gains are shared with stockholders.

These real incentives to do less lead to the fear that the fee-for-
service system, which does more than is required, will be replaced by
PGPs, which will do less than is necessary or desirable. The issue
would not be one of graft or corruption, which must and can be eliminated. Rather, the problem would express itself in subtle ways: long
waiting times for appointments, expensive tests or therapy postponed
a bit too long, hospital discharges a bit too early. The fact that PGPs
can and do cut costs must be coupled with the observation that each
prepaid group practice is different and has its own leadership, set of
objectives, and ways of meeting them. In turn, this means that just
as fee-for-service physicians cannot all be condemned for being profli-
gate, each PGP should not be extolled for being parsimonious. If we
ask why expenditures are high under fee-for-service, then we must
also ask why they are low in a particular prepaid group practice. The
quality of care must be assessed.

The independent practice association is another organizational form
whose economic relationships put the providers of care at financial
risk. In an IPA, a panel of independent physicians who continue prac-

ticing under fee-for-service arrangements guarantees to provide medical care to subscribers even if premium revenues prove insufficient to reimburse providers at predetermined fees for services rendered. Since physicians continue to practice in their existing locations, IPAs offer familiar arrangements (especially to individuals whose personal physicians join the IPA panel). Furthermore, since decisions are decentralized to independent physicians who continue managing their own practices and offices, IPAs require far less planning, construction and other capital expenditure, and central administrative control. They are far easier to organize and to administer.

The corollary is that IPAs cannot exploit the advantages of group association and practice or maximize system (as contrasted with individual) efficiency. Furthermore, IPA physicians who continue to treat patients who do not join the IPA insurance plan confront multiple and different incentives associated with the various forms of insurance coverage. In such cases it is both more difficult and less rewarding to learn to practice a new and leaner style of medical care. That may also be true even if all patients are IPA subscribers. Since the individual physicians continue to be paid on a fee-for-service basis and earn more by doing more, they may conclude that they are competing with other IPA physicians for their share of the fixed pool of dollars available. Such a view is hardly likely to lead to changes in behavior.

Keeping as many things as possible the same offers distinct advantages to patients and physicians. Yet the more features that are kept the same, the fewer structural and organizational changes there will be and the less likely it is that behavioral norms will be modified and efficiency savings realized.

Even so, IPA financial arrangements represent a break with more traditional insurance arrangements. They alter the expectations of both physicians and patients and increase their awareness about the need for, and utility of, control mechanisms. This is especially the case when the IPA is organized as a defense against the encroachment of expanding PGPs in order to enable physicians to retain their patients and their patient load or insurers to preserve their share of the insurance market. Under both conditions, appreciation of the presence of and need for constraints moves from the abstract to the concrete. If competitive pressures are maintained and are accompanied by IPA utilization review and monitoring of physician performance, physician behavior is likely to alter. The world of and around medicine is changing, and the IPA contributes to physicians' greater understanding of the new realities.

Federal legislation may have made possible the expansion of HMOs, but it was not sufficient to assure it. The HMO faced a competitive environment and had to meet its competitors in the marketplace. That it did so successfully can be attributed to many factors (such as perceived quality of care, a desire for one-stop medicine, and consumer awareness), but the largest single factor undoubtedly has been the PGP's economic performance, that is, its ability to contain medical care costs and premiums. It is less expensive to belong to a PGP than to pay private insurance premiums and additional out-of-pocket costs. The PGP saves money, largely by reducing the utilization of hospital care, and is able to do so without any apparent reduction in the quality of care.

The future growth of HMOs is likely to be even more rapid as a result of four factors. First, an increasing proportion of the population and of physicians will become acquainted with the way PGPs and IPAs function. As HMOs become more widely dispersed geographically and develop a critical mass, their accessibility and acceptability will increase. Furthermore, their present perceived defect, the closed physician panel arrangement, which exacts an economic penalty if the patient seeks services outside the HMO plan, is likely to become less critical as an increasing number of Americans find themselves covered by insurance programs with similar restrictions. Under one such arrangement, the preferred provider organization (PPO), the patient is reimbursed at a higher rate (say, 100 percent) for visits to a physician who has agreed to a reduced fee schedule and at a lower rate (say, 80 percent) for visits to a physician who is not a "preferred provider." In the future, similar restrictions and constraints are likely to apply to hospital care.[10] As PPOs spread and more Americans face restrictions on their choice of providers, HMO closed panel arrangements will not appear as wrenching.

Second, the projected large increase in the number of physicians will make individual independent practice less financially rewarding. It will be more difficult and take longer for a physician to build up his or her practice and will cost more to buy into someone else's. Even aside from the advantages many physicians already perceive in the PGP (such as increased collegiality, comparatively regular hours, and time for advanced training and continuing education), the desire for greater financial security will tend to increase the number of physicians who will seek an HMO relationship.

Third, as the costs of medical care increase, employers and employees will search for ways to economize without reducing the quality of care. If the costs of HMO membership and of more traditional insurance continue to diverge, HMO membership will be marketed more aggressively and will become more attractive. This is especially likely to be the case if both employers and employees share in the resulting benefits through lower contributions and/or more comprehensive benefits.

Fourth, pressures and inducements designed to increase enrollment of Medicare beneficiaries and Medicaid recipients in organized systems of care (such as HMOs) that yield cost savings will continue. These are likely to become increasingly effective as HMOs are perceived as part of mainstream medicine rather than as radical innovations.

Even though the further growth of HMOs seems assured, it would be foolish to expect HMOs and the competitive pressures they exert to carry the full burden of creating a more efficient and more cost-conscious health sector. For years to come most medical care will continue to be offered outside of PGPs or IPAs. Many physicians will prefer to be independent and will search for opportunities that meet their preferences. Many patients will resent and resist the economic pressures to join HMOs, assuming that the economic advantages of the HMO derive from cost-cutting behavior that offers a different and more restricted product than that available from the rest of the health care system. Few Americans feel comfortable with what they perceive as "bargain-basement" medicine. In the health arena, Americans, though influenced by costs, are likely to seek nonprice rationales for their behavior. HMOs will grow more rapidly when Americans feel attracted to them by noneconomic considerations (such as quality) rather than pushed to them by economic ones. Thus, although the growth of HMOs will be influenced by cost differentials, there will be a large role for social psychologists and marketing experts.

And there will also remain a need to monitor performance, for just as fee-for-service may lead to doing more than is necessary, so PGP fixed compensation may lead to doing less. Peer review, the group setting, medical ethics and attitudes—and the patient's freedom to leave the plan—help guard against this danger. Nevertheless, it would be the height of folly to assume that every organization that calls itself a prepaid group practice is, or will be, an embodiment of virtue. Equally, it would be folly to assume that individual members are fully able to judge subtle shifts in quality. Careful monitoring and appraisal of performance by disinterested evaluators will always remain necessary.

There will also be a role for government. Since HMOs may restrict as well as foster competition, government will have to monitor the interplay of HMOs with the total health care system. HMOs that are dominated by physicians who are not especially interested in growth and expansion may eschew vigorous price competition. Furthermore, HMOs, like other organizations, may be tempted to enroll younger and healthier subscribers and to compete around risk selection, to exploit the advantages of experience rating, and to make a sham of open enrollment requirements, namely that all who would join be accepted without discrimination. Since new HMOs (and especially PGPs) cannot be started quickly and since patients do not easily change providers, the ease of entry and the shopping behavior that help make competition work to lower price and improve quality in other areas of economic activity may well be missing. Today, HMOs are young and vigorous. Tomorrow, they may grow rigid and complacent. The prepaid group practice—shorn of its earlier ideological component and missionary zeal and, instead, viewed as an efficient and potentially profitable business enterprise—may, depending on its sponsorship, ownership, and control, prefer to follow the rest of the health care system rather than to lead it.

Even were government to define its responsibilities in narrow terms, involving only the individuals whose care it pays for and its own expenditures (rather than the health of the total population and the level of national expenditures), it would have to assume an active role in gathering and analyzing HMO performance data. But a narrow role will not suffice. The fact that efficient HMOs match resource inputs (such as the number of physicians and hospital beds) to the needs of an enrolled population inevitably increases the redundancy in the rest of the health care system. When, for example, HMO patients use fewer days of hospital care, total hospital bed requirements decline. The excess of hospital beds must be of concern to government. Unless unnecessary beds are eliminated, per diem hospital charges will rise in an effort to spread the fixed costs. If government and other third parties pay these increased hospital rates, little will be gained. The HMO member will be part of an efficient system, but the taxpayer and the non-HMO patient will be forced to finance the excess capacity created by that efficiency. Although economic pressures may eventually make themselves felt in the rest of the health care system, that result will be long in coming and is hardly a certainty.

Finally, government will retain its traditional responsibility to seek equity. The HMO is not designed to solve the health care or financing problems of those who lack the resources with which to buy in. Like traditional insurers, it seeks its subscribers primarily in the employment setting, must increase premiums if it enrolls a disproportionate number of members who are very sick or need chronic care services, and cannot give its services away but must charge a premium, even to the poor. In other words, it operates in a competitive market, and that market is not constructed to achieve equity.

The HMO can do much to help contain ever-increasing health care expenditures and to promote a more efficient delivery system. Rising costs, however, are only one part of the American health problem and efficiency only one of the desired goals. The other goals are access, fairness, justice, and equity. By reducing the costs of care and by demonstrating the benefits of planning, organization, and budgets, the HMO may make it easier (less expensive) for government to achieve equity. But that is all the HMO can do to promote that goal. The equity issue belongs to government; only it represents all the people, can muster the resources required to address the needs of all members of the society, and, through redistribution, can address the needs of members of the community who cannot make it on their own.

The HMO is not only an organization but also a concept. There is ample opportunity to apply the ideas of budget constraints, incentives to economize, matching input resources to health needs, and planning, to existing organizations and practitioners. Indeed, there is a need to do so. The number of physicians is growing rapidly. If this increasing supply functions in an open-ended payment and reimbursement system in which third parties pay on a usual and customary fee-for-service basis (a system without cost containment incentives), today's health care expenditures will continue to grow more rapidly than personal incomes. An increasing proportion of the population will be priced out of the insurance market or will find that in order to contain premium increases, insurance will cover a smaller proportion of health care costs. While economists may argue that the system will reach a new equilibrium, that prices will stabilize before all of us are rationed out, economic theory does not permit us to assume that the process will be quick and painless or even that the final result will fit reasonable standards of equity.

8

Health Care Costs: A New Constraint

Institution building takes leadership, energy, effort, and dollars. Above all, it takes time. Even the most zealous supporters of HMOs had to concede that PGPs and IPAs would not soon become important forces in health care delivery. Whatever advantages might accrue from new and more efficient health care delivery systems, they would not be gained quickly. In the short run, system reform would not increase access or contain health care costs. It could not substitute for the extension of insurance protection to those without it. Even as Congress directed its efforts to legislation that would stimulate change in the delivery system, the need to expand access to care and to health insurance coverage remained on the public agenda.

The 1972 Social Security Amendments provided Medicare Part A coverage to persons under sixty-five who had been entitled to Social Security disability benefits for twenty-four consecutive months (like other Medicare beneficiaries, they could elect to purchase Part B coverage). The amendments also provided benefits to persons who needed maintenance dialysis or a kidney transplant because of end-stage renal disease.[1] Although these were steps of great importance and value to the individuals affected, they were not steps toward national health insurance—unless, starting with the kidneys, they provided a model in which the nation would move to NHI organ by organ.

There remained a need, as some saw it, for a universal and comprehensive program. Pressures mounted on President Nixon to respond to a climate of public opinion that took for granted the enactment of some form of national health insurance. As of May 1971 some 13 NHI bills had been introduced in the 92nd Congress. In the 93rd Congress the number grew to 17 as of February 1974 and to 22 by July of that year. The American Hospital Association, the American Medical Association, the Health Insurance Association of America, the Chamber of Commerce, and the AFL-CIO each supported a different measure. So, too, did the administration. In 1974 the White House replaced the extremely modest and limited insurance proposal it had favored in 1971 with the much more extensive Comprehensive Health Insurance Program (CHIP).[2]

Departing from the social insurance approach, CHIP mandated coverage for the employed (through their employers) and set up a separate program for those not covered under the mandated approach. The program was financed by employer-employee premiums (with limited and temporary federal assistance). Patients were required to pay a deductible of $150 and faced a 25 percent coinsurance rate, but in an imaginative new departure the program set a maximum liability of $1,050 per individual and $1,500 per family per year.[3] Although this limit implied a potentially high family liability unrelated to family income, the concept of a maximum was both novel and appealing. The CHIP proposal was not a mere political ploy, to be dismissed out of hand.

Now all the leading proposals were on the table: Senator Kennedy's social insurance approach, the president's mandated program, and a catastrophic insurance bill submitted by Senators Long and Ribicoff.

The Long-Ribicoff measure provided insurance for events requiring very expensive treatment; for example, hospital coverage would begin *after* the first sixty days, and physician services would be covered *after* the family incurred $2,000 in medical expenses in the year (almost 15 percent of the median family income).[4] The early growth of hospital insurance had set a different pattern: provision of benefits up to defined limits specified in terms of units of service or dollar amounts. Following established and familiar patterns, similar limits for days of hospital care were set under Part A of Medicare. A benefit structure that provided "first-dollar" protection (sometimes, however, with a deductible) served the interests of hospitals by assuring payment for the bulk of the medical care they provided. A benefit structure that offered little or no protection beyond a defined limit served the interests of insurers by limiting their liability. It also was attractive to insurees, most of whom were concerned about the expense of unexpected hospitalization but few of whom would encounter the rare event that led to extraordinary medical care costs.

Furthermore, this pattern of basic protection maximized the number of individuals who would actually collect benefits for a given premium.

Employers and union officials who negotiated and legislators who en
acted health insurance programs were fully aware of the political advantages and the increased reelection possibilities associated with
programs that reached and assisted a maximum number of individuals
and constituents in a clear and tangible manner.

It is self-evident that protection against extraordinary expenditures
is of critical importance to individuals who face large bills. Nevertheless, though important, catastrophic insurance could not be considered
a substitute for first-dollar insurance. First, as a result of advances in
medical science and increases in health care costs, large expenditures
were no longer associated solely with rare events. Few families could
finance an average hospital stay out of current income. Second, insurance that covered expenditures above a defined amount would not avail
persons who were unable to meet the expenses that fell below the
limit. At the same time, catastrophic insurance and the guaranteed
payment of large bills could lead to (unnecessary) duplication of costly
facilities and stimulate the purchase and use of high technology. The
result could be both increased costs and misallocation of resources.

Third, individuals not only seek the peace of mind that comes with
protection against unexpected medical expenses (especially since illness often also leads to a decline in income) but also wish to guard
against having their medical care decisions influenced by monetary
considerations. Most of us want to make certain that when we are ill
we will not have to ask ourselves whether a physician's visit is really
worth the fee that will be charged and whether we can afford the
necessary care. We are willing to pay for first-dollar coverage in order
to avoid being forced to that thought process. Important as catastrophic insurance is in protecting against the financial impact of events
that we do not really believe will happen to us, it does not provide the
psychological security we seek.

Fourth, since incomes, debts, and savings are unequal, one person's
inconvenience or even hardship might be another's catastrophe. For
some, paying a $3,000 medical bill would require a change in vacation
plans or reduce the sum they have in stocks and bonds; for others, it
would mean a drastic cut in living standards or a revision of their
children's plans to attend college. Given an unequal income distribution, no single definition of financial catastrophe could apply equally
to all. As structured, catastrophic insurance had little to commend it
to those who were concerned with equity.

There is a logic to basic health insurance coverage. Consider an analogous situation in public education. Free public education would not be as socially meaningful if parents were required to pay full tuition for elementary and high school while university and graduate education were provided at no cost to the student. The ticket of admission to higher education would already have been rationed to those who could afford the price, and fewer individuals would enter the "free" universities. Inevitably, social and political support for quality education at the elementary and high school would weaken, and the nation would end up with a less-educated population.

The same logic applied to basic health care (including prevention and early diagnosis) and to catastrophic health insurance. In response to increasing public awareness of the frequency and impact of high-cost interventions, insurance companies had aggressively and successfully marketed major medical insurance to those who already had basic coverage. Although coinsurance required patients to bear a percentage of the medical care costs (often without an upper limit on their out-of-pocket liability), "major medical" provided significantly higher limits on health care benefits (either as a supplement to or integrated with basic coverage). By 1973 perhaps as many as 125 million persons were covered by major medical policies.[5] These plans did not help those without any health insurance. Nevertheless, they did help fill—though, because of cost-sharing, not entirely remove—one of the important gaps facing individuals who otherwise had adequate insurance.

The combination of the growth of private major medical insurance, the failure to address basic benefits or deal with equity, and the lack of political appeal for a program that defined catastrophe at such a high level that few would receive benefits helped doom the Long-Ribicoff proposal. Since then there have been various attempts to raise or entirely remove the limit on hospital days of care under Medicare but at the same time to cut basic coverage for hospitalization by increasing beneficiary copayments. These, too, have failed to elicit support either from aged and disabled beneficiaries or from Congress. President Reagan's efforts, like President Nixon's before him, have been rejected. Despite its importance, catastrophic health insurance, when offered as a substitute for basic coverage, has evoked little political support. There are important lessons in that history.

Without a constituency for Long-Ribicoff, the Kennedy and the Nixon proposals occupied center stage. Once again, favorable action on a compromise was expected, particularly after Senator Kennedy and Congressman Mills announced they would join in a new proposal that

built upon CHIP. This latest version of national health insurance pro
vided a fiscal intermediary role for the private insurance industry (not
unlike its role in Medicare). It included the same deductible and coinsurance payments as the administration's proposal but also set a
maximum liability limit of $1,000 per family (with reduced limits for
low-income individuals). Unlike the Nixon program, the Kennedy-Mills
compromise was financed through taxes that took account of income
and required larger payments by the more affluent. The difference
between the administration program, which required that employees
pay 25 percent of the premium, and the Kennedy-Mills bill, which
geared employee contributions to income, was significant. Nevertheless, the proposals shared many features. Since the Kennedy-Mills bill
was sponsored by two powerful legislators and would be acted upon
in the House Ways and Means Committee, which Mills chaired, and
since it was a compromise measure that included elements of Kennedy's
original Health Security Act and of CHIP, it seemed reasonable to
anticipate favorable action: national health insurance was an idea whose
time had finally come, and the summer of 1974 appeared to be that
time.[6]

The committee did not produce a bill; Congress did not act. There
are many possible explanations: the president offered his proposal for
the political record and did not support it vigorously; the president
would have been active, but Watergate occupied his (and the nation's)
attention and sapped his (and the nation's) energy; Republicans who
backed the administration were a minority, and the Democratic majority was split into three parts—those who supported Kennedy-Mills,
those who supported the original Health Security Act, and those, including advocates of Long-Ribicoff, who did not support either measure. When organized labor deserted Kennedy (arguing that he had
deserted real "health security" by adopting a mandated rather than a
universal social insurance approach and by including deductibles and
coinsurance) and decided to wait for the election of a more liberal
Congress in November, it became clear that no proposal could command the votes of a majority of the committee. The differences between
the various factions were simply too great to be compromised. Coalitions were formed to defeat each proposal; no coalition could be
mounted to produce a bill.

Proponents of NHI did not know it at the time, but the summer of
1974 marked a watershed. In the years since, no proposal has gone as
far as Kennedy-Mills and CHIP. Events (including changes in Con-

gress) have had their impact. It is unlikely that an amended Kennedy-Mills bill could have become law in 1974. The most that might have happened is that it would have passed the House of Representatives. But that would have assured its place on the political agenda. That would have been the point of reference for continued efforts.

The heavier Democratic majorities that labor counted on were elected in the fall of 1974. The number of Democrats in the House increased from 239 to 291 and in the Senate from 56 to 60.[7] Nonetheless, the opportunity for action had passed. Senator Kennedy saw little purpose in submitting a bill that labor would not support. He also saw little purpose in submitting a bill that only labor would support. Having revealed his negotiating position in Kennedy-Mills, he could hardly propose a measure that offered even less compromise and would not be taken seriously by his colleagues. Organized labor, in turn, was afraid that a compromise bill, offered too early, would become the departure point for further compromises. It was unwilling to reveal at the very beginning of the long legislative process what it might ultimately settle for.

Nor were the differences between Kennedy and labor the only problems NHI faced. Congressional attention was increasingly focused on other matters—including the aftermath of Watergate and the rapid increases in the costs of energy. NHI was becoming an increasingly expensive proposition as a consequence of the rising costs of medical care. The prevailing attitude seemed to be that if a national health program had not been passed by now, perhaps that was because it was a bad idea. In any case, Congress wanted a rest from the tiresome and divisive issue.

Furthermore, the nature of the debate had changed. The arguments concerning NHI had become strikingly complex. Growth of private insurance and the flow of dollars in the private sector, expansion of Medicare and Medicaid expenditures and their implication for federal and state budgets, continuing escalation of health expenditures, the growing awareness that a permissive insurance system without controls would feed further escalation (but the lack of consensus on desirable controls), the fear of national health insurance's potential budgetary impact, all these raised issues that called for data and analysis. There was an abundant supply of both.

The growth in congressional staff, in executive branch personnel, in Washington-based health care interest groups (attracted by the flow of dollars), and in the number of health economists and health care researchers meant that national health insurance would be debated, considered, analyzed, and argued about in a new and increasingly quantitative language. In this as in other policy areas, the need for data and for analysis inevitably slowed the legislative process. Position papers and policy analyses are handmaidens to enlightened legislation. They also can be bottlenecks, a prescription for paralysis.

The blame did not lie with analysts or with analysis, with statisticians or with statistics. Analysts and health care experts responded to changes in the social sciences and to opportunities created by the computer. They also responded to felt needs that arose from the greater complexity of the health economy. Dealing with complexity meant constructing a national health insurance program that was detailed, attempted to deal with every possibility, anticipated every constraint that existed or might arise, meshed the existing private and public programs, dealt with costs and system reform as well as equity, and still could be administered. Each construct had to be based on research and on data. Each construct had to estimate and project costs in a detailed fashion.

It was not sufficient to argue that the program could be amended as new knowledge was gained and as conditions altered. If NHI were that "experimental," why not support a series of small-scale experiments that would provide additional data for analysis (as in fact was later done)? Meeting the criticism of opponents meant anticipating all possible objections and, most especially, casting the argument in quantitative terms. For many, NHI remained a moral issue. But vision had been replaced by fine-tuning. For those who designed possible programs and debated how to implement them, or even whether they could be implemented, the national health insurance debate called for equations not emotions, for symposia not sermons.

National health insurance bills and their accompanying reports had changed since the days when Medicare was debated. They were far more detailed. They contained far more precise cost estimates and were more "useful" (though less understandable) to legislators. But, shorn of ideology and reading like engineering manuals, NHI reports hardly were manifestos around which people would rally and march to the voting booths.

National health insurance was and remains a political issue; yet it came to be discussed in a technical language that is incomprehensible to those who would have to rally to its political support. Those who continue to speak the language of the political marketplace are accused of being simplistic, of painting things in black and white; those who speak the language of the technician, who do address the shades of gray, are understood only by their colleagues. In part because their arguments are about things at the margin, in part because their words are gray, in part because it is difficult to be passionate about nuances, the words, articles, and reports tend to transform and limit the debate.

By 1977, when President Carter was inaugurated, the NHI agenda had changed again. Equity was still important and so was system reform. Now, however, the dominant theme was costs and cost control.

On one side were those who argued that, whatever the virtue of NHI, the nation simply could not afford the program, at least until health care expenditures were contained through system change and legislated cost control. Their focus was on the impact on the federal budget and they were unimpressed with the argument that, in largest measure, public dollars would substitute for private dollars already in the system. On the other side were those who, citing British and Canadian experience, argued that a national health program with budget controls was the only effective way to contain costs. They were willing to concede that during its first few years NHI would increase access to care and, therefore, total health expenditures, but they projected a crossover point after which health expenditures, while still increasing, would fall below the costs of a non-NHI insurance and delivery system. NHI, they suggested, was the nation's best, indeed only, hope for effective and equitable cost containment.

Concern about rising costs and expenditures was justified. In 1960 national health expenditures accounted for 5.3 percent of GNP; by 1965 the share had risen to 6.1 percent, and by 1970 to 7.6 percent. In 1975 it stood at 8.6 percent; in 1977 it was at 8.8 percent and still increasing. Expenditures for personal health care services (both in absolute terms and as a share of GNP) grew even more rapidly. In 1965 they totaled $36 billion; in 1977, $149 billion. Per capita expenditures rose from $181 in 1965 to $663 in 1977. Private health insurance was expanding. Medicare and Medicaid had been implemented. Yet per capita out-of-pocket payments increased from $91 in 1965 to $203 in 1977.[8]

The rising share of the nation's productive effort that was being absorbed by the health sector and the impact of rising prices and expenditures on private health insurance premiums and individual out-of-pocket expenditures were not the only problems. Congress was well aware of the ever-increasing impact of medical care on federal, state,

and local government budgets. Public financing of national health ex
penditures had totaled $11 billion (the federal share was $5.5 billion)
in 1965. In 1977 it was $70 billion (with $47 billion coming from the
federal government).[9] Medicare expenditures had increased from $5
billion in 1967 to $23 billion in 1977, and Medicaid had increased from
$3 billion ($1.4 billion federal) to $18 billion ($10 billion federal) in the
same period. The two programs together had risen from $7.7 billion
to $40.2 billion. Federal health expenditures, 4.4 percent of all federal
expenditures in 1965, were 11.3 percent in 1977.[10] The pressures of
Medicare and Medicaid on the federal budget were real and mounting.
The pressures on the private insurance sector, though different from
those the public sector faced, were no less real.[11]

Building on its early history in which health insurance was offered
as an employment-related fringe benefit, private health insurance remained largely a matter of group enrollment provided through the
employment relationship. Over 80 percent of total health insurance
premiums went for the purchase of group coverage and over 95 percent
of all group insurance was provided in the employment context. Furthermore, almost 90 percent of all U.S. employees worked in firms
that provided health insurance plans and over 90 percent of employees
in those firms were eligible for the insurance. Thus most employees
were covered by an employer-sponsored health insurance plan, and
that type of plan accounted for most of the dollars that purchased
insurance coverage. Health insurance was an institutionalized part of
collective bargaining and of labor-management contracts.

The availability of insurance and, importantly, the level of employer
contribution to premiums was dependent on factors such as the firm's
geographic location, industry characteristics, number of employees,
level of wages, and union strength. In 1977 over 99 percent of workers
in firms with over 1,000 employees had an employment-related health
insurance plan, compared with only 55 percent of workers in firms with
25 or fewer employees. The problem, therefore, was not simply that
employment-related group insurance tended to leave out individuals
who were not employed but that it was distributed unequally even
among those who were employed. In general, workers in smaller and
nonunionized firms were less likely to have employment-related group
coverage.

In addition, there were wide disparities in the cost of insurance. In
part these reflected geographic differences in health care prices (such
as per diem hospital charges and physicians' fees); in part they reflected

geographic differences in patterns of practice (such as length of stay in hospitals and frequency of surgery). Part of the variation, however, stemmed from the fact that insurance is an inclusive term covering a wide range of policies with substantial differences in benefits and coverage. The fact that an employer offers insurance does not tell us as much as we should like to know. We are no better served by the statement that there is insurance than is a prospective employee who, in assessing a job opportunity, knows that he or she will receive a salary but not how large, that there is a pension plan but not what it provides, or that he or she can accrue vacation days but not how many.

A measure of the variation in cost (and coverage) of employment-related insurance is reflected in data on employer-employee premium expenditures. In 1977 the average annual premium per eligible employee was $590. While 2 percent of employees had far more expensive protection costing over $1,750 per year, 25 percent of all employees worked in firms where the average annual premium was $250 or less. In general, higher-wage firms (firms with a smaller percentage of workers at or near the minimum wage) tended to offer policies with larger premiums. Employees in lower-wage firms who did have group insurance (and many did not) generally were covered by policies that cost less and that provided less protection (for example, by not covering dependents or by offering fewer benefits or requiring a higher level of cost-sharing).

A substantial part of the cost of employment-related health insurance was met by tax-exempt employer contributions. In 1977 employers paid an average of 80 percent of total premium costs. Over one-third of all employees had employer contributions of over $500 per annum and almost 10 percent had employer contributions of over $1,000, but another third had employer contributions of $250 or less (and 13 percent received no employer assistance). The pattern of differences between low- and high-wage firms again repeated itself: low-wage firms paid a smaller percentage of premium costs. Thus employees of those firms had cumulative disadvantages: lower rates of pay, less likelihood of group health insurance protection, poorer protection when it was available, and less tax-exempt employer assistance (in both absolute and percentage terms) to help defray premium costs.

When considered in terms of family income, the data reveal patterns that are equally disturbing. In 1977 poor and near-poor families had private policies (excluding Medicare supplements) whose annual premiums averaged $645, with employers contributing 54 percent. Premiums for middle income families averaged $901, with 67 percent contributed by employers; and high-income families had policies that cost $1,046, with employer contributions of 71 percent.[12]

The tax-exempt nature of employer contributions needs to be underscored. That the private sector distributes fringe benefits in a manner that favors higher-income individuals is hardly cause for pride; but that the federal government provides tax benefits in a similar manner is clearly cause for shame. The private sector has its own ethic and constraints: profitability, competition, market power, labor turnover, wage scales. Government's ethic and role are different: in part, its responsibility is to assist the weak. Yet today (as in 1977) those employees who have more comprehensive coverage and who receive larger employer contributions toward their health insurance gain the most from the tax-exempt nature of the employer contribution. Because these employees have higher incomes and are in higher marginal tax brackets, they receive more tax assistance for the purchase of insurance. A tax-exempt fringe benefit of an insurance policy that costs $1,000 saves the employee in a 40 percent tax bracket $400 in federal income taxes. The employee who is in the 20 percent tax bracket saves only half as much.

Whatever the merits of a tax subsidy for the purchase of private health insurance, it is difficult to support a system whose design gives less help to those who have lower incomes, less insurance, and less employer assistance and provides no assistance to individuals who must pay their total premiums out of their own incomes. A tax deduction (rather than tax credit) system that provides more help to the manager than to the secretary (although both receive the same employer contribution to premium) and more to either of them than to the short-order cook without insurance can hardly be considered a model of fairness and equity.

The system also creates distortions. Recently I met the owner of a firm that was only a few years old and had only two employees. The hard-working owner, who designed, made, sold, and delivered wooden outdoor chairs and tables, was trying to build his business. Nevertheless, confronted by the need for health insurance and facing the large cost of individual enrollment without a tax benefit, he was looking for part-time work where he might receive the fringe benefit of an employer-paid premium. He was angry at being forced to take time from his own business but saw no other way to deal with the consequences of our tax system. The private initiative that our political leaders glorify in rhetoric was being destroyed by the American health care financing system.

Different public agencies and private organizations using different methodologies have developed estimates of the number of individuals who have public and/or private third-party protection, who are covered only by private health insurance, and who are without any insurance. Although these estimates differ, the consensus is that by 1977 almost 85 percent of the population had some private or public protection for the whole year, that 70 percent was covered by private health insurance plans (not including those Medicare beneficiaries who also carried private insurance), that 9 percent of the population (19 million) had no coverage or protection for a full year, and that another 8 percent was without insurance at some time during the year.[13] The data, it was often suggested, told an American private-sector success story. With about 180 million persons covered, the 35 million without insurance for part or all of the year presumably represented only a "small" unsolved problem.

It is true that the average American had some financial protection and that the average health dollar flowed through a third party. But what if we were not average? A person drowning in the Mississippi would derive small comfort from being told that the average depth of the river is only two inches. Similarly, the individual who cannot pay for his or her prescription, physician visit, or hospitalization remains unimpressed by what others may term "the American health insurance success story."

It was not only the 35 million individuals without any insurance who made up the unsolved problem. Many Americans with insurance had little more than minimal protection. Although the data on coverage were impressive, they did not discriminate, for example, between the individual whose hospital insurance policy provided a cash indemnity of $30 a day, beginning after the third day of hospitalization, for each day of hospital care for a covered illness (excluding preexisting conditions) and the individual whose comprehensive prepaid group practice membership provided unlimited and complete care. Both were counted as "insured." It was as if the person caught in a torrential downpour with only a newspaper for shelter and the individual watching the rain from the comfort of his living room were both classified as "protected."

Many subscribers were aware that some insurance policies left wide gaps in benefits. They tried to deal with the problem by purchasing more than one insurance policy. For example, it was estimated that the 168 million Americans (including those covered by public programs) who had private health insurance hospital care protection in 1977 held 208 million different policies. Thus 40 million enrollments represented multiple coverage.[14]

As a consequence, America's health care financing system, with about 1,000 private insurance companies, 69 Blue Cross/Blue Shield plans, and numerous health maintenance organizations and independent plans, hardly represented a model of efficiency.[15] Multiple coverage not only was a burden on the individual but also added to enrollment costs, operating expenses, the staffs required to bill and process claims. That was especially the case with nongroup enrollment. Operating expenses for all private insurers totaled $5.4 billion or 12 percent of the 1977 premium income of $45 billion. While operating expenses as a share of premium income were 7 percent for the Blue Cross and Blue Shield system, they reached a high of 46 percent for individual policies purchased from insurance companies. The average individual who purchased insurance on his or her own, without employer or government assistance, received only 54 cents in benefits for every dollar paid in premiums.[16]

Every arrangement for health care financing must entail some administrative costs; they cannot be reduced to zero. But the financing arrangements that have developed in the United States are especially costly. The system is complicated and incomplete, encourages duplication, inevitably increases administrative expenses, and exacts its largest toll from those with the least adequate protection. Billions of "health expenditure" dollars go to pay not for health care but for the countless pieces of paper (whose manufacture denudes our forests)— the premium bills, claim forms, and benefit checks—that flow through the system. Even if each component of our health care financing system operated in an internally efficient manner, the system as a whole would be inefficient and wasteful of scarce resources.

Yet the fact that there was a structure (insurance companies, employees, computers, negotiated agreements between labor and management, employer contributions, and tax benefits) could not be disregarded. In 1977 the $40 billion of private health insurance payments represented 27 percent of the $149 billion total expenditure for personal health services.[17] Given the system already in place and the large money flows involved, the Carter administration searched for a national health insurance structure that would retain what already existed and extend its benefits more widely. Such an approach would minimize the disruption that a fully government program would entail. It was also hoped that it would minimize political opposition.[18]

Another advantage of retaining the private insurance sector instead of shifting all expenditures to the federal government was that the impact of health care inflation on the federal budget would be reduced. Even if NHI expenditures did not increase the federal deficit because the program would be self-financed, there was no escaping the arithmetic: they would increase the share of federal expenditures relative to GNP (22 percent in 1977). President Carter had pledged to reduce that percentage, not expand it. Moving funds and expenditures from the private sector into government would hardly assist in meeting that commitment.

If the dollars involved in NHI were not to flow through federal coffers, another body would have to receive the funds involved in the insurance program. The obvious candidates were the private insurers and the Blues. Thus there was an additional justification for their retention and for assigning them a large role in any future program.

In 1976 the Subcommittee on Health and the Environment of the House Committee on Interstate and Foreign Commerce published *A Discursive Dictionary of Health Care*, a volume explaining various terms used in the health care field. The entry for "national health insurance" read: "A term not yet defined in the United States."[19] In fact, of course, there were multiple definitions that kept changing as new programs were proposed and as the goals that NHI was designed to achieve were modified. The Carter administration rejected the definition of NHI as a single universal social insurance program. Instead, national health insurance was conceived of as a series of programs, each covering different groups in the population. Minimizing the impact on the federal budget was so important that it was worth the consequent administrative complexity. Universality, it was hoped, would be assured by elimination of any cracks; every American would be a member of a group that was included in one of the various programs.

Under such an approach, most Americans would be covered by an expanded private insurance sector that would require employers to offer the protection (presumably, no one would notice that the mandated premium would really be a poorly disguised tax). Federal financial assistance would be offered to individuals who did not qualify for coverage under the mandated approach.

The fiscal advantages (in terms of the federal budget) of relying on the private sector and mandating private insurance coverage were clear. Even so, an increase in federal expenditures would be necessary in order to provide assistance to those who were not employed, worked in low-wage industries, or faced unusual risks. The lower the cost-sharing requirements and the broader the scope of benefits, the greater the costs borne by employers, the more disruptive the effect on the labor market, and the more federal assistance and associated expenditures would be required. On the other hand, a program that reduced these various impacts by setting minimal standards for insurance could hardly be considered a significant advance.

The search for a way out of this dilemma led the administration to advocate a "phasing" approach. The secretary of HEW, Joseph Califano, testified that "with few exceptions, the consensus among legislators is that the 96th Congress cannot and will not digest a complete National Health Plan in one bite. The overwhelming number of those who favor eventual adoption of a National Health Plan urged me to bring this message back to the President: Ask the President to limit his legislative recommendation to the first phase of a National Health Plan and to describe his vision of a total plan so we can put that phase in context."[20] The Democratic president had replaced "national health insurance" with a "national health plan" that would be enacted and implemented over (an unspecified) time. Benefits and coverage would be limited at first but, if Congress saw fit, expanded in the future.

Senator Kennedy and organized labor, working through the Committee for National Health Insurance, had been encouraged to develop their own proposal that met the president's requirements (minimal impact on the budget and a role for private carriers). Hoping to develop a program that would be supported by the administration, they set to work. Inevitably, they found that the construction of a partly private and partly public program that was "affordable"—a concept that related to the burdens that might be placed on government and on employers, rather than to the level of total national health expenditures—was a complex and time-consuming undertaking.

The designs that emerged, one submitted by the administration and another (without a phased-in approach, which he considered ill-advised) by Senator Kennedy, were very different but had two things in common: both were worthy of Rube Goldberg and neither was as liberal or inclusive as the Kennedy-Mills bill submitted in 1974. President Carter, the leader of the Democratic party, and Senator Kennedy, the leading exponent of national health insurance, could not (or would not) compromise their differences. Prospects for national health insurance, which in any case were dim, were extinguished when it became clear that those who favored NHI could not agree among themselves on a single bill that could command their support.

Inaction could be considered politically prudent. True, health care costs and expenditures would continue to increase. Employers and employees with health insurance would face higher premiums; costs of care for those who could not pay would continue to be shifted to individuals with health insurance; Medicare beneficiaries would note a widening gap between physicians' actual fees and those approved by Medicare; state legislators would feel the budgetary effects of rising Medicaid expenditures. Although increases in both Medicare and Medicaid had implications for government budgets, most of the expenditure growth would be financed in the private sector.

There were those who argued that a Kennedy-like national health insurance program with a tight budget would help contain costs, but few legislators felt at ease with a budgeting system that Secretary Patricia Harris, Secretary Califano's successor, had testified "is beyond our technical capability . . . could work only in a highly structured health system which places severe limits on consumer access . . . would inevitably result in an arbitrary rationing of health care services."[21] Acting on NHI would require a choice between lax and tight budget control. In either case, NHI would inject government into matters that now lay in the private sector and for which physicians, hospitals, and insurance carriers were held responsible. Far better, from the point of view of the individual legislator, that the private sector continue to be viewed as the culprit.

In the late 1970s there were numerous public policy issues that had to be addressed; national health insurance was not among them. The climate of opinion was turning more conservative, and Congress both helped form that climate and responded to it. For Democrats, the place to vote for national health insurance was at the party convention, not on the floor of Congress. The party platform was the way to keep in touch with old values and commitments. Republicans, never enthralled with NHI, did not face the problem of inconsistency. The debate that would have helped educate the nation did not take place.

An examination of the various proposals offered in the 1970s calls into question the conventional view that the difficulty with national health insurance is that times and conditions have changed but that the answers have not. In fact the various NHI proposals have been quite different and some have represented sharp breaks with past efforts. They have utilized different mechanisms to raise the necessary funds, different administrative structures, and different methods of enrollment. Some have employed deductibles and coinsurance and have assigned major insurance functions to existing insurers in order to reduce premiums, taxes, and budgetary impacts. All have attempted to build in cost-control features, and many have attempted to reduce the impact on the federal budget and have departed from the government as sole insurer. In substituting a variety of enrollment patterns, generally via employment, they have become overly complex, difficult to understand and to administer. They also have run the risk of being less universal than earlier proposals.

The problem with NHI was not that its proponents were intransigent or unimaginative: that they would not discard outmoded answers or that they lacked new ideas. Even aside from the possibility that the traditional solutions had not been wrong (Medicare is a working example of the "old" social insurance approach), they had been modified to place greater emphasis on system reform and cost control. New and very different proposals had been submitted to deal with perceived new constraints. National health insurance's difficulties were not technical in nature.

Nor were the problems solely institutional: the way Congress works, the failure of presidential leadership, the lack of a well-organized citizen constituency, the complex nature of the health care system. By the latter 1970s the health care system had grown and its costs had exploded. Undertaking a new venture in an atmosphere of retrenchment seemed inappropriate. Yet it is not enough to ascribe NHI's fate to this fact.

Although we could easily list a hundred factors that help explain each of the successive failures to enact a national health insurance program, something more fundamental was involved. National health insurance ran counter to long-standing American attitudes toward government and deep-seated beliefs—made more explicit in the late 1970s— in the efficacy of market solutions to social problems. Its enactment would require a major shift in public opinion.

We act and choose only when we are forced to. Only when the broad middle class is being hurt and when it becomes clear that private solutions will not suffice—as in the case of Social Security and Medicare—does America turn to universal programs addressed to all its citizens. For most Americans that time had not yet come.

9

Cutting Back on Health Insurance: Competition and the Free Market Ideology

A modern Rip Van Winkle who had been asleep for the last decade would hardly recognize today's health sector or health care debate. In the early 1970s health insurance was considered a cure for much that ailed America's health system; the nation was considering how to structure a national health insurance program and extend the benefits of health insurance to all the population. Today there is a different agenda: concern focuses on costs rather than on access, and sensible, reasonable, and responsible persons are contending that insurance is not the cure but the cause of our difficulties; the debate is about the "advantages" of reshaping existing health financing programs and reducing health insurance benefits. The awakening citizen would be confused by the shift in priorities and by the new policy proposals. He would not understand how having less insurance and requiring larger out-of-pocket payments would be extolled as beneficial and meritorious.

Until recently, the story of American private health insurance was one of growth, of expansion of both coverage and benefits: more and more persons enrolled and more and more protection. Many Americans had no insurance, but their proportion was declining; many had only minimal protection, but benefit packages were becoming more comprehensive.

Although it was clear that private health insurance could not reach all the people, it was generally assumed that its growth and expansion would continue and that it would offer more assistance to an increasing number of Americans. In doing so it would help define the have-nots and those left out, the sicker and the poorer part of the population. It was recognized that those whom private insurance could not cover would need assistance. It was assumed that in a growing economy they would receive that help through programs in the public sector.

The projection of continued growth was based on an implicit assumption that the health sector and its costs would not expand more rapidly than the general economy and overall price levels. That assumption has proved fallacious. Rapidly rising medical care expenditures combined with periods of economic sluggishness resulted in substantial increases in the share of GNP allocated to and absorbed by personal health services.

The concern with rising health care costs is related to the fact that a major share of health expenditures is financed by government and industry. Since health insurance premiums have grown more rapidly than revenues, these large payers have been less and less able or willing to finance the seemingly inexorable increases.

Federal expenditures on Medicare and Medicaid total over $90 billion. The programs are therefore hostage to the need to reduce the federal deficit. The current administration wants to cut back on social programs both as a matter of political philosophy and because it wants to limit budget growth while increasing defense expenditures. The goal is that much harder to achieve if Medicare and Medicaid are growing rapidly.

Medicare and Medicaid add to congressional frustrations because Congress does not appropriate sums that represent limits on program expenditures. The financial commitment is of another kind: in Medicare, to pay the bills as rendered; in Medicaid, to provide the formula-determined share of state Medicaid expenditures. An examination of the ways the necessary sums could be further reduced highlights the difficulty Congress faces. Except for savings generated by a slowing of the rate of increase in medical care prices in general and hospital prices in particular, all other savings would come from unpalatable measures: reducing the number of beneficiaries and recipients, restricting covered services, or paying less for them. The latter is a tempting approach, but there are limits to tight federal reimbursement policies. These limits are set by the fact that Medicare and Medicaid operate in a much larger medical market to which they must respond. Thus a solution to the impact of health expenditures on the federal budget is more effective—and less harmful to individual beneficiaries and recipients—if it is part of a broad approach to general cost containment. But the federal government has little control over the costs of the total health care system.

Private third-party payers face similar problems. Annual premium payments have increased dramatically even when benefit packages have remained fixed. Potential wage increases have disappeared into larger employer payments for unchanged health benefits. Attempts to cut back on coverage in order to reduce the ever-larger health insurance payments that often bought little or no more this year than last, did not help smooth the collective bargaining process or buy goodwill on the shop floor.

As health care expenditure increases took their toll, individual employers searched for ways to contain the cost of health insurance benefits. Some supported health system reform and planning efforts and controls on hospital capital investment as well as state regulation of reimbursement rates (in order to reduce cost-shifting from Medicare and Medicaid). There was an expansion of employer-sponsored health education efforts and in-plant behavior modification, exercise, and other health promotion programs. Individual firms, however, reap the benefits of these activities only in the course of time (and, in the case of programs for individual employees, only if the employees stay with the firm).

The onset of the major recession in the early 1980s, the most severe downturn since the Great Depression, increased the pressure for more direct ways to cut corporate health expenditures. The decline in the relative strength of labor in the collective bargaining process provided many employers with an opportunity to achieve the desired reductions. Although many individual firms understood the importance of containing the growth in the nation's total health care costs, their immediate priority was to shift as much of their own costs as possible onto employees. They pressed for reductions in coverage for dependents, higher deductibles and coinsurance by beneficiaries, and larger premium contributions by employees. In a number of cases they were successful.

The cuts in coverage and benefits were not viewed as temporary measures designed to save on employer premium costs during an economic downturn and to be abandoned when recession turned to recovery. Rather, they stemmed from a view that belt-tightening would help create a "leaner" health sector, one that would make available necessary health care services at lower costs and without reductions in quality. The actions to cut back on health insurance protection were not only a pragmatic response to reduced revenues and profits but the operational accompaniment to a theoretical structure. An old economic argument concerning the importance and benefits of economic incentives was now applied to the health sector. As the nation entered the 1980s, a new debate began.

What is the nature of the new debate? How is it possible for the general population to be better off with less health insurance, larger deductibles, and higher coinsurance rates? What rationale suggests that Medicare beneficiaries would benefit if proposals requiring larger out-of-pocket payments for hospital care were enacted? What arguments are advanced for taxing employees on health insurance premium payments by employers?

These and similar questions are part of today's health care debate. As in earlier times, the debate is laden with values and is ideological. And yet there is a difference. In the past, the arguments and the language in which we cast our disagreements about the proper role for government at various levels came from political theory. Today the language and the arguments come from economics.

At heart, however, the new language and the new formulations of the conflict are simply the latest intellectual weapons to be brought to an old battle. Although the subject of debate is health sector financing, it is not too much to claim that, in its most basic sense, the battle is still over the appropriate roles for private markets and for government. We remain divided by very different value-laden images of American society. We still differ on the relative emphasis to be accorded to the community and to the individual. We should not be surprised that economists, like other social scientists and like the general public, do not all share the same vision.[1]

THE MARKET AS CONTROL MECHANISM

The argument that new patterns of financing might contain rising health care prices and expenditures begins with a set of observations about the health economy. It then invokes economic theory to explain the observed data on the basis of existing economic arrangements and economic behavior. Finally, in a leap of faith often found in proclamations about the virtues of a "new economic order," it offers a simplistic solution to a complex issue. Unencumbered by doubts or misgivings about what people seek and how they would behave in the real world, it sketches its version of Utopia, assures us that it is attainable, and reassures us that it can be achieved with little pain. Were the prescription a new pharmaceutical, the Food and Drug Administration would be suspicious. The criteria for social policy are less exacting.

We begin with the observations. Health care prices have been rising steadily despite significant increases in the supply of hospital beds, in the number of physicians and other kinds of health workers at all levels, in the quantity of health care services delivered. In other areas of economic activity, substantial increases in supply tend to restrain rapid price increases: a bumper grain crop, an Alaskan oil field, new apartment dwellings, all are weapons in the war against inflation. Not so in health care, or at least, not to a significant extent.

If prices for health care were set in a competitive market place and determined by the forces of supply and demand, a further and continuing increase in supply might bring an answer to the vexing problem of health care inflation. If the demand for care were constantly expanding (say, because of an increase in medicine's ability to cure illness, reduce pain, or improve the quality of life; because the population is growing or is aging and therefore needs more care; or because of rising incomes and increasing affluence), prices might continue to move up even though supply was growing. Nevertheless, although supply might not expand sufficiently to bring price reductions or even price stability, the pressure for price increases would be moderated.

Unfortunately, there are many problems with a supply-side solution to health care price inflation: the market may not operate smoothly, there may be collusion about prices, the health care economy may not be sufficiently competitive, supply increases may turn out to be very costly. Furthermore, even if the increased supply of facilities and manpower did lead to price restraint, we might find ourselves facing an even more serious problem, that of rising expenditures for health care.

It is quite possible that an increase in supply would lead to higher levels of total health care spending. If hospitals are paid when beds are occupied and there are more hospital beds, there will be an incentive and an opportunity to admit more patients and keep them in the hospital longer. If there are more physicians there will be fewer patients per physician and an incentive to maintain income by increasing the number of visits and procedures per patient. If there are more surgeons there may be more surgery. More medical services would be delivered, but more may be neither necessary nor better. More care will mean more dollars.

Prices count. The prices for physician visits and hospital days are important data. They are visible and measurable. We talk and complain about them. They enter into the consumer price index. When they increase, and they have been increasing much more rapidly than the general inflation rate, they contribute to inflation and irritate presidents who have pledged to restore stable prices.

But expenditures count even more. The sums that government, employers, and individuals spend on health care do not depend on price alone. They are determined by both the prices paid and the quantities used. Thus we do not deplore the intervention that is costly but that cuts the length of the expensive hospital stay, and thus the total health care bill. Conversely, we are disturbed if, by filling hospital beds with patients who do not have to be there and who need less care, we reduce hospital per diems but increase total hospital expenditures. We do not want to spend more on health care even if each extra (but unnecessary) visit, test, and procedure can be obtained at bargain prices.

Supply increases that reduce prices but raise expenditures are not a boon. Presidents who have pledged to submit tight budgets (and all presidents do) find health expenditure increases disconcerting.

The explanation for the seemingly perverse behavior of the health economy, in which supply, prices, utilization, and expenditures all increase, is that it is not perverse at all. Part of it can be explained by the fact that the product called medical care is constantly changing and being redefined as a consequence of scientific advances. Today's health care is not the same as yesterday's. It is also true, however, that patients, physicians, and hospital administrators are responding in appropriate fashion to the prevailing set of institutional arrangements. Until recently there have been few incentives to contain costs and prices and numerous incentives to increase utilization. It is not surprising that, absent effective controls, the way we pay for care has created an ever-expanding health care industry and has yielded ever-growing expenditures.

The situation, some suggest, is analogous to one in which four individuals, upon entering a restaurant, decide to divide the check equally. "A" would not spend $10 extra for lobster if the checks were to be paid individually. Yet he realizes that, when the price is divided by four, the dish will cost him only an additional $2.50. He takes advantage of the "bargain." Each member of the group faces similar price distortions and orders items that otherwise would be rejected. Why not consume more when others provide a subsidy? The result, of course, is that the total bill increases.

Like many analogies, this one is flawed. Some individuals, after all, may order less rather than more, not wanting to take advantage of their friends. Nevertheless, the analogy is provocative, and the more so if, as in collective sharing of costs under health insurance, there are thousands at the table, they are strangers, they do not know who ordered what, and the provider—interested in increasing his income—encourages reliance on his judgments.

The story is a familiar one. Insurance, the complex third-party arrangement that characterizes America's health care financing, insulates both providers and consumers from a concern about prices and costs and from normal market forces. As insured patients we are not forced to engage in the calculus by which we weigh other purchases: is it worth it, is there a less expensive substitute, shall I seek care elsewhere or make do without it? Prices have not been particularly important data for millions of Americans whose health care was paid for in full or in large part by a third party. That has been especially the case for hospital care, where, since charges quickly exceed the level of the deductible (if any) and are not subject to coinsurance payments by the patient, over 90 percent of the cost is paid for by third parties.[2]

Furthermore, patients are not the only ones whose behavior is influenced by third-party payment. Physicians have not been forced to act as other sellers do. Not only does their expertise enable them to influence demand, but the presence of insurance means they are less impelled to consider whether patients will pay or search out less expensive competitors. Medical care providers, aware that prices are no longer as important in determining utilization, feel little pressure to economize, to search for efficiency, to compete vigorously by offering more for less. The failure to economize increases costs, expenditures, and insurance premiums, but most Americans are at least partially insulated from those effects by public insurance programs and by non-taxable employer contributions to group insurance. Thus, under existing fee-for-service and hospital reimbursement arrangements (excluding HMOs and DRGs, which, after all, do not apply to most Americans) insurance permits and fuels the increase in health care expenditures. Collective payment, which reduces individual concern with price, transforms private insurance, Medicare, and Medicaid. Once considered our protectors, they are now cast as villains.

Though incomplete, the story does ring true. Each of us knows friends and relatives who we believe visit the doctor more often than is necessary or at least more often than they would if they had to pay for care out of their own pockets. Many of us can remember that our physician ordered one more test that he or she told us was of only the slightest value. We remember, as well, that we did not discuss cost or consider it especially relevant. We are aware that physicians sometimes keep the patient in the hospital an extra day in order to suit their or the patient's convenience. As one physician put it before DRG reimbursement was implemented: "What should I do? How can I refuse my Medicare patient who asks to be discharged on Saturday rather than Friday because it is easier for her son-in-law to pick her up at that time? How tough can I be? But if her dollars rather than Medicare's were at stake she, not I, would make the decision to go home." Casual observation and individual memory are not the most powerful research methodologies, but we do not need to rely on more advanced techniques to know that insurance does increase the number of visits, tests, procedures, hospital days, and hospital investment.

We should not be surprised. Third-party payment was developed in order to protect us, to do just what it does: insulate us from price. We purchase health insurance not only to regularize our health payment expenditures but also to free ourselves from the cost-benefit calculus and to gain access to medical care that otherwise we could not afford. The fact that insurance increases utilization and, by assuring payment and a flow of income, permits upgrading of facilities (and, presumably, of quality) is one of insurance's predictable, desired, and desirable outcomes.

The restaurant analogy is suspect after all. It encourages us to accept its implied standard that the appropriate level of expenditures is the sum of what each of us, individually, is willing *and able* to spend. But is that the correct standard? It is not the one the nation used when it adopted free public education or when it chose to develop systems of subsidies and differential prices that take account of ability to pay.

It is true that we are spending much more on health care than we once did. Personal health expenditures rose from 3.8 percent of GNP in 1950 to 5.2 percent in 1965 (an increase of 37 percent). During the same period the share of personal health expenditures paid for by third parties rose from 34.5 percent to 48.4 percent (an increase of 40 percent).[3] Third-party payment permitted or encouraged escalation of expenditures. Yet it is also true that cost increases stimulated the purchase of insurance.

Americans were spending more on health care in 1965 than in 1950, yet even as late as 1965, 78 percent of personal health expenditures were private and 66 percent of private expenditures were paid for on an out-of-pocket basis.[4] There is no evidence that Americans (individually or collectively) were spending more on health care than they deemed desirable. The share going for health was growing, but most Americans felt that they were getting something (indeed, quite a bit) for their money.

From 1971 to 1981 expenditures for personal health services increased from $72 billion to $255 billion. Yet two-thirds of the increase was accounted for by economy-wide factors (57 percent attributed to general inflation and 8 percent to the growth in population). Seven percent was attributable to increases in health prices in excess of overall inflation, and the remaining 28 percent was explained by "intensity," changes in use and/or kinds of services and supplies (including an upgrading of quality).[5] Again, it is not clear that the expenditure increase is not supported by consumers and is simply the consequence of widespread health insurance.

Moreover, the health care system does not operate without constraints. The presence of insurance does not convert all medical care into a free commodity. Health insurance (collective payment) accounts for only a portion of personal health care expenditures. True, of the $158 billion spent for hospital care, only 9 percent (for some patients the percentage is far greater) is accounted for by direct consumer payments. Yet 28 percent of payments for physicians' services (and an even greater part of payments for office visits) is paid for on an out-of-pocket basis.[6] Furthermore, many Americans pay part (in some cases a substantial part) of the cost of insurance, and many more are aware that there is a tradeoff between insurance and wage and salary increases. In addition, patients bear monetary costs (transportation, loss of wages, deductible and coinsurance charges) when they receive care. People do not seek unlimited amounts of care; it is not a source of pleasure. We all know individuals who are afraid of physicians, who associate doctors' offices and hospital rooms with pain and anguish, who postpone the visit and behave as if the physician's diagnosis will convert the suspected illness into reality, who are afraid of information. Nor are those who deliver care bereft of moral standards. They do not simply seek to maximize their revenues and incomes. Finally, third-party payers do try, and with increasing diligence, to police the system, to question fees and the need for particular procedures.

Insurance does increase utilization, costs, and expenditures, but even in an uncontrolled or minimally controlled insurance and payment system there are limits. We will not spend all of our time seeking care, and medicine will stop short of absorbing all of the nation's resources. At no time will health expenditures equal 100 percent of GNP. But the knowledge that there is some upper bound hardly provides sufficient comfort. Nor should it. Existing insurance and payment mechanisms do help individuals but we know that, as now constituted, they have encouraged the health sector to grow beyond our needs, to make medical care more costly than it need be, to misallocate resources and dollars. We pay a price for redundancy, duplication, and waste. Sometimes the price is poorer quality care. Sometimes the price is the exclusion of individuals, who cannot afford and thus do not receive the care they need. Always the price is denial of the opportunity to use those dollars spent on unnecessary or unwarranted medical care for other worthwhile private and public purposes.

Few of us would dare to face the world without the protection that health insurance provides. We do not envy those of our fellow citizens who are forced to do so. Nor do we desire insurance simply because in a world in which others have and use it we too need it. We do want to contain health expenditures and recognize that insurance has helped and helps to increase them but we do not press for a constitutional amendment prohibiting its sale and purchase. It is true that if each of us had to pay for all of our medical care out of his or her own pocket, the utilization of medical services and the health sector's share of GNP would decline precipitously (as would the incomes of physicians, the revenues of hospitals and other health care facilities, and the wages and the number of health workers). It is also true that the elimination of third-party payment would mean that medical care would be distributed on the basis of income to those who felt they needed it and who—given their incomes—wanted it more than they wanted other things. That is an allocative principle on which we are willing to rely in many but not in all areas of life.

Americans do not want to put an end to insurance and the pooling of risk and money by the potential patient population. Our ethical values (and self-interest) preclude limiting access and the availability of costly medical procedures (some of which are the products of our collectively financed research efforts) only to those who can afford to pay. We reject the abolition of third-party payment because, as in other areas (such as education, food, and housing), we speak and think of needs instead of preferences. As a consequence, we are unwilling to let the existing unequal income distribution play too large a role (although there is disagreement about how large is "too large") in the determination of who does and who does not receive needed medical care services (there is also disagreement about what needs are really "needs"). We fear the unpredictability of illness and know we (and others) may require help in meeting the costs of care. Since most Americans reject government provision of medical care through a national health service, we seek protection (and offer it to others) through the purchase of insurance and the enactment of public programs that pay for care produced privately.

And so we support and retain an insurance system that has served us both well and badly. In the past its shortcomings were of much less consequence. Medical costs were lower and health care expenditures absorbed a much smaller share of GNP. Furthermore, we needed and wanted to expand America's health care resources in order to make more care available to more people. Today we face a different set of facts. The impact of waste, inefficiency, and misallocation is greater and less readily absorbed. The nation no longer needs a greater number of physicians or hospital beds. The cost-benefit calculus has changed, perhaps most poignantly for those of our neighbors who face an insurance-fed health sector but who themselves lack third-party coverage. Their situation—though of greater consequence—is similar to the one many of us face when we are asked to pay high restaurant and entertainment prices, generated by expense-account demand, out of our own pockets.

In the latter part of the 1970s the rapid increases in health care costs led various levels of government and private-sector payers to search for mechanisms that would control medical care inflation and counter the undesired consequences that seemed inevitable corollaries of widespread third-party payment. President Carter proposed legislation that set limits for increases in hospital rates. Successive attempts to enact the measure failed, but the American Hospital Association and American hospitals committed themselves to a voluntary effort to contain costs. The federal government pressed the states to restrict new capital formation, arguing that an excess of hospital beds added to health system costs and provided an incentive for unnecessary hospitalization. Employers and insurance underwriters announced that they would monitor service utilization patterns and require second opinions for surgical procedures. There were public- and private-sector efforts to stimulate the growth of HMOs. The emphasis was on regulating, constraining, and changing the behavior of those who delivered care, who hospitalized the patient, ordered the tests, wielded the scalpel, read the X rays, and purchased the technology. Patients were viewed as playing an innocent and somewhat passive role. It was not their behavior that had caused the expenditure explosion; most dollars were spent as a result of decisions by physicians. Regulatory attention was therefore focused on physicians, the system's gatekeepers and decision makers, and on the hospitals in which they practiced.

The growth of regulations in the 1970s is often read as evidence of government's strength and power. It can also be read as evidence of government's weakness. Unable or unwilling to alter basic structural components and incentives created by existing hospital reimbursement and fee-for-service patterns, government was forced to try to regulate prices and behavior in order to contain costs and keep providers from responding to the economic incentives placed before them. Government could not address its real concern, total health care expenditures, directly. There was no central budget or budgeting mechanism. Since providers continued to be paid on a piecework basis, government and private payers were forced to concentrate on price and quantity, on the price per piece and the number of pieces.

The contrast with Great Britain is revealing. Under the National Health Service government has restructured health system incentives. Thus, although government funds almost all health care services, it has fewer regulations and is less intrusive in clinical decisions than is the case in the United States.

Regulatory activity has its problems and its limits. Regulations by their very nature deal with details, but because they attempt to define and constrain normal behavior (that is, the behavior that responds to the system's incentives) they are often viewed as interference. They are of vital concern to a minority of individuals and organizations to whom they make a very substantial difference and of little or no interest to most of the rest of us. They appear to be technical and nonideological, the outcome of purely objective consideration, but in fact are imbedded in the political world. Rules and regulations are necessary, but those affected by them view them as nuisances at best and as unwarranted interference at worst.

As in other fields of economic activity, there was a call for deregulation. Some felt that regulations represented the arbitrary use of power by nonelected officials and civil servants. Others felt that the regulatory process was costly and ineffective, that clever people could always circumvent the system. Observers pointed out that in many areas of economic activity those who were being regulated perverted the regulatory process so that it served their interests rather than those of the general public. Still others argued that regulations and rules had a basic flaw: either they were general and did not apply to every situation and take account of the vast differences inherent in a heterogeneous health sector or they were so detailed that few could understand, apply, or police them. In one case they would be inequitable and would inhibit change, reduce flexibility and experimentation, freeze whatever was in place and ossify the system. In the other they simply would not yield the desired results. As regulations grew more detailed and cumbersome, there was pressure for an alternative. Since rising health care expenditures were of real concern and since we were committed to retaining health insurance, the task was to find a different control mechanism, a less intrusive and more effective way to retain third-party financing but to reduce its unfavorable side effects.

As America entered the 1980s the focus shifted to the search for a nonpolitical, nondiscretionary, nonregulatory control mechanism. What was wanted was something that would work automatically to contain costs and reduce misallocations, maximize producer and consumer freedom, encourage change, be responsive to new discoveries (both technological and organizational), and allow for diversity. Many economists were able to describe just such a mechanism.

Many who argue that regulatory agencies and regulations are unnecessary or at least can be substantially scaled down place their faith in what they perceive as a less costly and more workable alternative. That alternative is market competition: the market instead of government as allocator, the market instead of government as regulator, the market rather than government as the mechanism that monitors tastes and desires and assures appropriate responses. Knowledgeable and cost-conscious consumers, interacting with producers who compete vigorously and who face the threat of new entrants lured by the opportunity for profits, provide the governing structure that presumably yields desired outcomes. Regulations are replaced not by anarchy but by competition. The heavy hand of the bureaucracy gives way to the invisible hand of the market.

The model has an elegant simplicity. It is one with which millions of Americans are familiar, not because we encounter it in its pure and perfect form in our daily lives but because we have met it in our courses in economics and have heard it extolled in rhetoric. It is a model in which price-conscious consumers who act to maximize their satisfactions face sellers who compete vigorously to maximize the difference between their costs and revenues. Prices are set by the market, not by regulatory intervention or monopolists. This self-regulating model of market competition is one in which the consumer is knowledgeable and sovereign and in which only responsive and efficient producers are assured of survival.

Economists have elaborated the competitive model and defined its characteristics: many buyers and sellers none of whom can wield undue market power, no price distortions as a consequence of subsidies, no excess market power associated with restrictions on entry of new producers, relatively homogeneous commodities and knowledgeable consumers able to recognize differences in quality, no situations in which one person's or firm's decision based on private costs and benefits confers costs or benefits on others. These conditions, elaborated in textbooks, are seldom found in the real world. But the fact that the model does not describe reality does not diminish its importance.

For many economists the model of pure competition has a normative character. Competitive markets, if we could but construct them, would provide optimal answers to (what have been defined as) the central questions of economics—questions concerning the allocation of resources (what, how, how much should be produced). Given the prevailing distribution of income, the market also determines who will have access. Any departures from this market economy would misallocate resources. Noncompetitive markets and price distortions would lead to over- or underproduction of particular goods and services (relative to their true resource costs), and thus to reduced total satisfaction. In this way the competitive market becomes not only a standard against which other markets can be measured and compared but also a goal to which we should aspire.

It is legitimate for theologians, social reformers, and prophets not only to describe a better world, but also to call upon us to organize and behave ourselves in ways that would help attain it. Similarly, it is legitimate for economists who believe that a health care system characterized by competition makes for a better world, to try to convince us to take steps to reach or at least approach it. But it is important that we understand that all definitions of "a better world" stem from sets of values that we are free to share or to reject. When we turn from descriptions of what is or what (under certain conditions) might be, to consideration of what we want and are willing to give up to attain it, experts and laypersons all have one vote. Our democratic institutions presume that each of us has an equal voice.

Americans—including economists—do disagree. We do not all sing the same free-market hymn. While some deplore the minimum wage as an interference with the market, others see its effects as salutary. While some would weaken occupational safety and health standards, others would strengthen them. In the vigorous competition that some seek, others see the potential destruction of the small businessperson and family farm. We welcome the benefits that an increase in competition would bring (greater efficiency, lower prices, newer products). At the same time we wonder: can we devise rules so that the competitive battle is fought cleanly, can we make certain that those who survive do not use their power to exclude potential new competitors, can we make certain (if size itself increases efficiency) that the one or two or three large winners do not simply carve up the market? The American ethos favors competition; the American experience suggests that free competition is not easily attained or without costs (is our more competitive telephone service really better?).

The argument in the health field is that the health marketplace is distorted by the presence of traditional insurance and payment mechanisms (which alter our assessment of costs and benefits), licensing, accreditation procedures, and capital controls (all of which inhibit or prevent entry and thus protect existing institutions), lack of data on performance (which prevents us from being knowledgeable consumers). If that is the diagnosis, the treatment follows: free the market to be free. Even as most economists recognize that the health care market is not the same as other markets and cannot be reconfigured to include all of the characteristics of pure competition, many believe that more price competition is both feasible and desirable. While most also believe that a major restructuring of existing arrangements would not be easy, many (but not all) are convinced that safeguards could be erected to protect individuals during the period of transition.

If you and I are not sufficiently aware of and concerned about health care prices, reduce the support mechanisms that protect us. Increase price consciousness by making prices count. If they count, we will care; if we care, price competition will begin to flourish. True, depending on our incomes, some of us will care more (and be able to buy less) than others (who will be able to buy more). That, however, is defined as an equity issue, a separate and different question—one that some economists contend is part of the "softer" disciplines of ethics and moral philosophy.

But the question remains whether a free, unfettered, competitive market in the health field would yield a better world. Am I not concerned and affected by your illness and you by mine? Do we not care about today's sick children, tomorrow's adults and the nation's future, who are without Medicaid? Is the competitive solution optimal? Does it reflect our collective wants and needs? Is it attainable, and at what price and within what time span?

LESS INSURANCE, THE WAY TO PRICE CONSCIOUSNESS

If the need is to increase consumer price consciousness, one way to do so is to require or induce us to have less insurance than we now carry. If we had to pay for more of our medical care out of our own pockets, we would want to know more about both the costs to be incurred and the benefits we might derive from the utilization of various medical services. Theory suggests that as we were affected by and considered price we would begin to shop. Presumably, those who needed appendectomies would avoid institutions that charged high prices because they were equipped to do open-heart surgery. We would seek and limit ourselves to institutions that could meet *our* needs. Producers of care would specialize and offer different levels of care at different prices.

It is not necessary to imagine a world of surgeons of different abilities (as reflected in patient mortality rates) offering their services at widely different prices. The competitive model need not assume unrestricted and vigorous price competition directly related to performance: the able practitioner at a $500 fee and the hack who endangers the patient's life at $25. Such a world is not what those who favor competition seek. Few observers seriously endorse the abolition of all regulations, licensing and accreditation requirements, and safety and quality standards. In health care *caveat emptor* has its limits.

It is within those limits that those who would seek more price consciousness and competition erect their model. In a world with less insurance and less pooling of resources by the potential patient population, medical care would be distributed to those who felt they needed and, given their incomes, wanted it more than they wanted other things. Patients presumably would not do without the care they needed but would define their needs more carefully and responsibly. The problem of those whose lack of income would influence their decisions too heavily, of those who would be rationed out of the market by their inability to finance the care they needed on an out-of-pocket basis, would have to be dealt with. The purpose of competition is not to reduce health care expenditures by denying care to those who cannot pay the price. Its goal is a more modest one: to induce us to consider price and thus to stimulate and reward efficiency.

Increased cost-sharing would reduce utilization. Theory also suggests that it would induce us to shop and seek lower cost providers. However, in this as in other areas of life, theory is not a substitute for data.

The largest single study of consumer behavior, by the Rand Corporation, "found little evidence that increased cost-sharing did lead consumers to shop for lower priced providers." The study concluded:

> In sum, increased cost-sharing is one solution offered to the problem of the high cost of health care. This strategy would have significant effects on total health care expenditures because it would substantially affect the demand for care. Many argue that it would also provide the incentive for consumers to search for the lowest price of medical care and so encourage greater competition in the medical market . . . Though our results are tentative and might be altered with increased fee information available to consumers, the results give little reason to be optimistic that increased cost-sharing will also lead to greater price competition.[7]

This is a severe indictment of the structure on which much of the argument for competition is based. We are left with a decline in utilization and a drop in demand, but these are due to the price rationing of care, to the fact that some could not afford or would not choose to buy the product. Of course, as utilization fell prices might drop (except if the supply of services also decreased, as providers who found the need to engage in price rationing distasteful left the field). In a competitive world in which producers could not increase prices to make up for declining utilization, expenditures on medical care would decline. So, too, would health status.

Few Americans would find explicit price rationing of care socially acceptable. Such rationing, of course, is acceptable in other areas: theater seats, airplane tickets, automobiles, sirloin steaks, gasoline. But medical care is viewed differently. Few of us think of it as a luxury good or service and few of us believe that there is an abundance of close substitutes. Quality and prices differ for theater seats as well as other forms of entertainment. Similarly, one can travel by train or bus, buy a new or used car, eat more or less expensive protein foods. The fewer the substitutes and the more necessary the particular good or service for the sustenance and quality of life, or for life itself, the more distressed we are by free-market solutions that allocate only to those whose income permits them to translate their wants and needs into effective demand. It is illuminating that during the Second World War price rationing for gasoline (for which there was no substitute) was rejected in favor of a distribution on the basis of need through a new currency (ration stamps) that could be distributed more equitably. It is revealing that most of us do not decry the existence of multiple tiers or classes of hotels but that many of us are troubled by the existence of two-class medicine.

Our views cannot be ascribed solely to our awareness of the risk of epidemics and contagious diseases, and thus to the fact that each person's physical health may be affected by the health status of his or her neighbor. That factor plays some part, but the issues go far beyond your not wanting to catch my cold. The health of others affects our psychological well-being. Decent people—and we are a decent people—are offended by unnecessary pain and suffering, that is, by pain and suffering for which there is a treatment and for which some (who are affluent) are treated. We are troubled by the notion that relief from the pain and suffering caused by ill health (perhaps even the postponement of death) should be available only to those who can pay for it out of their own means and who, after weighing matters, choose to do so. We fear that as medicine advances and new and more expensive interventions are developed, we will be rationed out of the market. Once we admit that price rationing of care is proper, we put ourselves at risk.

When medicine could do little and when the costs of care were minimal, private charity (often provided by physicians) sufficed. Today, when medicine can intervene successfully and when some interventions are and will remain beyond the resources of the individual patient and his or her physician, collective action and cooperation are accepted as necessary. A larger, more urbanized, more heterogeneous society, a society of strangers, requires the expansion of third-party payment (including public funds) as the expression of those views.

No one has proposed the prohibition of the sale and purchase of insurance, one of the ways we act collectively. Nor has there been a proposal to eliminate all public third-party payments. Collective private and public programs are seen as necessary. Proposed instead are changes at the margin: a little less private insurance, Medicare, and Medicaid, a little more price consciousness, a little price rationing, but not too much. The goal is to structure insurance benefits and payment mechanisms in ways that would offer the benefits of protection when that is required and yet achieve the benefits of control and constraint.

The various proposals that have been put forward to move the health sector toward competition reflect the views and priorities of their proponents. Accordingly, they differ in both emphasis and timing. Aware that we do not want to debate price at the moment when we need care and seek service, most proposals are directed at decisions that are one step removed from that emotional event. Instead we are invited to consider the breadth and coverage of the insurance we purchase and to take the protection package that, at the price, we deem most suitable. Our decision, of course, will have important consequences on later sets of choices in seeking care and on behavior. The virtue of directing our attention to various insurance packages is that we are encouraged to think about coverage (not about necessary or desirable care) and to think at a time when we can be more objective.

One suggested mechanism to increase our concern with the selection of an insurance package derives from the argument that the failure to tax employer-paid health insurance premiums induces individuals to expand their health insurance coverage and makes that coverage more comprehensive. It simply is more economical for individuals to shift health care expenditures that otherwise would be made with aftertax dollars into insurance paid for with nontaxable dollars provided by the employer. The effective price of insurance is reduced below its actuarial value. Subsidized to do so, we buy more insurance than we would if we had to pay its full price. We then end up using (and abusing) it.[8]

Suppose an employee is considering the purchase of a health insurance policy that would cover additional health services whose average cost is $1,200. Because insurance protects the individual if his or her needs exceed the average (and because insurance helps in budgeting), the employee may be willing to pay $1,300 for such a policy. If, because of the costs of administration, the insurer charges $1,400 for the additional coverage, the policy will be seen as too expensive and will be rejected.

If the employer agrees to pay the cost of the $1,400 policy with pretax dollars (in lieu of wages), the effective price of the insurance is changed. Suppose the employee is offered a choice: a $1,400 wage increase or the policy that costs $1,400. If the employee is in a 30 percent marginal tax bracket, the $1,400 pay raise will leave him or her with $980 after federal income taxes (and even less after payment of state income and applicable Social Security taxes). Thus, in choosing the $1,400 policy the employee loses $980 in aftertax income but gains a policy for which he or she was willing to pay $1,300. The second option (effectively a $1,300 policy for $980) is preferred. Because of the tax code, more insurance is purchased than would otherwise be the case.

Although the particular example depends on the numbers chosen for illustration, the general point is clear. If all of us received an extra dollar in wages (and less than a dollar in take-home pay) and, at the same time, lost a dollar's worth of employer-financed insurance, we would not all turn around and replace the insurance. The advantage of a dollar's worth of insurance would remain but its real cost would rise. Some of us would choose to do with less protection.

If employer contributions to the purchase of health insurance were treated as employee wage and salary income and thus were fully taxable, the effective price of insurance would increase. Although the degree to which we would make do with less insurance or less of other things is unclear, there would be some inducement to search for a better insurance buy—the same protection but at a lower price—as well as to make do with less comprehensive coverage and accept higher levels of cost sharing. How various individuals would react depends upon many factors, including income and perceived health status. If those who felt they were low-risk individuals who could make do with less insurance dropped out (or, say, accepted a very large deductible), the premium for those who remained would rise. Over time, the process of self-selection would effectively deny insurance (because of high premium costs) to those who need it most. The tax subsidy is one way to encourage healthy people to buy insurance. It partially offsets the negative effects of experience rating. Without it our private health insurance system, which increases access to care for many who would otherwise be denied access, would be much weaker.

Two other arguments have been advanced in favor of taxing the health insurance fringe benefit. The first is that the Treasury would gain substantial additional revenues (estimated at $21 billion excluding Social Security taxes in fiscal year 1985 and projected at $42 billion in fiscal 1987).[9] The corollary, however, is that Americans (including low-income workers with comprehensive insurance) would pay considerably more in taxes. Even though the nation faces continuing large deficits (and may elect to increase taxes), there is no groundswell of support for full taxation of employer-provided health insurance.

The second argument relates to tax equity. Employment-based insurance is more likely to be available to higher-wage employees. As a consequence, it is estimated that in 1983 the tax exclusion provided benefits to 73 percent of American households with incomes between $50,000 and $100,000 but to only 31 percent of households with incomes between $10,000 and $15,000 and to a mere 13 percent of households with incomes under $10,000.[10]

Furthermore, those with higher incomes are more likely to have larger employer contributions and to be in higher marginal tax brackets. Thus their tax savings are greater: the average federal tax benefit (including Social Security taxes) for households in the $50,000 to $100,000 income bracket who received a benefit, amounted to $857 but was only $269 for beneficiary households with incomes between $10,000 and $15,000 and only $129 for those with incomes of less than $10,000.[11] One does not have to be overly sensitive to equity considerations to conclude that a tax system that gives more help to the rich than to the poor is highly unfair. Were the billions in "tax expenditures" to be voted upon as budget expenditures for health care, few of us would select this particular distribution of benefits, this distribution of assistance in meeting health care costs.

But the fact that current health insurance tax benefits are distributed inequitably does not necessarily suggest that the tax benefit should be eliminated. It can instead be argued that the nature of the tax benefit should be altered to increase its progressivity (for example, by substituting a sliding tax credit for the tax deduction as well as a refund to those whose credit exceeds their taxes and by permitting a credit for individual payments for insurance). Such a proposal, however, has not been made. Nor are we offered a menu of items, each involving $21 billion (today's figure is much higher than this 1985 estimate), and asked which we would choose. Instead we are asked to give up something useful, but hardly perfect, for an unspecified alternative.

Furthermore, the equity issue is not as simple as it first appears. While upper-income groups receive more dollar help both from employers and from the government, the dollars received by low-income families represent a higher proportion of their family income. For high-income families ($50,000 or more in family income) the new tax would represent 0.85 percent of income ($576), while for low-income families (under $10,000) it would be 3.17 percent ($174).[12] Although low-income families would pay fewer additional tax dollars and although it would cost them fewer dollars to replace the employer's contribution, it would be harder for them to do so. The effect of the new tax would be to reduce coverage and access to health services for those who (because of both lower income and lower health status) need that coverage the most. It is their utilization that would be most affected.

Consider an analogy. Imagine that there are two neighbors, one with a freezer full of food, the other with a bare cupboard. Under the prevailing system, the first receives a weekly shipment of the finest meats and produce from his legislators. The second receives a few pounds of fatback and bruised vegetables. Concerned about this inequity, legislators agree not to give either party anything. The neighbors return to fending for themselves. The first continues to eat well; the second starves.

Of course, this analogy is incomplete. Perhaps the resources saved are used to help those who are starving. Perhaps the story does end happily. We do not know. Absent information on other policy measures, we are left with a curious situation, one in which we are supposed to congratulate ourselves on reducing a program inequity even as we increase starvation. Of course it is unfair to give more tax relief to those with higher income than to our neighbors who are poor, to chief executives than to blue-collar workers. But the cause of justice is not advanced—unless one has a curious definition of justice—by eliminating support for everyone.

The proposals to change the tax-exclusion provisions are more modest and do not involve the full taxation of employer-supported health insurance. One approach, embodied in the tax-simplification program presented by then secretary of the Treasury Donald Regan in November 1984, would have imposed a tax on employer health insurance premiums in excess of $70 a month for individuals and $175 a month for families. It was estimated that only 30 percent of those who benefited from employer contributions received assistance in excess of these amounts. Because the tax would be directed toward comprehensive rather than basic coverage, it would not affect an appreciable proportion of low-income individuals.

The second approach was contained in the tax program offered by the administration as a replacement for the Treasury proposals. This taxed the *first* $10 a month paid by employers for individual health insurance and the *first* $25 a month for family coverage. This proposal was not directed against large employer contributions that finance extensive coverage. It hit at the first rather than the last dollar and affected everyone who receives employer assistance.

This second approach was a tax-revenue measure pure and simple. Whatever the validity of the argument that cost control requires us to cut back on insurance and to increase out-of-pocket costs, the program did not in fact discriminate against extensive (presumably unnecessary) coverage. Nor did it enhance equity. At the proposed new tax rates high-income employees with substantial employer assistance (say, $2,100 per annum) would pay a maximum of $105 in new taxes on the $2,100 employer contribution. Low-income individuals receiving more limited assistance might pay as much as $45 for $300 worth of help. To the degree that the tax raised the price and reduced the purchase of insurance, it would hit heaviest those who are convinced that they are healthier and need less protection and those who already have less coverage. The upper-income employee could convert one-seventh of his insurance to salary to pay the tax (retaining $1,800 of insurance), while the low-income wage earner would have to give up half of his insurance (retaining only $150 of protection). It is not difficult to understand the program's appeal: it would increase tax revenues. It is also not hard to understand why, since it would do little else and what it would do is undesirable, it aroused opposition.

It was not surprising that in September 1985 the staff of the House Ways and Means Committee proposed that the committee reject the first-dollar approach in the tax-simplification measure it was considering, in favor of the tax method embodied in the original Treasury proposal, but with higher limits: $120 a month for individuals and $300 a month for families.

Taxation above a "cap" has a certain elegance. By exempting the first $3,600 per annum of family coverage and the first $1,440 for individuals, the staff proposal focused on the upper end of the insurance spectrum and affected relatively few individuals (the corollary, of course, is that it would have raised relatively little money). Yet it also had its problems. It would hit especially hard at low and middle-income workers with extensive insurance. Furthermore, it would have different consequences on individuals and families at different income levels and with different health status. Again, the dynamics of self-selection would come into play.

Moreover, a cap does not take account of the very substantial differences in health care costs (and therefore in insurance premiums) as a function of geography and of risk factors of group members (often heavily related to age). Not permitting variation in the exclusion limit would mean that less effective assistance would be provided to (or a higher tax exacted from) those whose insurance was most costly because of age, state of health, or location—matters largely outside the individual's control. A new inequity would replace the old. Conversely, adjustments to the cap would require classifying health care and other data by place of employment and residence (exacerbating the impact of experience rating) and would represent a significant departure both from the way the tax code now operates and from proposals for tax simplification.

Furthermore, the tax cap would have an unpredictable effect on HMO enrollment. It is true that as health insurance becomes more expensive because of the required tax payment, better shopping should induce individuals to enroll in HMOs that offer better value for the health care dollar. Conversely, HMOs offer a more comprehensive benefit package and sometimes do require large premiums. Employees who want or need to save tax dollars may prefer less coverage at lower premiums and may opt out of HMOs. The need to spend more dollars (even if to get much more value) might therefore lead to an unfortunate side effect in which the tax cap inhibits the expansion of more efficient health care.

If the cap is not indexed to health sector inflation, an increasing number of individuals will be affected as premiums increase. Conversely, if it is indexed, its impact on insurance and on health sector behavior will remain marginal.

This should not surprise us. Hospital care consumes the largest single part of the health dollar. It is likely that Americans will give up other parts of their health insurance package (such as physicians' service benefits) and retain hospital coverage. Individuals who do not seek out a physician will be less likely to be hospitalized, at least in the short run. But will this reduce expenditures? It is unclear whether persons would enter the hospital later and stay longer, or even whether, as the hospital census dropped, the empty beds would be filled by others and by extended patient stays. Indeed, since hospital insurance would continue to cover expenses incurred, it is easy to imagine a return to the situation in which total health expenditures would rise as physicians substituted costly hospital services for less expensive ambulatory care. The dilemma is clear. Small actions that would cause relatively little pain on average (though much pain to the most vulnerable) would yield small benefits; large actions, in turn, would be associated with substantial pain and dislocation.

These are not the most serious problems raised by the tax proposals. The unfavorable impact on labor relations would be temporary; after a time, the parties would adjust to the new rules of the game. Difficult as it might be to adjust the tax bite to take account of differences in health care costs, this, too, could be done (although doing so would add to administrative and research expenditures). Unfavorable distributional effects could be mitigated (though, again, by increasing administrative costs and complexity). No, the most severe problem is of another kind. Selling the tax cap as a revenue enhancer is one thing; advancing it as health care reform is quite another. If the taxation of employer premium contributions is accepted as a health care expenditure control it will delay more meaningful and necessary actions. The enactment of a tax change that does not have the support of the public, of providers, of insurers, of labor, or of management would require overselling its potential health system advantages and expending considerable political energy. Such an expenditure is justified when the prize is sufficient and when no greater prize is available for an equivalent expenditure of effort. That is not the case with the tax cap proposal.

Many employer, labor, health insurance, medical care provider, and citizen groups have opposed the various tax proposals. They fear the distributional aspects of cutbacks in health insurance protection, the precedent-setting nature of the proposals, and the impact on existing labor-management contracts (as employees would attempt to recoup the loss of perceived benefits). They have been joined by members of Congress—including Senator Robert Packwood, Republican from Oregon and chairman of the Senate Finance Committee—who believe that the encouragement of the private purchase of health insurance has weakened the pressure for a government national health insurance program. They believe that taxation of employer-provided premiums for private health insurance would revive the pressure for publicly funded health insurance. Perhaps therefore it is not surprising that the tax bill as reported out by the Ways and Means Committee and as enacted by the House in December 1985 did not tax health insurance premium payments by employers.

The proposals to tax employer payments toward health insurance would do little to help create a competitive health care market. Most supporters of the market-control approach recognize that other actions would be necessary if health care costs are to be contained. They would offer a multipronged approach: encouraging employers to offer more insurance options with different costs to employees (and tax-free rebates if the employee selects a plan costing less than the employer's standard contribution), increasing the proportion of the insurance premium paid for by the employee, reducing first-dollar coverage and increasing deductibles and coinsurance rates, increasing the ease with which employees can convert to HMO enrollment, stimulating negotiated agreements between insurers and providers who offer less expensive care.

These approaches are based on the assumption that if the consumer has more options in his or her selection of an insurance policy and if the individual is made to feel a greater financial burden as a result of selecting a more expensive option, insurers will compete vigorously. If they can gain a market advantage by associating themselves with providers who control costs and if an increased proportion of providers organize themselves efficiently, reduce prices, and are more deliberate in their prescribing behavior and use of tests and days of hospital care, then expenditures will be contained. Efficient producers will capture a greater share of the market; the inefficient will be forced to become efficient or go under as they are priced out of the market. Similarly, as insurers introduce more cost-sharing and thereby attract subscribers by offering lower premiums, more and more Americans will become increasingly cost conscious. As a consequence health care expenditures would decrease.

If all this, and only this, would occur, the benefits of competition could be gained with few dislocating effects. But is this all that would happen? The history of the competition between Blue Cross and commercial health insurers serves as a powerful reminder that differences in premiums arise for reasons that have little to do with provider efficiency and clinical behavior or with insurer motivation to question costs. Premium differentials, we recall, arose because, under experience rating, insurers were able to offer lower premiums to groups with lower-risk factors and because individuals and groups were free to self-select. The consequence of creaming behavior was that low-risk groups were able to purchase insurance at substantially lower premiums than were high-risk groups and individuals. Over time the latter groups, older, sicker, poorer, and no longer assisted by their more fortunate fellows, were priced out of the private health insurance market. It was that process that led society to design and enact the Medicare program as a mechanism that would provide protection to aged individuals with high projected utilization.

A similar selection process would take place under the competitive model. Insurers are likely to reap higher rewards from careful risk selection than from efforts at inducing system change (the former gains are captured in their entirety by the insurer; the latter are shared with one's competitors). Different market prices reflecting market segmentation rather than differences in insurer efficiency would appear. HMOs and other producer groups would compete to attract healthier subscribers. Indeed, the effect of experience rating would be far more pronounced than at present, since individuals within a group (the plant, the firm) would each have the opportunity to choose from among many plans and from among numerous options. The greater the number of competitive options in the purchase of insurance, the more the self-selection; the more the self-selection, the less risk-sharing and help for those in our community who need and use more health services. Individual concerns would have created a segmented community.

Recognizing the incentive toward creaming and its harmful consequences, advocates of the competitive model have stressed the need for open enrollment, the requirement that the insurer accept anyone who cares to enroll. This would reduce the opportunity for insurers and providers to discriminate against higher-risk individuals. Unfortunately, requiring open enrollment is not the same thing as achieving it. Insurers could be more diligent in seeking low-risk subscribers (say, by using more advertising and opening more branches in some areas than in others). Perhaps policing the system would be easier than policing equal employment opportunity behavior, but certainly it would not be easy. We should not be surprised: pure competition does not come easily or cheaply.

The problem would be magnified if insurers offered high and low options and if, as the competitive model suggests, there were frequent opportunities for individuals to exercise their choices. Under those conditions, individuals could "game the system," purchasing more insurance when they anticipated a need for greater utilization and less insurance (such as insurance with much higher deductibles) at other times. Although the timing of much medical care utilization is nondiscretionary, some is, such as that for elective surgery. Full and frequent opportunity to change coverage would inevitably result in even greater market segmentation. It would also have two other consequences. The first is that, even though we recognize that our future health status is in no small measure unpredictable, we would be encouraged to spend time weighing and considering which of the numerous options was the best buy. Whether this is how we want to or should spend our time is questionable. The second is that some of us will make choices which will turn out to be unfortunate. We may select the high deductible and become unemployed or be the victim of an accident. If we then find we cannot pay for our medical care, it is not only we who are put at risk. Surely it is unhealthy for a society to turn away from its sick, telling them they should have thought of the future when they were well. During a crisis, the larger society may elect (be forced by its value system) to subsidize them. Recognizing that possibility, some among us will choose to rely on a magnanimous society and will carry less insurance. The burden of uncompensated care will grow, the power of insurance will decline, and neighbor will be set against neighbor.

Competition among delivery systems does benefit some prospective patients. It has its place. We should not discount the stimulus provided by HMOs, ambulatory and surgical care centers, and other delivery innovations. At the same time we must recognize that the health system has been built on a system of cross-subsidies that, though not fully equitable, has served us well. All of us have paid for the standby capacity of the hospital emergency room and have derived benefits from its presence even if we have not used it. Similarly with high-technology equipment, research, and education. Fragmentation that destroys cross-subsidies and erects nothing to assure the continued survival of structures that each of us wants but hopes the next person will pay for will hardly serve us well. Yet that is one of the consequences of competition. As we seek the lower-cost HMO, surgi-center, shopping mall emergency room—whose lower costs may result in part from the fact that they do not subsidize education or research, or care for patients who cannot pay, or stand ready to perform expensive procedures—we destroy the ability of the health sector to respond today and in the future.

Like most things in life, competition should not be sought to the exclusion of other goals. We do need competition but in moderation. Whether we can contain the forces of competition once we unleash them is a question that cannot be answered. The outcome will depend on the public's understanding of the benefits and costs of the changes competition will bring and on actions by federal and state government. Nevertheless, it is important that we not underestimate the difficulties that competition will create and those it already is creating. As the health sector undergoes a radical transformation, an increasing number of for-profit health care delivery institutions are entering what once was a not-for-profit arena.

These institutions are able to compete because they have access to capital markets through which they raise the funds necessary for expansion. In the competitive battle they may also gain advantages from careful selection of patients and market segmentation. Accountable to their stockholders rather than to the total community, they may refuse to serve those who are not insured. A number of these for-profit chains are developing their own insurance companies. By tying subscribers to their own hospitals, they may reduce premium costs. In turn the not-for-profit sector is developing its defenses, its own ties to a particular insurer (who will offer lower premiums but limit the free choice of hospital). Some observers suggest that health care in the future will be delivered by a dozen or so large national conglomerates. That hardly sounds like competition. Even if such a development does not take place, it seems clear that there will be more and stronger ties between particular insurers and deliverers of care and an increased pressure to limit free choice. Such limitations on selection of practitioners also inhibit competition. It is true that there will be an opportunity to change delivery systems once a year. But selecting a new health care provider is not the same as selecting a new insurance carrier, and changing providers is rather more difficult than changing supermarkets, gas stations, or hardware stores.

Those who would welcome competition and rely on medical ethics and the sector's ethos to protect the patient and assure quality must be aware that those protections are growing weaker. As medicine becomes more commercialized, what was defined as unscrupulous behavior is redefined as normal business. Where once we took pride in institutions that served the public and served it well, we now measure status by the bottom line. Will we be better off when we view our health care providers as simply profit maximizers and when, as a consequence, they also begin to view themselves that way?

Relying on competition and the free market to control costs raises serious problems that cannot be wished away. Some can be dealt with but only by incurring additional data collection and administrative costs and by enforcing—but with questionable efficacy—a variety of rules designed to keep competition working. When we are through we may have simply substituted one set of regulations for another.

The most severe indictment, however, relates to competition's basic propositions: that competition is an appropriate way to organize all our activities, that consumers can control the health system and its costs, that they should be encouraged to do so by putting their pocketbooks at risk, and, above all, that this can be done without violating equity.

Competition does not promote increased access for those unable to afford prevailing prices; indeed, because of segmentation, it reduces access. None of this is surprising, except perhaps to those who see health care as just another commodity and who have not considered the complexity of the health care delivery system, the importance of continuity of care, the variation in illness patterns and need for medical care exhibited by different individuals, and the special relationship between the health care professional and the patient. Competition assumes ease of entry of new producers (hospitals as well as physicians), an absence of collusion, and above all, sovereign and knowledgeable consumers. Surely these are heroic assumptions.

Furthermore, competitive markets cannot be built quickly, if at all. Even those who are most optimistic about the benefits that competition would bring have to face a problem in the dynamics of institution building: how we get from here to there. How would we cope during the period in which private insurance coverage had been cut back but before the forces of competition brought the potential changes in behavior and organization that would presumably protect us?

Of course, no mechanism exists, or can be imagined, that can answer all our questions and concerns. In the absence of control mechanisms, existing insurance and financing arrangements can contribute to, or permit and validate, high expenditures, some of which neither reflect medical need nor represent the most effective or efficient use of scarce resources. The competitive market system, while creating more individual choice and furthering more self-regulation, leads to its own difficulties, many of which are related to our desire to build a sense of community and achieve greater equity in the face of an unequal distribution of income. The special characteristics of health care make it difficult for us to behave as economic men and women. Most of us believe that health care is "different." More than that, many of us want it to be different. In health care as in other areas (such as education or legal services), we recognize that the distribution of income, of economic and political power, and of information is likely to yield a market distribution of services that is at variance with our value system.

And many of us believe that it is useful to have parts of our society and economy that are organized in ways that strengthen our solidarity with others, our charitable instincts, our sense of cooperation. Even as those who would nurture such sectors recognize that America cannot be a Brook Farm or Israeli kibbutz writ large, they would strive to keep health care from turning into just another industry. Those who believe that competition expresses an attitude and value system and does not merely describe a form of economic organization are distressed to see the free market invade one more sanctuary.

Yet we do need a control mechanism, a way of deciding how much is enough. If not the market (the sum of individual decisions), what other construct can we turn to? What can we erect that captures some of the virtues of competition but minimizes its unfavorable side effects, assists us in allocating resources in wiser fashion, and reflects our concern with efficiency and with equity? If we can no longer support a health sector governed by an uncontrolled insurance system and if we reject competition as unattainable and/or undesirable, what should we seek?

10

Controlling Costs, Achieving Equity: The Case for Government

In earlier periods the search for a mechanism that could contain rising health care expenditures and at the same time increase equity focused on public payment programs that relied on nonmarket government controls involving regulations, expenditure limits, and prospective budgeting for hospitals. Today policymakers are increasingly reluctant to consider such approaches, many of which were embodied in various proposals for national health insurance.

Yet the rising costs of care, together with growing inequities in its distribution as a result of increases in private premium costs, reductions in employer contributions to health insurance, and cutbacks in government health programs (even in the face of growth in the number of Americans living in poverty), require a reconsideration of national health insurance and its control mechanisms. We are forced, if not by a belief in equity, then by the need to contain health care expenditures, to seek a program that, though meeting new constraints and therefore different from earlier versions of universal health insurance, would strive to attain similar goals.

Conceptually, a comprehensive and universal national health insurance scheme is not synonymous with a nonmarket control mechanism. After all, it is possible to create a universal health insurance program without budget control, an open-ended program that simply paid the bills—a larger version of the early years of Medicare. Alternatively, one could create a budgeting system that set an upper bound to health care expenditures but did not provide for universal access or coverage. In fact, however, universal insurance and budget control have come to be intimately related, and for good reason. National health insurance without a mechanism to control expenditures would be both an irresponsible and unstable solution. The costs of inaction to control rising expenditures would be concentrated and highly visible. Eventually we would recognize our profligacy and would be forced either to cut back on universality and comprehensiveness or to adopt budget limits.

Conversely, meaningful expenditure controls without universal protection implies reductions and cutbacks without a mechanism to assure an equitable distribution of the health care that is available. Such a system may receive short-term support from those whose incomes encourage them to believe they would have access to desired resources and that the system would continue to serve them. It is likely to be opposed by those who fear that cutbacks would not be shared fairly and might severely affect middle-class as well as low-income persons and other disadvantaged individuals. A budget limit without assurance that resources will be allocated equitably is not a politically sustainable solution. If enough of us are rationed out and if enough of us understand the issues, Americans will seek another answer, one that does not negate the long-expressed view that health care is a right.

Earlier formulations of the right to health care were concerned solely with the distribution of care and presupposed an open-ended claim on resources for medical care. It was assumed that only modest resources would be needed to sustain the health sector and that economic growth would make those (and additional) resources available. Since those assumptions are no longer valid, a new formulation of rights is called for. That new formulation need not abandon the earlier ethical precept. Nor need it rely on a vague and nonoperational phrase that circumscribes the right to care—as, for example, when the "right to care" is coupled with the injunction that resources should be used "wisely and responsibly."

In that new formulation, the right to health care can be defined as consisting of two parts. The first is the right of citizens to expect that the dollars and resources allocated to medical care will be consistent with their perception of the benefits that care confers and the alternative benefits that might be generated by using some of those dollars and resources in other ways. That right assumes we are a community and is similar to our expectations in areas such as national defense, highways, education, fire and police protection. It is a concept with which we are familiar. It calls for a decision about the appropriate level of expenditure; it calls for budget targets.

The second part is the right to an equitable share of total health care resources, where equitable means that the distribution of care reflects medical need and the costs and benefits of care rather than individual income, wealth, political power, or social status This right is similar to our expectations in areas such as access to education, parks, and a basic level of sustenance. It, too, is a concept with which we are familiar. It calls for a decision about the way to pay for care; it calls for allocation criteria.

The first right speaks to the need to determine a level of expenditure, to macro health care policy. The second addresses distribution issues, how we divide the pie, the micro questions.

Neither right, by itself, would be sufficient or socially responsible. Cuts in health insurance and the erection of price-competitive markets can encourage or force us to spend less on health care. They can control expenditures and thereby give the appearance of conferring the first right. But the level of expenditures does not represent the collective perception of all the citizenry. Rather, it is the sum of the individual perceptions of those who have the dollars to enter the market and thus to indicate their tastes and preferences. In health care as in education, such an allocation would lead to outcomes at variance with the values many of us espouse when we help others in order to offset the consequences of an unequal income distribution.

The second right (equity) without the first (cost control) would hardly meet our needs or serve us well. A health sector grown bloated at the expense of housing, food, or education would represent a misallocation of scarce resources. We do not need nor should we want an ever-growing health sector (in no small part, because we enjoy and desire other things as well).

Both rights are necessary. To achieve them requires a structure that can address both macro and micro health policy, that can determine the citizenry's perceptions and translate them into an effective program, that enables us to make collective decisions. Such a structure operates at various levels. It is called government.

Reliance on government to ensure that the health sector utilizes an appropriate share of the nation's resources is not based on a misguided belief that the process of government decision making is smooth and without controversy. Nor does it assume that the various levels of government are always wise and responsive to the public interest or the public's desires. Government is cumbersome and is influenced by small but powerful and vocal groups. Because government is large, if it errs it can cause grievous damage. It is naive to turn to government on the basis of an unbounded faith, hardly sustained by empirical evidence, that it is always wise and beneficent.

The strength of government lies in another area. In the marketplace each of us votes with dollars, and that fact inevitably means that some have more votes than do others. In the political realm, conversely, each of us has no more or fewer votes than the next person (indeed, we are disturbed when we find that dollars invade and influence the electoral process and political decisions). There is little reason to think that the two voting systems would yield the same results. There is much reason to think that, though imperfect, the democratic method would more appropriately reflect the health needs of the total population.

The two-part formulation of rights has an operational counterpart: a universal health insurance program with budget control. It does not require that government produce medical care, but it does require that government be concerned with how much care will be produced. It does not require that government run the delivery system, but it does require that those who run it be held accountable. It does not require that government make medical or clinical decisions, but it does require that government set appropriate incentives and a framework for those decisions in order that they more adequately reflect medical and other needs.

A universal and comprehensive program does not negate the importance of individual choice (indeed, without equity, individual choice is constrained, since each of us would be free to choose only from among alternatives that are within our means). It can and should permit the individual to select from among health care providers and provider arrangements. It can and should provide incentives that encourage providers to respond to consumer tastes and priorities. Nor does a universal and comprehensive program bar competition or the use of economic incentives to encourage utilization of care in more efficient settings (such as HMOs). Although economic inducements may admittedly lead to preferred-risk selection, the potential abuse of market segmentation is reduced because the primary burden of cost control rests on predetermined budgets rather than on price competition.

The rest of this chapter outlines the basic characteristics of a universal and comprehensive health insurance program that would meet these multiple goals. The focus is broad because the national health insurance debate is not yet at the stage that requires the skills of legislative draftsmen or a product so detailed that it would lead to discussions about its various refinements and deflect attention from the basic issues. The details, though important, should be filled in when the debate over broad principles has been resolved and when a program is closer to enactment. At this level the description is general, like the initial stages of planning a house; it involves only the number of rooms and their functions. Consideration of the design of the exterior and interior space must wait. At present and for some time to come, both citizens and policymakers must further define and discuss the concept of universal health insurance with budget control. We are far from a consensus on broad principles that would give national health insurance its shape and form.

In defining important characteristics we can draw on broad historical patterns, bearing in mind that to every pattern there are exceptions. Earlier efforts, successful and futile, have shown the influence of strongly held attitudes and basic processes that have helped shape our health care financing system and that are likely (though not certain) to constrain it in the future. Past behavior and debates can further our understanding of tomorrow's possibilities, even though the earlier patterns and constraints may be changed.

Any description of a universal health insurance program must outline its basic administrative structure, method of enrollment and financing, types of benefits, forms of payment and reimbursement and the incentives they provide, as well as the nature of cost containment initiatives. In all these areas we can choose among numerous options. The selection process should be responsive to two constraints. The first is that the choice be related to the American experience and attitudes. The second is that it be related to existing health financing and delivery patterns and the institutional framework now in place. We are not a new nation with an underdeveloped health sector. We are the United States in the mid-1980s with a $400 billion health industry. New times and new conditions compel us to reconsider and reexamine earlier national health insurance proposals, lest they no longer be appropriate. We need a national health insurance program that is responsive to our present condition.

The two constraints and their interpretation will disappoint some readers. There will be those who argue that tying the future to the American experience and to today's health sector will yield only the most minimal of change. They will criticize what they perceive as conservatism. Others will say that some of the changes called for violate the constraints and that the resulting program represents too sharp a break with present patterns and deeply held attitudes. They will criticize what they perceive as radicalism. Such differences in point of view are inevitable. The development of a program that is feasible and implementable dares not ignore reality. But reality must be interpreted, and that interpretation cannot yield conclusions on which we must agree.

The two constraints reflect a point of view: that the American health sector, like health sectors everywhere, is a part of and not apart from the society in which it is embedded. It is no accident that American health care delivery is organized and financed differently from that of other countries. It is not that our physicians, nurses, health care administrators, insurance executives, economists, sociologists, lawyers, public-policy analysts, and elected officials are either more or less intelligent than their counterparts elsewhere. We Americans behave differently because we have a different history, set of attitudes, and values. Our public dialogue contrasts with the dialogue in other countries. We assess benefits and costs and balance conflicting objectives differently. We prize different traditions. It is true that we face different facts and intersect with different institutions. It is even more important that we see those facts and institutions through different eyes.

Just as we are not British or Canadian or Japanese, so, too, we are not what we once were. There is a continuity with our past, but yet there is also a difference. We are constantly being shaped and reshaped, our newness intertwining with our oldness. As facts change and as the attitudes we bring to them and the context in which we place them alter, so does the context and, therefore, the content of our national debate. Our agenda and our policy discussions address the future, reflect the present, and are responsive to the past.

The two constraints, that proposals be tied to the American ethos and to the fact that there already is a health care system in place, rule out two widely differing options: a national health service and an unbridled free market. The first, a socialized health care delivery system, is too distant from the American perspective. There are lessons to be learned from the fact that it has performed well in Great Britain both in furthering equity and in controlling health care expenditures. In 1977 health care expenditures in the United Kingdom represented 5.2 percent of GNP (the comparable U.S. figure was 9 percent).[1] Furthermore, in the five ensuing years the average annual rate of growth in the percentage of national resources devoted to health care was 3.1 percent in the United Kingdom and 3.9 percent in the United States.[2] Nevertheless, it is unlikely that the United States, which has not nationalized its transport of energy systems and which occasionally discusses turning its postal service over to the private sector and contracting out its prisons, would begin to socialize its health sector. The fact that we do provide various services such as education, libraries, and fire and police protection through government is noteworthy but, in my view, not compelling.

Nor are we likely to opt for a pure free-market health system. Government (at all levels) is deeply involved in paying for care, in setting reimbursement rates, in financing medical education and research, in monitoring quality and performance standards. Whatever our irritations with government, we are not prepared for nor would we accept its withdrawal from the medical care arena. We look to government for protections that we cannot provide by ourselves and that we do not believe can be provided by the market. The lessons available from the performance of competitive markets can be built upon without destroying the complex web of existing public initiatives.

Over the last half-century most proposals for NHI have called for a federal program and for federal controls. Central authority and responsibility seemed both necessary and desirable. In the last two decades many observers drew important lessons from the contrast between Medicare (a federal program) and Medicaid (a series of state programs). One inescapable fact was that the various states exhibited wide differences in administrative capacity. A second was that, under Medicaid, individuals in essentially similar circumstances were treated differently depending on their place of residence.

Many policymakers concluded that a federal program with single standards would best assure that Americans would be treated as Americans and not as, say, New Yorkers or South Carolinians. It is undeniable that the federal government has been more diligent than some of the states in protecting civil rights and in combating discriminatory behavior. It was far easier to make the case for a federal program than for another alternative.

Yet arguments for state control (with federal standards and oversight) are not without merit. The political climate has changed and there is a turning away from centralized government. Even if that trend is temporary, we should not ignore the fact that some of the states have developed administrative knowledge and capacity, particularly in the important arena of cost containment. We must also recognize that even as individual states have improved on their performance, the federal bureaucracy has grown weaker. It will take years to rebuild what has been eroded, and that process is not yet under way. Some states' capabilities now exceed that of the federal government.

Furthermore, as the health sector has changed, the different states have developed and face widely disparate patterns in the organization and delivery of care. Homogeneity has given way to differential enrollment patterns in HMOs and PPOs, to different degrees of competition in ambulatory and hospital care. The individual patterns found across the land are best understood and best addressed at a locus of control that is closer to those delivery systems and to the people they serve. California is not the same as West Virginia, and the systems and incentives that would best suit the one are not necessarily appropriate for the other. Given the different patterns of medical care delivery and the very different costs across geographic areas, there is a need to erect different incentives and different types of cost control mechanisms.

An NHI program that deals with the delivery system and its incentives and that is more than an underwriting of what already exists requires a measure of fine-tuning. It is difficult to imagine that such a task can be performed from Washington or that if it were it would be found acceptable. State government is certainly not responsive to all its citizens, but it may be more responsive to the inherent differences that prevail. It may be better able to explain how various changes might affect at the local level the care that people seek and/or their pocketbooks. It may be better able to set appropriate incentives, educate the public about the implications of various choices, and respond to different tastes and priorities.

The importance of the cost containment component of a universal health insurance program argues for greater rather than less state participation. A large participatory role for the states also responds to economic and political realities. While the states cannot finance an NHI program by themselves, the size of the current and projected federal deficit hardly suggests that the federal government could do so without their help. Furthermore, there is more pressure for and interest in new patterns of financing at state levels. The more distant Congress can more readily ignore the problems of those without protection, of cost-shifting and of uncompensated care, and of the burden carried by local institutions who serve the under- and uninsured. The needs of those individuals and institutions are increasingly being articulated in state capitals.

There is no doubt that a program with major administrative responsibility delegated to states will be complex. It will exhibit wide variation. In the past that was considered its fundamental weakness. And yet, perhaps that is its strength. If we want to maximize innovation and flexibility we may gain much from multiple and smaller programs. If, further, we recognize that there is no guarantee that government will always act wisely and appropriately, we may want to act as risk averters. Multiple state programs are like a diversified portfolio: we will not do as well as we might if we bet on a single winning program, but neither will we do as badly if we were to commit a blunder.

State control of the administrative and cost containment structure does not preclude an important role for the federal government. Whatever the enrollment method, Congress must make certain that all residents are insured. If the program is based on state rather than federal enrollment, there must be a federal backup program for individuals who live in states that elect not to participate (and perhaps for employees of national corporations). Furthermore, in order to assure that all residents are treated equally, benefit standards must be set centrally and must apply in all jurisdictions. Because we are a highly mobile population these benefits must be portable across state boundaries. Finally, the federal government will have to assist the various states in meeting their financial obligations.

There is much to commend a universal health insurance program with a single central enrollment mechanism. Nevertheless, the arguments for state enrollment appear stronger. If we choose to rely on the states to monitor their health delivery systems and to provide incentives for efficiency and cost control, they must have a financial stake in doing so. It is administratively cumbersome to organize an insurance program that is federal and at the same time puts the states at financial risk. It is far simpler to require states that want to participate in the program (and receive financial assistance) to certify that all their residents are enrolled in an insurance program that meets defined federal standards.

We can expect the various states to develop different enrollment mechanisms. Some may elect to move to a mandated system requiring all employers to purchase a defined private insurance benefit package for their employees and their dependents. Employers for whom this new obligation would exceed a given percentage of total payroll would receive assistance. Special enrollment programs would be developed for individuals not covered through employment. Other states might set up a state insurance system and rely on insurers to fill a fiscal intermediary role. Thus, insurance companies would not be underwriters who bear risks. As under self-insurance (where the employer bears the risk and the insurance company administers the program), insurers would process and review claims and pay bills and be compensated for this activity. The fact that self-insurance is growing rapidly suggests that many insurers find the limited administrative role attractive and financially rewarding.

One approach that might appeal to employer, employee, and insurer groups within a state would involve a state authority that collected all premium payments on the basis of ability to pay, that is, in relation to payroll for employers and income for individuals. These funds, together with those provided by the federal government, would be used to purchase insurance from the particular insurer (including HMOs) selected by the individual. The rates charged would have to reflect actuarial risk and be monitored in order to protect against skimming. The individual would still have a relationship with a particular carrier, and carriers would still have the incentive to compete for subscribers. If HMOs and new modalities of care could operate at lower cost, their savings could be shared with employer and employee groups in the form of expanded benefits, rebates, or lower deductibles and coinsurance payments (if these are part of the basic program).[3]

This construct has an important characteristic: it breaks the existing link between insurance coverage and premiums that cannot and do not take account of income. That link is inherent in today's private financing system because private insurers do not and cannot adjust their rates to take account of an individual's economic status. A public program such as Medicare, of course, can do so. But many states might feel that a purely public program would not fit well with their desire for insurance company involvement in more than a limited fiscal intermediary role. Instead, they might choose to develop a public-private financing mix.

Still other states could and would develop additional patterns and programs that they felt responded to their own needs and situations. Similarly, they would use different tax mechanisms to raise the funds required to enroll all their residents. The fact that both enrollment and a portion of the costs would be matters of state jurisdiction should provide incentives to seek efficiency both in administration and in health care delivery.

Federal financial assistance should be related to the economic and demographic characteristics of the individual states. States with more low-income individuals and with greater unemployment will need more help. But it would be important to apply one of the lessons learned from the Medicaid experience: federal funds should not be provided as a percentage of state expenditures. The open-ended *ex-post* allocation system should be replaced with one of *ex-ante* annually determined fixed amounts; the states should operate within predetermined budgets.

There is little question that a program combining the public and the private sectors as well as the various levels of government, will appear and will be complicated. Yet if we are to erect a system that responds to our needs and to existing structures, that is as it must be. Less than that will not suffice. Of course we could strike different compromises and design a simpler and, in that respect, more appealing program. But a simpler program could not retain the flexibility that we should seek. Our complicated health care system is still evolving (and at different rates in different places). Permitting variations that build on local experience and respond to local conditions (while meeting federal standards and advancing equity) is desirable. It is not clear that a simpler program would accomplish all our objectives. Nor can we assume that design simplicity would increase the probability of enactment.

There is an important lesson to be learned from the fact that in the long history of national health insurance each successive proposal has grown more complicated. In part that has been because we have recognized the importance of new objectives: system change and cost control. In part, however, it is because proposals presented in the last decade have shifted from enrollment through a universal social insurance program to a mandated approach (embodying the continuation of employment-related insurance and the coverage of other individuals through separate programs). The added complexity and administrative costs inherent in mandated insurance have been justified on two bases. The first is that it is simply impossible to undo the structure and the institutions that exist. The second is that a mandated approach permits most of the health care insurance dollars to stay within the private sector. As the number of dollars flowing through the private insurance sector has grown, the second argument has assumed increased importance.

Proponents of national health insurance in both parties have shied away from a social insurance program that would move approximately

$110 billion in private premiums and some portion of the $100 billion in private out-of-pocket payments into the federal budget. The shift of funds would not represent a new burden on the private sector, since there would be an equal decline in private expenditures. Nor would the new program increase the federal deficit, since health insurance expenditures (as in Medicare) would be financed out of earmarked taxes. The issues, rather, are ones to which all presidents and legislators are sensitive: the size of the federal budget in relation to GNP and the rate of taxation. The body politic does not view visible public expenditure increases and taxes as desirable.

Nor do presidents or members of Congress look with favor on a large new federal program requiring them to become involved in controlling expenditures at the local level, where medical care is delivered. The fact that national health insurance would require meaningful and socially equitable budget control is hardly a plus in the legislator's personal cost-benefit calculus. It is not a responsibility that he or she seeks. A mandated program that seemingly delegates responsibility to the private insurance sector is preferable.

Today, except for Medicare beneficiaries, who look to Washington, and Medicaid recipients, who turn to their state capitals for relief, most Americans focus their irritations about rising premiums on insurance companies, hospitals, or physicians. We may be angry, but we are not quite certain where to vent our ire. We may complain, but not at or to our representative in Washington. Only occasionally are some of us likely to say, "Government ought to do something about it." Even then, since care is delivered and financed in the private sector, we do not know quite what that "something" is. Thus, a mandated program that leaves most people insured as they are at present provides the legislature with some breathing room.

A fully federal national health insurance program that enrolled individuals through a social insurance mechanism (like Medicare) would create a far different situation. If Congress ignored its responsibility to control costs, we would complain about government mismanagement, about rising premiums, taxes, or contributions to the health insurance fund. It would not avail our representative to argue that these premiums would have risen by a greater amount had we left the current system in place. Nor would it necessarily avail to argue that increased costs may be a small price to pay for greater equity. The focus of our anger would no longer be the insurer, the hospital, the physician. Instead, it would be the legislature and our legislator.

If Congress, conversely, did control cost increases— and, even under tight controls, costs would continue to increase because of general inflation, increased utilization of services by a growing and aging population, and welcome advances in medical science—our irritations would not subside. We would complain about the cutbacks and the closure of institutions and facilities. We would wonder whether general cost control measures were responsive to our local situation. We might not see the immediate benefits of cost containment but would complain about the standards set in distant Washington. We would want more health care, less government control, and lower taxes. Legislators would be the focus of our irritation when they could not meet our inconsistent desires and demands.

Small wonder then that members of Congress, aware that public irritation is diffused and directed toward various elements of the private delivery or insurance system and toward state regulatory bodies, are not eager to take action that will focus our discomfort and put them at risk on a continuing basis. The temptation is to attempt to control Medicare and Medicaid expenditures by service cutbacks and cost-shifting onto beneficiaries, recipients, and other insured and uninsured individuals and to postpone—for as long as possible—action on a comprehensive approach to health care costs and health insurance. If Congress is forced to act, it is likely that it will develop a complex mandated insurance program and try to fill in the gaps with additional enrollment systems.

While the temptation to postpone may also be found in state legislative bodies, the costs of postponement are greater. The viability of local institutions is at risk; the plight of one's close neighbor is more discernible. It is no accident that a number of states have taken action to reduce cost-shifting and to create pools of funds to pay for uncompensated care. The pressures on the various states are such that they are likely to be more responsive and more innovative than the federal government. Furthermore, state governments may see less need for mandating arrangements and those that did would have to respond only to local employment patterns. It would be much easier to fashion and administer a mandated program within a state than to do so for the entire nation.

I recall being asked whether the mandated program proposed by Senator Kennedy in 1979 would work. I answered with a story: when I was a child my father told me that if I wanted to scratch my left ear with my right hand I would find it easier to be direct and to do so by putting my hand across my face rather than by putting it behind my head. I continued with the observation that nevertheless, if President Carter set mandating constraints that precluded doing things in a simple fashion, it was worth engaging in complexity as long as we could still reach the objective. Yet there was a nagging fear that we might be forced to scratch the left ear with the right hand by putting an arm behind and under the left knee. Doing that requires standing on one foot. Even then the arm might not be long enough to reach the ear. And there is the danger of falling on one's face. A construct might become so complex that we fail to reach our objective. It is quite possible that a federally mandated program that enrolls most beneficiaries through their employers will be cumbersome and miss the very individuals who are most at risk.

Those who would argue that NHI's time has passed may really be saying something far different: that the time has passed for the kind of programs once put forward. We must accept the fact that any system we would enact will be complicated. The program that I suggest would not be as simple in its enrollment patterns as a universal social insurance program, but it would be simpler and far better than a federally mandated system of enrollment.

A series of state-run programs requires more from the federal government than financial assistance. To achieve equity among the states and their residents, the federal government will have to define the benefit package and make certain it is made available to all without discrimination. Benefits should include physicians' services as well as hospital care. Special attention should be directed toward procedures that encourage early diagnosis and care, enhance health status, and prevent disease. Again there is a lesson to be learned from Medicare: a benefit program can be so oriented toward acute care that it negates efforts at prevention. It can also be made so complicated that it engenders confusion and fear. We pay an unnecessary price in both complexity and dollars for a two-part program that also encourages individuals to purchase supplementary private insurance.

A realistic appraisal of the American perspective and of experience regrettably suggests that any health insurance program we erect will be encumbered with cost-sharing provisions (deductibles and coinsurance). Such cost-sharing does help reduce premium costs and may reduce utilization. But unless the cost-sharing is significant and the resulting decline in utilization is large the savings are only an illusion: what we do not pay in premiums we will pay at the time that we seek care. Conversely, if we reap real savings from restraints on utilization, we do so because the deductibles and coinsurance payments are large enough to interfere with equity. As long as we have a widely unequal income distribution, we cannot use a single deductible or coinsurance rate without affecting some individuals and families more severely than others. But using multiple rates tied to income and local or state health system costs may add significantly to the costs of administering a program. Both equity and administrative efficiency suggest that the economic stick is not the best way to control the use of services and health care expenditures. In seeking cost control we would spend our time more usefully if we worried more about controlling the supply and reforming the organization of services and setting health care budgets and less about affecting demand through cost-sharing.

But cost-sharing has an appeal. Americans do not believe in a free lunch; sharing of costs has a symbolic value. It would be a pity indeed if an NHI program failed of enactment because those who support and those who oppose cost-sharing defined their positions as ones of principle. Those who believe that cost-sharing has virtue and those who feel that it impedes equity should be able to find room for compromise. It is possible to find a rate that is high enough to create the necessary illusions, yet low enough not to hit with undue force on low-income individuals and families. It is also possible to use tax credits through the federal tax mechanism to redress inequities that do arise.

A universal and comprehensive health insurance system will have to concern itself with payment and reimbursement incentives and with cost containment programs. To eliminate cost-shifting, it should require that all payers pay the same rates. It should encourage hospital budgeting on a prospective basis. Fortunately, there is an increased understanding of these issues among all affected parties: employers, employees, provider groups, and the various levels of government. Measures that once might have been rejected as unnecessary or too difficult to implement (such as the DRG system or second opinions for surgery) are now considered acceptable. If some of them prove less effective than we desire, we will experiment with new and different programs. The need for cost containment will continue; the support for meaningful policies will not abate.

We will continue to develop data systems that permit closer monitoring and control of provider performance and that provide reassurance (to both providers and patients) that reduced utilization does not translate to lower quality. Greater attention will be devoted to educating practitioners about the economic and medical implications of variations in styles of practice and to encouraging (through both rewards and penalties) behavior patterns that conserve resources.

The large growth in the number of physicians will increase the economic pressures they face. It will be easier to develop, negotiate, and implement more rational fee schedules. HMOs and new patterns of organization (often involving salaried arrangements for physicians) will proliferate and become increasingly attractive. An ever-larger proportion of physicians will practice medicine in settings that are not organized on a fee-for-service basis. As a consequence, they will face different payment and reimbursement systems and new kinds of incentives and controls and will develop new practice patterns. At the same time, the shift from hospital to ambulatory care (combined with more active monitoring and control of hospital admissions) will force institutions to economize in their use of resources.

The health care delivery system is changing rapidly to respond to new imperatives. More and more providers are adapting to budget constraints; more and more payers and subscribers are searching for new arrangements that can assure quality while reducing outlays. We cannot predict which specific cost containment programs will be appropriate in an evolving health sector and might be erected in the future. But it is important to build an insurance system that does not relax the pressure to economize, is sufficiently flexible to respond, and offers visible positive inducements to do so.

A series of state programs, financed in part (but only in part) by a fixed federal contribution, can do all that. The fixed contribution puts employers, employees, and state treasuries at financial risk. It is they who would have to pay the price for inefficiency and unnecessary utilization. Most important, they would be aware of the price, since a large proportion of health sector services would continue to be financed locally and would be tied to local conditions and behavior. As long as some Americans continue to equate cost containment with lower quality and higher spending with better care, the savings associated with control of costs will have to be shared in order to induce people to make what they believe to be a sacrifice. The individual states can do that by rewarding (through more comprehensive benefits or smaller premium or tax payments) those who pursue and those who are affected by cost containment efforts. The gains associated with rationalization can be made palpable. Indeed, it is far easier to do this through a system of state enrollment and state taxes than through a federal system with a single national tax that applies equally to the efficient and to the inefficient.

A system that places responsibility upon the states has an additional advantage. That advantage lies in the area of budgets. A federal program that limits total health care expenditures at the local level (in an effort to achieve economies and to promote efficiency) is at variance with American political traditions. Telling a "rich" state to spend less than it desires is far more difficult than giving it less financial assistance and putting it at risk if it wants to be spendthrift. Furthermore, it would be difficult to arrive at a budget figure that would be found acceptable at the place where medical care is delivered. It is easy to use today's expenditures as a starting point or to provide a set sum per person (adjusted for key variables such as age and gender and using existing model delivery systems as standards). But it is hard to imagine that federally imposed budgets at the state or local level would be seen as responsive to local tastes, desires, wishes, and priorities.

If we are to move to a budget control mechanism for health care—and if we want effective cost control we will be required to do so—these budgets should be determined at the state (or in some cases substate) level. Such a step does not negate the importance of federal assistance designed to help equalize conditions among the various states. Federal assistance, however, is not the same as a federally imposed budget. State budgets, arrived at with participation of the affected citizenry, are likely to fare better politically. The sums agreed upon are also likely to be more appropriate.

It will not be easy to move to a system that involves more comprehensive budgeting. It will take time and will have to be phased in gradually. If the limits are tight, that is, if it is determined that as a society we cannot or will not pay for any and all procedures and advances however marginal their impact, then the limits must have an impact on provider behavior. Providers will have to learn how to economize and how to adapt to new resource constraints. If society will not make available the resources required to do everything possible for everyone who conceivably might benefit and if we reject price rationing of scarcity, providers will need allocation criteria. We will need to develop socially acceptable standards and guideposts (something looser than guidelines) to help determine what and how much shall be done and for whom. Society, and that includes consumers as well as providers, will have to help develop a general understanding regarding collective behavior, and those who render care will have to learn how to apply those guideposts in individual cases.

This can be done. It is already being done (unfortunately, often with input only from health care professionals) in numerous hospitals, HMOs, and salaried practice settings where physicians have learned how to develop and live within budget constraints. It is true that HMO physicians and patients are self-selected and that HMOs (and especially prepaid group practices) do not rely on fee-for-service and, therefore, face a very different incentive structure. Nevertheless, the fact that an increasing proportion of America's health practitioners are learning to constrain resource use will increase the competitive pressure on other practitioners.

With effort we can develop budgets and a social consensus (albeit imprecise and not promulgated in legislation) on how to spend those budgets. We need not feel threatened that such budgets will replace standards of abundance with those of scarcity. A call for dieting is not a call for fasting. If Americans accept the need for constraints in health care, that acceptance and the necessary belt tightening will come gradually. That is as it should be and is all that is required. There is no reason to believe that the nation can or should move from an uncontrolled system to severely limited budgets. Neither patients nor physicians will accept budgets that require cutbacks in worthwhile services to which they have grown accustomed. Nor need they. The most that can and should be expected is a restraint on future expansion.

The differences between a state-controlled and federal program are great. Although there are numerous advantages to a program that delegates heavy responsibility to states, the inherent risks to equity should not be minimized. Not all states will administer their programs efficiently. Nor will they all be equally diligent in protecting the rights of all their residents and in guarding against the dangers of creaming and self-selection. Some will finance their programs in a more (and others in a less) progressive manner. Some states may want to pay for new technologies (such as artificial hearts) not in the federally defined benefit package. There will be individuals who would have reaped larger benefits (and/or paid smaller premiums) had they lived elsewhere.

But a federally administered program would not eliminate all disparities. A single program legislated in and administered from Washington is not the same program in every locality. Because medical care is a service, the local delivery systems exhibit great variability. As long as local health systems and costs differ, as long as health resources are not distributed equally, as long as incomes and living conditions differ, some Americans will receive better medical care and will have a better health status than others.

What is incumbent on the federal government is to work to reduce disparities and promote equity in the provision of services. That task may be more difficult in a program administered by the states, but it is doable. Indeed, it is quite possible that the federal government will protect equity more diligently in the type of program outlined than it would in a purely federal program. We would not be forced to rely on self-monitoring and self-evaluation, on what we know is suspect. Nor would we be lulled into a false sense of security derived from the assumption that centralized administration assures equitable access at the point of service delivery.

A universal health insurance program is not an untested idea; the United States already has Medicare, and other nations (including our neighbor Canada) have even more extensive programs covering their entire populations. Adding cost containment features to insurance is also not a novel venture; individual states, private insurers, and Medicare are moving in that direction, albeit haltingly and, because there are multiple payers, without a well-conceived, coherent plan that eliminates cost-shifting. Nevertheless, it would be foolish to argue that universal health insurance is only a minor change that should arouse no opposition. Consequently, even some who favor a universal and comprehensive program might argue that to implement a complete plan would be too large a single step. They would suggest that we move in incremental fashion, in a series of small steps.

It should be clear that phasing in a national health insurance program involves a different approach from previous implementations of health care policy. Deliberate phasing stands in sharp contrast to the hurried enactment of inconsistent legislation designed to address interrelated problems as if they were separate and compartmentalized. It is to have a goal and purpose against which the various interventions and legislative initiatives can be assessed and their mutual consistency examined. It is to require that measures reinforce (or at least not negate) each other and that each serve as a step toward the agreed-upon goal. It is to know the distance we have come and what remains to be accomplished. It requires much more than Secretary Califano suggested when he discussed the first phase of a national health plan and the "vision of a total plan."[4]

To phase in a comprehensive program does not mean merely to enact each step separately. A phased-in program defines the times at which its various components would be implemented, thus reducing the number of unknowns. Uncertainty about what the next step might be and when it would be taken does not make for effective and efficient planning or administration. Nor, since the nation faces many problems, is it desirable to adopt a strategy that forces us to engage in a national debate on health insurance at periodic intervals. True incrementalism requires a plan of action. It is not something we discern after the event.

It is useful to consider the possible risks and benefits to be derived from phasing in universal insurance over a defined period. The benefits seem clear: the fiscal impact would be spread over a number of years and the shock in any given year would be reduced. In addition, the necessary administrative capability could be built up gradually. A phased-in program would appear to be more responsible and therefore might be more appealing to the body politic. But there are costs associated with such a strategy. The most obvious, of course, is that we would postpone full implementation of the program, and thus the attainment of equitable access and the development of both effective and equitable cost control measures. Our health care system would grow more complex and engage in more and yet more creaming. The health financing problems faced by an expanding number of our citizens would increase. The longer we take to reach our goal, the more difficult our task becomes.

But if political timidity forces us to adopt a phased-in program, we should make every effort to minimize its disadvantages and negative side effects. We should adopt a program that sets forth a timetable when each of the various phases would take effect. Each future Congress could adjust and amend the program as a result of monitoring efforts but the gain in flexibility would not preclude effective planning. A timetable would permit but would not require periodic debate. Most important, it would require that a full program be designed even while permitting it to be achieved in a series of incremental (but mutually consistent) steps.

There are only a limited number of ways that a universal health insurance program can be phased in. It is tempting to begin by filling

In the gaps and providing coverage to those whose needs are greatest. the unemployed, the poor, individuals with inadequate or no insurance. Nevertheless, that approach—the equivalent of an expanded and enhanced Medicaid program—does not provide a building block for a more universal structure. Nor does it erect the necessary conditions for more effective cost containment. A second approach would phase in the various benefits, say, beginning with hospital care and moving on to physicians' services. While that is one of the ways in which other nations have moved to their own comprehensive programs, policymakers could raise serious questions about its desirability. It can be argued that because hospital care is so expensive it would have to be included in the first phase but that doing so would lead to an unnecessary and undesirable expansion of the hospital sector. That argument, however, may be incorrect. Our hospital sector has already undergone its period of growth (in no small part because private coverage did begin with hospital insurance). A universal hospital insurance program, enacted with cost control features, need not translate into a large number of new dollars. Furthermore, the commitment to phase in ambulatory service coverage within a very few years would help contain expansionary pressures. It is possible to envision a phased program of benefit expansion that would not be irresponsible.

Yet another approach to universality would be to enroll different age groups at predetermined intervals. We could begin with children under a given age (it would be sensible to include their mothers and pregnant women) and, on a fixed timetable, expand the age of coverage. Such an approach would first address the needs of the growing number of uninsured dependents and households headed by a single parent. It would automatically help rationalize the Medicaid program. Since few children require hospital care or have many physician visits, such a program would not be especially costly. It would therefore not exert significant leverage on the health care system. Nevertheless, it would be a beginning and would represent a commitment. Given the long-term benefits of care for children, mothers, and pregnant women, it would be an especially wise investment.[5]

Like any other complex public program a universal and comprehensive health insurance program can be structured in many different ways. We can and should debate the locus of administrative responsibility, the different roles to be played by the various levels of government, the mechanisms of enrollment, the nature of the benefits, the patterns of payment to hospitals and care providers, the nature of state and federal budgeting, and the types of cost containment efforts. That debate can be illuminated by the experience in Canada. Health care spending as a percentage of national income in the United States and Canada was quite similar from 1950 to 1971; "but the completion of universal public coverage [in Canada] in 1971 initiated a period of stability, in sharp contrast to previous Canadian or concurrent American experience."[6] The percentage of national resources devoted to health care in the two countries has diverged sharply in the ensuing fifteen years.

In Canada each province has a health insurance program that meets national standards and is supported in part with funds from central government. All residents are covered, and the comprehensive benefits include hospital and physicians' services. Although the program provides little encouragement for the development of HMOs (a regrettable deficiency), Canadian health care expenditures are far below those in the United States. It would be foolish to imagine that our nation could simply adopt the Canadian system. But we could learn from it and adapt it to our needs.[7]

Thirty years and more of participating in the national health insurance debate, helping design programs, and searching for compromise make me feel a certain sadness at the loss of an old friend: a federal social insurance approach to NHI. Yet it is clear that the social insurance component has long departed—all the major proposals in the last decade have built on mandating. It is also clear that if the only thing that remains of the old friendship is the word "federal," we are left with a hollow shell. The lessons of Medicare and Medicaid need to be applied, but that does not mean we should spend our time fantasizing about a Medicare-like program writ large or having a nightmare about a Medicaid-like program (or problem) for all Americans. Instead, we should try to build a workable program that captures the advantages of Medicare and avoids the pitfalls of Medicaid. That task can be accomplished if both those who favored and those who opposed national health insurance in the past give up their fantasies and nightmares, eschew their comfortable and familiar rhetoric, and confront reality: the problems that Americans and America face today, how we have come to this point, and, given that history and the present, where we can go.

It is time to resume the debate about the principles that should govern a national health insurance policy. As that debate moves forward it will become necessary to provide the detailed characteristics of the program. Those specifications will have to mesh and be consistent. Developing them thus requires that we first develop a consensus around principles. Only then will we be able to judge whether this or that change or compromise in specifications (and the inevitable side effects) can be accommodated or would do violence to the basic character of the program. Since this is not the way our legislative process usually works, the American people will have to understand the issues and make their voices heard. Those in the executive and legislative branches will have to know what we want. Nothing would be sadder, both for the financing of health care and for the democratic process, than to enact a program that cannot and is not designed to meet its goals.

A universal and comprehensive program could help achieve a more equitable distribution of care. It could also provide a structure for responsible cost containment. If, as I believe, we cannot have the one without the other, its appeal is broadened. In the past much of the support for NHI derived from its equity component while much of the opposition was based on its potential for cost increases. Today those who would emphasize equity and those who would emphasize cost control should recognize they need each other. Only if both goals are sought can a sustainable program be erected.

If we lack the political will to begin to move toward a system of universal coverage coupled with budget control of hospitals and physicians, it is time to stop the charade that there is a real support for effective cost control or for a more equitable distribution of care. It is time, instead, to face the fact that by cost control we really mean control of expenditures, to be achieved by defining people out of the health system and by shifting costs among the various payers. But shifting costs is hardly equitable, and cutting back on Medicare, Medicaid, and private insurance is a form of rationing. The fact that access is allocated by an impersonal market and invisible hand may make it more acceptable. It hardly makes it virtuous.

11

Agenda for Action

The American public is not pressing for a national health insurance program with budget limits. We do not relish a larger role for government. Nor is there pressure to erect a program that strengthens competition through increases in individual cost-consciousness. We do not relish more cost-sharing or larger personal payments for health insurance. There is no widespread sense of national crisis that compels immediate and comprehensive action. It is not difficult to conclude that America is willing to wring its collective hands about the costs of medical care, but is not yet prepared to act effectively to control them; that it is willing to talk about the need for equity, but not prepared to legislate its enhancement.

American health care is not at the turning point that defines a crisis. Yet forces are at work that, in time, will compel us to make a fundamental choice. Health care costs continue to increase more rapidly than other prices. Health care expenditures will continue to exact an ever-larger toll from government budgets and from the private sector. Medicare and Medicaid will offer less protection. Members of the middle class, now largely exempt from health care price rationing, will face a world with less insurance and larger deductibles and coinsurance. The reaction of large payers to ever-increasing expenditures, of the public to reductions in coverage, and of institutions to the growth of "uncompensated care" will force Congress to consider what it now ignores: the development of a comprehensive public policy toward health insurance and toward medical care costs. The nation will be forced to choose between market rationing and growing inequities on the one hand and health budget ceilings and universal insurance on the other.

In the early 1970s conventional wisdom held that national health insurance was an idea whose time had come. Today the prevailing view

Is that it is an idea whose time has passed. The first view was in error: reality changed more rapidly than attitudes formed a decade earlier. I believe that today's perception, a product of yesterday's conditions, will prove equally fallacious. Inflation in health care costs, once an obstacle to national health insurance, will become its catalyst. We will move from the view, held by some, that inflation means we cannot afford NHI and the view, held by others, that NHI must wait until we control costs. We will come to recognize that NHI is necessary if we want equitable cost containment. As with all changes in understanding, the shift in view will take time. Tragically, many Americans will suffer in the process.

The elements of the scenario are clear. A growing aged population, further advances in medical science and clinical practice, and the need for major capital investment to renovate an aging hospital sector, all mean a continuation of cost increases, which will be translated into higher health insurance premiums. Offsetting factors, such as the growth in HMOs, will slow down but not halt the growth in health expenditures. Inevitably the increases in premiums will lead to cutbacks in coverage, particularly for individuals who purchase their own policies and for employees whose employers limit their contributions to fringe benefits. These reductions in private insurance will be accompanied by cutbacks (in real terms) in Medicare and Medicaid coverage and in other federal health programs as federal and state governments try to limit the growth in their expenditures for health activities.

Rising costs and inadequate coverage are only one part of the story. The second part involves the differences in market power among various insurers or payers. Medicare and Medicaid are sufficiently large to be able to limit their reimbursement of fees. They receive discounts below prevailing charges to other payers. Although some of the reduction in price may reflect savings in collection costs, the bulk of the discount is shifted onto other payers with less market power.

As a consequence private insurers will seek to make arrangements with hospitals that serve only a small proportion of Medicare and Medicaid patients, since those facilities will have less costs to shift. Hospitals will react by trying to minimize the number of Medicare and Medicaid patients they serve. Whether the DRG reimbursement system eases or exacerbates this problem will depend on the level of payment in general and for specific diagnoses. If hospitals believe the general or specific reimbursement level is too low, they will attempt to shift patients and costs elsewhere. Public hospitals will be forced to assume responsibility for patients who are sicker and who will require more resources and longer stays. The problem will be spread beyond the Medicare population if private payers shift to DRG reimbursement that is not adjusted for severity of illness. Market segmentation in the insurance sector will spread to the delivery of care.

As costs continue to mount, an increasing number of employers and insurers will institute preferred provider programs offering economic incentives to subscribers who select from an approved list of providers with whom the insurer has negotiated lower fees and whose behavior (as it reflects itself on costs) can be monitored. This trend will further segment the care market. Organized medicine will use its traditional argument against interference with free choice. Given abundant supply of physicians, it is not likely that the argument will succeed. The battle will be fought, if it is fought at all, between employers and employees.

Recognizing that expenditures depend upon both price and quantity, individual firms will also try to influence the utilization of medical services. An increasing number of businesses will move to (already rapidly expanding) self-insurance arrangements under which the employer provides the funds required to pay for medical services and contracts the administration of the program to an insurance company. These self-insurance arrangements may be accompanied by financial inducements (such as rebates or sharing of savings) to employees who use less medical care. Those employees who need and use more services will suffer financial penalties and will be pressed to reduce their utilization of medical care services. The thrust to economize will especially affect preventive care services. In some cases it will also affect interventions that improve health or the quality of life. The new economic pressures (on both employers and employees) will also impinge on labor markets and lead to hiring policies that give preference to younger and healthier workers. Individuals who are likely to use above-average amounts of medical care may face job discrimination.

Absent a comprehensive attack on the health cost problem, we are likely to see the erosion of insurance. The purpose of insurance is to spread risks and their financial impacts. As more and more people have less comprehensive coverage, as more and more employers develop arrangements that penalize individuals who use more care because they are sicker or suffer from chronic illness and need more services (such arrangements will be described as "rewarding individuals who don't abuse the system"), as both the insurance market and the delivery system become more segmented, in sum, as we move farther away

from collective risk-sharing and equity, we will increase the vulnerability of those who need help. Today, that may be someone else, someone who is sicker, less affluent, unluckier than we; tomorrow, or the
day or month or year after, it will be you and I.

Private philanthropy will not be able to fill the gap to meet the needs
of those whose third-party payment, if any, covers less than the full
cost of care. The costs of medical and especially of hospital care have
grown too rapidly. Furthermore, the hospital construction and reno-
vation that began in the 1970s was and continues to be financed with
borrowed money. The large debt-service requirements must be met.
Many of the trustees of not-for-profit hospitals, attracted by the opportunity to participate in community service, will wish it were otherwise but will agree that, in an effort to survive, the institution will
have to seek full-pay patients. Members of the boards of institutions
in the rapidly growing for-profit sector, governed by a different imperative and attracted by a different mission, will have no pangs of
conscience when they fill their beds with those who pay their way.
This, too, will segment our care system. A disproportionate share of
the sickest and the poorest will seek the hospital of last resort, the
public institution.

What is happening in the health care sector is a replay of our earlier
experience in which competition between experience and community
rating led to segmentation of the insurance market. Escalation of health
sector expenditures and growth in individual cost-consciousness will
increase the pressure for segmentation in the delivery of care, for the
deliberate creation of multiple- (and unequal) tier medicine. The collective sharing of costs will decline as groups try to dissociate themselves from those with above-average utilization. Inevitably, that
response will increase the burden on the part of the population that is
left out. Our earlier experience did lead (but only after years of sustained efforts) to the enactment of Medicare, a response to the failure
of voluntary cross-subsidy arrangements. The present situation will
create its own tensions and difficulties and will also call for legislation.
This time the problems will not be associated with the aged and the
poor alone but will affect large segments of the electorate. Legislators
who do not yet sense the need to intervene will find that the pressures
to do so will increase. Once again the nation will return to the issue
of insurance and access to care.

None of us can predict which public policy issues will compete for
our attention or the speed with which events in the health sector will

unfold. Although it is unlikely that state and federal efforts to contain costs and to increase access will cure our financing problems, they will help to relieve the fiscal pain and pressure and to postpone the crisis. We cannot know when the nation will begin its debate about a universal insurance program. Nor can we be certain how long the debate will take. All we know is that issues concerning the roles and responsibilities of government and the private sector are not resolved easily or quickly.

It should be clear that I do not imply that we should sit by passively and wait for things to get worse, accepting cutbacks in health coverage out of a misguided view that only if pain and suffering are increased will we get progress. There is much that can be done to prevent the further dismantling of our health insurance system. There are measures that would assist our sick and needy neighbors, policies that would help our most vulnerable institutions, and programs that would help contain health care expenditures. None of these alone, nor all of them together, can substitute for the type of comprehensive program discussed in the preceding chapter. But neither can or should a comprehensive program, to be enacted some time in the future, substitute for what can be done today. To be so infatuated with the immediate present that we devote no thought or energy to planning for a better tomorrow is irresponsible. To care so much about our dreams that we ignore today's realities and fail to improve them is immoral.

We can unite with those who share our views about our nation's values and who recognize that the federal budget is not only an economic but a social document through which those values are expressed. The expenditure and revenue numbers in the budget represent our collective decision about programs and priorities. They define the role of government and describe our national purpose. We can question the distribution of expenditures and of the tax burden. We can support those who seek equitable solutions to mounting federal budget deficits that constrain the nation's future possibilities. There is no more important way to voice our disagreements than to become knowledgeable about and to debate the budget.

We can support efforts to improve and simplify Medicare's financing, benefit, and payment mechanisms. The program can be restructured in ways that increase the equity of its cost-sharing provisions and that reduce the large costs associated with the purchase of private supplementary insurance. We can reject suggestions to means-test beneficiaries and to provide Medicare vouchers whose dollar value could be used to purchase private health insurance. Such proposals would destroy the program's universal character and lead to segmentation. We can rationalize the Medicaid program in order to reduce benefit and eligibility disparities among the states. We can encourage the development of private and public programs that address needs in the area of long-term care. Medicare, Medicaid, and programs for long-term care are vital, not only to those whom they would assist, but also to our nation's self-respect.

We can support efforts to retain sufficient funding for public health, nutrition, and other social programs that help protect our most vulnerable fellow citizens. We can work to extend health insurance to the unemployed, low-wage workers, dependents of insured individuals, and the growing number of persons whose protection is withdrawn as a result of divorce or death of a spouse. Payment mechanisms can be developed to take account of the special needs of those institutions that serve a disproportionate number of individuals with inadequate or no insurance protection.

We can encourage meaningful competition in the delivery of care, competition that does not reduce quality but that encourages efficiency and benefits the consumer. We can assist the development of HMOs and new delivery systems that foster budget control and that have an incentive structure that helps control costs. We can resist reforms that further segment the insurance and medical care market, recognizing that dividing the community does not help control total health care costs but alters the way we allocate the risks. We can support business, labor, government and third-party attempts to develop new reimbursement and cost-containment mechanisms that move to prospective budgeting and put providers' balance sheets, not patients' health or pocketbooks, at risk. Changes in reimbursement mechanisms mean that we must increase our efforts to assess the quality of care delivered to all patients and most especially to those whose care is paid for under DRG-like systems. The incentives of fixed payment may tempt some providers to cut costs by cutting corners. We must guard against such false economies by careful monitoring of performance.

We can become more knowledgeable and more involved, more discerning about pronouncements by professionals (be they physicians, economists, or legislators), and more discriminating about the difference between analysis and value judgments.

There is a rich agenda.

Health care and the way we pay for it is a matter of efficiency, and today's system is inefficient. Health care and the way we pay for it is a matter of equity, and today's system is inequitable. We can do better and, since we can, we should. Will we? It depends upon whether enough of us are concerned about costs, recognize that a less costly health care system will free resources for other private and public purposes, and support the notion of health care budgets. It also depends upon whether enough of us care enough to work at translating concepts of decency, humaneness, cooperation, universality, and justice into actions that would protect all members of the American family. At stake is not only our health care system but the very nature of our society.

Data Sources
Notes
Index

Data Sources

Extensive data on national and personal health expenditures can be found in publications of the Health Care Financing Administration (HCFA). Special articles and the annual review of health expenditures, with data on the sources and uses of funds, are found in the quarterly *Health Care Financing Review* (Baltimore: Health Care Financing Administration). The first issue appeared in the summer of 1979. Before that, similar data were published in the monthly *Social Security Bulletin* (Washington, D.C.: Social Security Administration), which continues to provide current data on the Social Security trust funds, including the Hospital Insurance Trust Fund and Supplementary Medical Insurance Trust Fund.

HCFA also publishes annual reports on Medicare and Medicaid operations: *The Medicare and Medicaid Data Book* (Baltimore). Additional data and program summaries can be found in *Social Security Bulletin, Annual Statistical Supplement* (Washington, D.C.: Social Security Administration).

The annual publication by the National Center for Health Statistics, *Health, United States* (Washington, D.C.: U.S. Government Printing Office), is the most complete single source of data on health status, health resources and their utilization, and general health statistics.

The National Center for Health Services Research publishes special studies of the health sector and expenditure and insurance patterns. Its Data Preview Series has released over twenty reports analyzing the National Medical Care Expenditure Survey, completed in September 1979.

Studies by the Congressional Budget Office and the congressional Office of Technology Assessment, as well as congressional hearings, often contain data and data analyses not readily available elsewhere.

Notes

1. THE ISSUES

1. *1985 Annual Report of the Board of Trustees of the Federal Hospital Insurance Trust Fund*, House Document 99–47 (Washington, D.C.: U.S. Government Printing Office, 1985), pp. 1–73.

2. Alicia H. Munnell, "Ensuring Entitlement to Health Care Services," *New England Economic Review*, November–December 1985, p. 32.

3. Pamela J. Farley, "Who Are the Underinsured?" *Milbank Memorial Fund Quarterly/Health and Society*, Summer 1985, p. 499.

4. Hewitt Associates Survey, cited in "Environmental Analysis" (Chicago: Blue Cross and Blue Shield Association, May 1985), pp. 18–19.

5. Calculated from U.S. Bureau of the Census, *Characteristics of Households and Persons Receiving Selected Noncash Benefits: 1984*, Consumer Income Series P-60, no. 150 (Washington, D.C.: U.S. Government Printing Office, 1985), pp. 10, 40.

6. Justin F. Kimball, "Prepayment Plan of Hospital Care," *Bulletin of the American Hospital Association*, July 1934, pp. 42–47; Sylvia A. Law, *Blue Cross: What Went Wrong?* 2d ed. (New Haven: Yale University Press, 1976), pp. 6–13; Katherine R. Levit, Helen Lazenby, Daniel R. Waldo, and Lawrence M. Davidoff, "National Health Expenditures, 1984," *Health Care Financing Review*, Fall 1985.

2. IN SICKNESS AND IN HEALTH

1. Robert Gibson and Daniel R. Waldo, "National Health Expenditures, 1980," *Health Care Financing Review*, September 1981, pp. 34–35; Levit et al., "National Health Expenditures, 1984."

2. Kimball, "Prepayment Plan," pp. 43, 45–46.

3. Calculated from U.S. Bureau of the Census, *Historical Statistics of the United States, Colonial Times to 1957* (Washington, D.C.: U.S. Government Printing Office, 1960), p. 185.

4. Harry Becker, ed., *Prepayment and the Community*, Report of the Commission on Financing Hospital Care, vol. 2, (New York: McGraw-Hill,

1955), p. 6; see also Paul Starr, *The Social Transformation of American Medicine* (New York: Basic Books, 1982), pp. 198–232. The latter provides a comprehensive treatment of the relationship between the American medical profession and the health care system.

5. Becker, *Prepayment and the Community*, p. 6; Bureau of the Census, *Historical Statistics*, p. 73.

6. Bureau of the Census, *Historical Statistics*, p. 139.

7. Selwyn D. Collins and Clark Tibbets, *Research Memorandum on Social Aspects of Health in the Depression* (New York: Social Science Research Council; reprint, Arno Press, 1972), pp. 146–149. This is one of thirteen volumes published in the series Studies in the Social Aspects of the Depression.

8. Health Insurance Association of America, *Source Book of Health Insurance Data 1984–1985* (Washington, D.C.: 1985), pp. 5, 11.

9. Herman M. Somers and Anne R. Somers, *Doctors, Patients, and Health Insurance* (Washington, D.C.: Brookings Institution, 1961), pp. 264–265.

10. Becker, *Prepayment and the Community*, p. 7.

11. Ibid., p. 8.

12. Ibid., p. 11.

13. Health Insurance Association of America, *Source Book*, p. 59.

14. Becker, *Prepayment and the Community*, p. 11.

15. Council of Economic Advisers, "The Economic Situation at Midyear 1951," in *The Midyear Economic Report of the President* (Washington, D.C.: U.S. Government Printing Office, 1951), pp. 235, 226, 233.

16. Becker, *Prepayment and the Community*, p. 11.

17. Gibson and Waldo, "National Health Expenditures, 1980," p. 35.

3. THE UNREALIZED DREAM

1. Accounts of the early efforts to enact national health insurance can be found in: Odin W. Anderson, "Compulsory Medical Care Insurance, 1910–1950," *Medical Care for Americans: Annals of the American Academy of Political and Social Sciences*, January 1951, pp. 106–113; Peter A. Corning, *The Evolution of Medicare: From Idea to Law*, Social Security Administration Research Report no. 29 (Washington, D.C.: U.S. Government Printing Office, 1969), pp. 3–28; Harry A. Millis and Royal E. Montgomery, *Labor's Risks and Social Insurance* (New York: McGraw-Hill, 1938), pp. 235–353; Daniel S. Hirshfield, *The Lost Reform* (Cambridge, Mass.: Harvard University Press, 1970), pp. 6–41.

2. Millis and Montgomery, *Labor's Risks*, p. 323.

3. Anderson, "Compulsory Medical Care Insurance," pp. 106–108; Corning, *The Evolution of Medicare*, p. 10.

4. Isadore S. Falk, "Some Lessons from the Fifty Years since the CCMC Final Report, 1932," *Journal of Public Health Policy*, June 1983, pp. 135–161; Committee on the Costs of Medical Care, *Medical Care for the American People* (Chicago: University of Chicago Press, 1932; reprint, U.S. Department of Health, Education, and Welfare, 1970).

5. Committee on the Costs of Medical Care, *Medical Care*, p. iii.

6. Ibid., p. 127.

7. Ibid.

8. Ibid., pp. 189–190.

9. Ibid., p. 196.

10. Cited in Anderson, "Compulsory Medical Care Insurance," p. 109.

11. From President Roosevelt's Social Security Message, June 8, 1934, cited in Edwin E. Witte, *Social Security Perspectives*, ed. Robert J. Lampman (Madison: University of Wisconsin Press, 1962), p. 4. A comprehensive treatment of the Roosevelt period is found in Hirshfield, *The Lost Reform*.

12. Frederick Lewis Allen, "Economic Security: A Look Back and a Look Ahead," in *Economic Security for Americans: An Appraisal of the Progress during the Last 50 Years* (New York: American Assembly, Columbia University, 1954), reprinted in William Haber and Wilbur J. Cohen, *Social Security: Programs, Problems, and Policies* (Homewood, Ill.: Richard D. Irwin, 1960), p. 36.

13. Edwin E. Witte, *The Development of the Social Security Act* (Madison: University of Wisconsin Press, 1962), pp. 111–173.

14. *Fiftieth Anniversary Edition: The Report of the Committee on Economic Security of 1935* (Washington, D.C.: National Conference on Social Welfare, 1985), p. 6.

15. Efforts to enact a national health insurance program during the Truman administration are discussed in: Eugene Feingold, *Medicare: Policy and Politics* (San Francisco: Chandler, 1966), pp. 96–101; Richard Harris, *A Sacred Trust* (New York: New American Library, 1966), pp. 31–57; Corning, *The Evolution of Medicare*, pp. 53–69.

16. Feingold, *Medicare*, p. 100.

17. Ibid., p. 99.

18. *National Health Insurance: Hearings before the Committee on Labor and Public Welfare, U.S. Senate*, 91st Cong. 2d sess. (Washington, D.C.: U.S. Government Printing Office, 1970), p. 85.

19. Harris, *A Sacred Trust*, p. 52.

20. Seymour E. Harris, *The Economics of American Medicine* (New York: Macmillan, 1964), p. 251.

21. *National Health Insurance*, p. 204.

22. Becker, *Prepayment and the Community*, p. 11.

23. Adlai E. Stevenson, *Major Campaign Speeches of Adlai E. Stevenson* (New York: Random House, 1953), pp. 201–202.

24. President's Commission on the Health Needs of the Nation, *Building America's Health* (Washington, D.C.: U.S. Government Printing Office, 1952), p. 48.

4. THE BATTLE FOR MEDICARE

1. U.S. Bureau of the Census, *America in Transition: An Aging Society*, Current Population Reports Series P-23, no. 128 (Washington, D.C.: U.S. Government Printing Office, 1983), p. 3.

2. Numerous sources provide detailed accounts of the political climate and the development of Medicare. Perhaps the most detailed is Harris, *A Sacred Trust*. This account first appeared as a series of four articles in *The New Yorker*. Additional valuable material can be found in Corning, *The Evolution of Medicare;* Feingold, *Medicare;* Theodore R. Marmor, *The Politics of Medicare* (Chicago: Aldine, 1973); Herman A. Somers and Anne R. Somers, *Medicare and the Hospitals: Issues and Prospects* (Washington, D.C.: Brookings Institution, 1967); James L. Sundquist, *Politics and Policy: The Eisenhower, Kennedy, and Johnson Years* (Washington, D.C.: Brookings Institution, 1968); and Irwin Wolkstein, "Medicare 1971: Changing Attitudes and Changing Legislation," *Law and Contemporary Problems*, Autumn 1970, part 2, pp. 697–715.

3. Corning, *The Evolution of Medicare*, p. 102; Bureau of the Census, *America in Transition*, p. 10.

4. Feingold, *Medicare*, p. 109.

5. National Center for Health Statistics, *Health, United States: 1975* (Washington, D.C.: U.S. Government Printing Office, 1976), p. 573.

6. Harris, *A Sacred Trust*, p. 139.

7. Theodore C. Sorenson, *Kennedy* (New York: Harper and Row, 1965), p. 343.

8. John F. Kennedy, *Congressional Record*, vol. 109 pt. 2, February 21, 1963, p. 2694.

9. U.S. Bureau of the Census, *Statistical Abstract of the United States: 1982-83* (Washington, D.C.: U.S. Government Printing Office, 1982), p. 478; Bureau of the Census, *Historical Statistics*, p. 691.

10. Bureau of the Census, *Statistical Abstract*, pp. 107, 114.

11. Clinton P. Anderson, quoted in Wolkstein, "Medicare 1971," p. 700.

5. MEDICARE

1. The general sources on Medicare noted for Chapter 4 also provide background for the discussion of the implementation of Medicare. For a comprehensive discussion of the implementation of the program see Judith M. Feder, *Medicare: The Politics of Federal Hospital Insurance* (Lexington, Mass.: D.C. Heath, 1977). For additional material see Theodore R. Marmor, "The Congress: Medicare Politics and Policy," in Allen P. Sinder, ed., *American Political Institutions and Public Policy: Five Contemporary Studies* (Boston: Little, Brown, 1969), pp. 3–66.

2. Congressional Research Service, "Medicare: FY86 Budget," in *Major Issues System: Issue Brief* (Washington, D.C.: Library of Congress, 1985), pp. 1–25; *The Medicare and Medicaid Data Book, 1983* (Baltimore: Health Care Financing Administration, 1983), pp. 16, 23.

3. Quoted in Wolkstein, "Medicare 1971," p. 698.

4. The summary is adapted from *Information on Medicare and Health Insurance for Older People* (Washington, D.C.: American Association of Retired Persons, 1985); *Social Security Benefits Including Medicare* (Chicago:

Commerce Clearing House, 1985), pp. 38–47; *Your Medicare Handbook* (Washington, D.C.: Social Security Administration).

5.   U.S. Senate, Special Committee on Aging, *Medicare and the Health Costs of Older Americans: The Extent and Effects of Cost Sharing*, S.Prt. 98–166 (Washington, D.C.: U.S. Government Printing Office, 1984), p. v.

6.   *Annual Statistical Supplement: 1983, Social Security Bulletin* (Washington, D.C.: Social Security Administration, 1984), p. ii.

7.   Senate Committee on Aging, *Medicare and Health Costs*, p. 4; Congressional Research Service, "Medicare: Physician Payments," in *Major Issues System: Issue Brief* (Washington, D.C.: Library of Congress, 1985), p. 18.

8.   Congressional Budget Office, *Changing the Structure of Medicare Benefits: Issues and Options* (Washington, D.C., 1983), p. 50.

9.   Senate Committee on Aging, *Medicare and Health Costs*, p. 5.

10.   Ibid., p. v.

11.   Congressional Budget Office, *Changing the Structure*, pp. 22, 24.

12.   Bureau of the Census, *America in Transition*, p. 4; U.S. Bureau of the Census, *Money Income of Households, Families and Persons in the United States: 1983*, Current Population Reports Series P-60, no. 146 (Washington, D.C.: U.S. Government Printing Office, 1985), p. 10; Congressional Budget Office, *Changing the Structure*, p. 71.

13.   Senate Committee on Aging, *Medicare and Health Costs*, p. v.

14.   Elliot Richardson in *Health Care Crisis in America, 1971: Hearings before the Subcommittee on Health, Committee on Labor and Public Welfare, U.S. Senate* (Washington, D.C.: U.S. Government Printing Office, 1971), pp. 11–12.

15.   Senate Committee on Aging, *Medicare and Health Costs*, pp. 7, 11.

16.   *1985 Annual Report of the Board of Trustees of the Federal Hospital Insurance Trust Fund* (Washington, D.C.: U.S. Government Printing Office, 1985), pp. 33–46.

17.   Bureau of the Census, *America in Transition*, p. 16; Levit et al., "National Health Expenditures, 1984."

18.   Joseph A. Califano, Jr., *Governing America* (New York: Simon and Schuster, 1981), p. 144.

19.   John Knowles in *The Federal Budget, Inflation, and Full Employment: Hearings before the Subcommittee on Fiscal Policy of the Joint Economic Committee, U.S. Congress* (Washington, D.C.: U.S. Government Printing Office, 1969), p. 224.

20.   For a discussion of the new payment system and its possible implications, see Office of Technology Assessment, *Medicare's Prospective Payment System: Strategies for Evaluating Cost, Quality, and Medical Technology*, OTA-H-62 (Washington, D.C., 1985).

21.   *Impact of Medicare's Prospective Payment System on the Quality of Care Received by Medicare Beneficiaries*, Staff Report to Special Committee on Aging, U.S. Senate, September 26, 1985.

22.   See Robert G. Evans, *Strained Mercy: The Economics of Canadian Health Care* (Toronto: Butterworth, 1984).

23. Congressional Research Service, *Medicare: Physician Payments*, p. 18.

24. Karen Davis, "Access to Health Care: A Matter of Fairness," in *Health Care: How to Improve It* (Washington, D.C.: Center for National Policy, 1985), p. 50.

25. Somers and Somers, *Medicare and the Hospitals*, p. 28.

26. Michael Harrington, *The Other America* (New York: Macmillan, 1962).

27. Lester C. Thurow, *The Zero-Sum Society* (New York: Basic Books, 1980); John Kenneth Galbraith, *The Affluent Society* (Boston: Houghton Mifflin, 1958).

6. MEDICAID

1. President's Task Force on Health, "Report to the President" (November 1964, mimeograph), pp. 27, 34.

2. *The Medicare and Medicaid Data Book, 1983*, p. 3.

3. For a comprehensive discussion on Medicaid in the recent past see Randall R. Bovbjerg and John Holahan, *Medicaid in the Reagan Era* (Washington, D.C.: Urban Institute Press, 1982); Robert Blendon and Thomas W. Moloney ed., *New Approaches to the Medicaid Crisis* (New York: Frost and Sullivan, 1983); Kathleen N. Lohr and M. Susan Marquis, "Medicare and Medicaid: Past, Present, and Future," Note N-2088 HHS/RC (Santa Monica: Rand Corporation, 1984). For additional material see *The Medicare and Medicaid Data Book, 1983;* and Karen Davis, "Access to Health Care."

4. Bovbjerg and Holahan, *Medicaid in the Reagan Era*, p. 2.

5. Bureau of the Census, *Characteristics of Households and Persons*, pp. 2, 7, 40, 42; U.S. Bureau of the Census, *Money Income and Poverty Status of Families and Persons in the United States: 1983*, Current Population Reports, Series P-60, no. 145 (Washington, D.C.: U.S. Government Printing Office, 1984), p. 25; "Health Care Financing Trends," *Health Care Financing Review*, Spring 1985, p. 8–9; U.S. Bureau of the Census, *Characteristics of the Population below the Poverty Level: 1977*, Consumer Income Series P-60, no. 119 (Washington, D.C.: U.S. Government Printing Office, 1979), p. 2.

6. "Health Care Financing Trends," pp. 8–9.

7. *The Medicare and Medicaid Data Book, 1983*, pp. 85–91; Bovbjerg and Holahan, *Medicaid in the Reagan Era*, p. 33.

8. Levit et al., "National Health Expenditures, 1984"; Robert Gibson, "National Health Expenditures, 1978," *Health Care Financing Review*, Summer 1979, p. 30.

9. Levit et al., "National Health Expenditures, 1984."

7. SYSTEM REFORM

1. See Wolkstein, "Medicare, 1971"; Karen Davis, *National Health Insurance: Benefits, Costs, and Consequences* (Washington, D.C.: Brookings Institution, 1975); Isadore S. Falk, "National Health Insurance: A Review of

Policies and Proposals," *Law and Contemporary Problems*, Autumn 1970, part 2, pp. 669–697; idem, "Proposals for National Health Insurance in the USA; Origins and Evolution, and Some Perceptions for the Future," *Milbank Memorial Fund Quarterly/Health and Society*, Spring 1977, pp. 161–191.

2. Cf. Committee on the Costs of Medical Care, *Medical Care for the American People*, pp. 105–134.

3. Health Insurance Association of America, *Source Book*, pp. 10–17.

4. Gibson and Waldo, "National Health Expenditures, 1980," pp. 36–38.

5. Quoted in Wolkstein, "Medicare, 1971," p. 700.

6. Falk, "National Health Insurance," pp. 174–177.

7. The following discussion owes much to Lawrence D. Brown, *Politics & Health Care Organization: HMOs as Federal Policy* (Washington, D.C.: Brookings Institution, 1983); Harold S. Luft, *Health Maintenance Organizations: Dimensions of Performance* (New York: John Wiley and Sons, 1981); and Alain C. Enthoven, *Health Plan* (Reading, Mass.: Addison-Wesley, 1980).

8. Paul Starr, *The Social Transformation*, p. 305.

9. Health Insurance Association of America, *Source Book*, p. 6.

10. "Strong Medicine to Cure Ford's Fever," *Business Week*, November 25, 1985, pp. 40–41.

8. HEALTH CARE COSTS

1. *Annual Statistical Supplement: 1983*, pp. 33–35.

2. *Analysis of Health Insurance Proposals Introduced in the 92nd Congress* (Washington, D.C.: Social Security Administration, 1971); *National Health Insurance: Provisions of Bills Introduced in the 93rd Congress as of February 1974* (Washington, D.C.: Social Security Administration, 1974); *National Health Insurance: Provisions of Bills Introduced in the 93rd Congress as of July 1974* (Washington, D.C.: Social Security Administration, 1974).

3. *National Health Insurance Provisions as of February 1974*, p. 4.

4. Ibid., p. 18.

5. Health Insurance Association of America, *Source Book*, p. 14.

6. See *National Health Insurance: Hearings before the Committee on Ways and Means, House of Representatives*, 93rd Cong. 2d sess., vols.1–9 (Washington, D.C.: U.S. Government Printing Office, 1974).

7. Bureau of the Census, *Statistical Abstract 1982–83*, p. 483.

8. Robert M. Gibson, Katherine R. Levit, Helen Lazenby, and Daniel R. Waldo, "National Health Expenditures, 1983," *Health Care Financing Review*, Winter 1984, pp. 7, 8, 14.

9. Gibson et al., "National Health Expenditures, 1983," pp. 3–4.

10. Daniel R. Waldo and Robert M. Gibson, "National Health Expenditures, 1981," *Health Care Financing Review*, September 1982, pp. 31–34; Mark Freeland and Carol E. Schendler, "National Health Expenditure Growth in the 1980s: An Aging Population, New Technologies, and Increasing Competition," *Health Care Financing Review*, March 1983, p. 55.

11. The data in the following five paragraphs are based on Amy K. Taylor and Walter R. Lawson, Jr., "Employer and Employee Expenditures for Pri-

vate Health Insurance," in *National Medical Care Expenditures Survey Data Preview 7* (Hyattsville, Md.: National Center for Health Services Research, 1981), pp. 2–13.

12. Gail Lee Cafferata, "Private Health Insurance: Premium Expenditures and Sources of Payment," in *National Medical Care Expenditures Survey Data Preview 17* (Rockville, Md.: National Center for Health Services Research, 1983), pp. 2–19.

13. Daniel C. Walden, Gail R. Wilensky, and Judith Kasper, "Changes in Health Insurance Status: Full-Year and Part-Year Coverage," in *National Medical Care Expenditures Survey Data Preview 21* (Rockville, Md.: National Center for Health Services Research, 1985), pp. 2–15.

14. Marjorie S. Carroll and Ross H. Arnett III, "Private Health Insurance Plans in 1978 and 1979: A Review of Coverage, Enrollment, and Financial Experience," *Health Care Financing Review*, September 1981, pp. 56, 59.

15. Health Insurance Association of America, *Source Book of Health Insurance Data 1977–1978* (Washington, D.C., 1978), p. 20.

16. Carroll and Arnett, "Private Health Insurance Plans," p. 72.

17. Waldo and Gibson, "National Health Expenditures, 1981," p. 23.

18. Joseph A. Califano, Jr., *Governing America*; *National Health Insurance: Working Papers*, 2 vols. (Washington, D.C.: U.S. Public Health Service, 1980) (no page numbers); Judith Feder, Jack Hadley, and John Holahan, *Insuring the Nation's Health* (Washington, D.C.: Urban Institute Press, 1981); James Morris, *Searching for a Cure* (New York: Pica Press, 1984); *Health Care for All Americans Act*, 96th Cong. 1st sess., *Congressional Record*, vol. 125, September 6, 1979.

19. Subcommittee on Health and the Environment of the Committee on Interstate and Foreign Commerce, U.S. House of Representatives, *A Discursive Dictionary of Health Care* (Washington, D.C.: U.S. Government Printing Office, 1976), p. 106.

20. Statement by Secretary Califano before the Committee on Finance of the U.S. Senate, March 27, 1979, in *National Health Insurance: Working Papers*, vol. 2.

21. Statement by Patricia Roberts Harris before a joint session of the House Ways and Means Committee and House Commerce Committee, November 29, 1979, in *National Health Insurance: Working Papers*, vol. 2.

9. CUTTING BACK ON HEALTH INSURANCE

1. There is an extensive and growing literature on competition in health care. Among the comprehensive treatments are: Enthoven, *Health Plan;* "Competition and Regulation in Health Care Markets," special issue of *Milbank Memorial Fund Quarterly/Health and Society*, Spring 1981; Mancur Olson, ed., *A New Approach to the Economics of Health Care* (Washington, D.C.: American Enterprise Institute for Public Policy Research, 1981). For a comprehensive treatment of market-competition and other reforms, see Eli Ginzberg, *The Limits of Health Reform: The Search for Realism* (New York: Basic Books, 1977).

2. Levit et al., "National Health Expenditures, 1984."

3. Waldo and Gibson, "National Health Expenditures, 1981."

4. Gibson et al., "National Health Expenditures, 1983," pp. 4, 14, 15.

5. Freeland and Schendler, "National Health Expenditure Growth," pp. 8–9.

6. Levit et al., "National Health Expenditures, 1984."

7. M. Susan Marquis, *Cost-Sharing and the Patient's Choice of Provider* (Santa Monica: Rand Corporation, 1984), p. 29.

8. For an interesting discussion on tax treatment see Alain C. Enthoven, "A New Proposal to Reform the Tax Treatment of Health Insurance," *Health Affairs*, Spring 1984, pp. 21–39.

9. Office of Management and Budget, *Special Analyses, Budget of the United States Government, 1987* (Washington, D.C.: U.S. Government Printing Office, 1986), p. G-45. Also see Congressional Budget Office, *Containing Medical Care Costs through Market Forces* (Washington, D.C.: U.S. Government Printing Office, 1982), p. 26; and Amy K. Taylor and Gail R. Wilensky, "Tax Expenditures and the Demand for Private Health Insurance," in *National Health Care Expenditures Study* (Hyattsville, Md.: National Center for Health Services Research, 1982).

10. Congressional Budget Office, *Containing Medical Care Costs*, p. 27.

11. Ibid.

12. Taylor and Wilensky, "Tax Expenditures," p. 20.

10. CONTROLLING COSTS, ACHIEVING EQUITY

1. Robert J. Maxwell, *Health and Wealth* (Lexington, Mass.: D.C. Heath, 1982), p. 37.

2. Brian Abel-Smith, "Who is the Odd Man Out?: The Experience of Western Europe in Containing the Costs of Health Care," *Milbank Memorial Fund Quarterly/Health and Society*, Winter 1985, p. 15.

3. In 1972 a colleague, Lawrence Kirsch, and I wrestled with the problem that Congressman Mills posed: how to achieve equity while preserving the private insurance system that charged premiums unrelated to income and without engaging in a "charade." The construct we developed bears a resemblance to the approach outlined here. A somewhat similar plan is discussed in Herman M. Somers and Anne R. Somers, "Major Issues in National Health Insurance," *Milbank Memorial Fund*, April 1972, pp. 177–211.

4. Statement by Secretary Califano, *National Health Insurance: Working Papers*, vol. 2.

5. See "The Maternal and Child Health Care Act (H.R. 12937)" introduced by Congressman James Scheuer (Democrat from New York) in *National Health Insurance Resource Book*, Committee on Ways and Means (Washington, D.C.: U.S. Government Printing Office, 1976), pp. 502–503 and testimony by Theodore R. Marmor before the House Committee on Ways and Means, February 26, 1976 (mimeo).

6. Evans, *Strained Mercy*, p. 10.

7. The interested reader can consult: Spyros Andreopoulos, ed., *National*

Health Insurance: Can We Learn From Canada? (New York. John Wiley and Sons, 1975); Evans, *Strained Mercy;* Judith Feder, John Holahan, and Theodore Marmor, eds., *National Health Insurance: Conflicting Goals and Policy Choices* (Washington, D.C.: Urban Institute, 1980); Victor R. Fuchs, *Who Shall Live* (New York: Basic Books, 1974), pp. 127–151; Gordon McLachlan and Alan Maynard, eds., *The Public/Private Mix for Health: The Relevance and Effects of Change* (London: Nuffield Provincial Hospitals Trust, 1982); Carl A. Meilicke and Janet L. Storch, eds., *Perspectives on Canadian Health and Social Service Policy: History and Emerging Trends* (Ann Arbor: Health Administration Press, 1980); Malcolm G. Taylor, *Health Insurance and Canadian Public Policy* (Montreal: McGill–Queen's University Press, 1978).

Index